Girls & Women,
　　Men & Boys

For David, with love

Girls & Women, Men & Boys

GENDER IN TARADALE 1886–1930

Caroline Daley

AUCKLAND UNIVERSITY PRESS

First published 1999

Auckland University Press
University of Auckland
Private Bag 92019
Auckland
New Zealand
http://www.auckland.ac.nz/aup

© Caroline Daley 1999

ISBN 1 86940 211 1

Publication is assisted by the Historical Branch of the Department of Internal Affairs

This book is copyright. Apart from fair dealing for the purpose of private study, research, criticism or review, as permitted under the Copyright Act, no part may be reproduced by any process without the prior permission of the publisher.

Cover design by Christine Hansen
Printed by GP Print, Wellington

Contents

Acknowledgements	*vii*
1 Introduction: Gender and the Taradale Community	1
2 Family and Community	12
3 The Household and Local Economy	31
4 Women's Work	46
5 Men's Work	73
6 Communal Leisure	91
7 Feminine Leisure	113
8 Masculine Leisure	132
Conclusion	158
Appendix A: Oral Informants	164
Appendix B: Occupational Categories for Men	172
Notes	176
Bibliography	200
Index	212

Acknowledgements

This book began its life many years ago when I was a graduate student in the Department of History at Victoria University of Wellington. Jock Phillips supervised the PhD from which *Girls and Women, Men and Boys* is derived. I remain extremely grateful to Jock for the support he offered me then, and has continued to offer. Many other people in Wellington influenced my work over those years. I would like to thank Dominic Alessio, Michael Eyes, Miles Fairburn, David Hamer, Ann Hardy, Richard Hill, Malcolm McKinnon, Malcolm McLean, Benjamin Morgan, Melanie Nolan, and Kim Sterelny for their encouragement and help.

After I joined the Department of History at the University of Auckland I began the slow process of turning my PhD into a book. When I became frustrated with the project Raewyn Dalziel and Barry Reay were always there to offer encouragement and help. My debt to them is enormous. Despite the onerous tasks of the modern university, they both read an earlier draft of my manuscript. Their encouraging response helped me bring this project to fruition. Others in the university have also been a great source of help and friendship, particularly Malcolm Campbell, Tim Dare, Deborah Montgomerie and Philip Rousseau.

I am grateful for the financial support I received to write the PhD and then turn it into a book: a University Grants Committee Postgraduate Scholarship, the F. P. Wilson Scholarship in New Zealand History, the Helen Stewart Royle Scholarship, the Jacob Joseph Scholarship, a Historical Branch Bursary, a grant from the Taradale and Districts Centennial Celebration Committee, and short-leave from the University of Auckland. I thank the Historical Branch, Department of Internal Affairs, for awarding this book a publication subsidy.

I would also like to thank the people of the Taradale area who have helped me over the years. I am indebted to the people who agreed to be interviewed for this project, to Irene Lister – Taradale's own local historian – and to May Davis, who shared her photograph album with me. I am grateful for the assistance offered to me by Joy Axford and Gail McGahan at the Hawke's Bay Museum, and the many librarians and archivists at the various institutions I did research in. The nature of the study meant I spent a lot of time working in non-governmental archives, and I extend my thanks to the many unpaid archivists who went out of their way to assist me. I would also like to thank the Registrar General for giving me free access to Birth, Death and Marriage records.

The staff at AUP has been supportive of this project from a very early stage. I thank Elizabeth Caffin for always believing in Taradale, the Press's anonymous reader who made me rethink some of my work, Anne Else for her sympathetic editing, and the rest of the AUP team.

Finally, I would like to thank my family – especially my mother, Pat, and my grandmother, Sally – for the support and encouragement they have given me and my work over the years. From always welcoming me home when I came to do research, to buying me a leather jacket (thank you, Sarah), they were and are always there for me. As has David. He has read drafts, made me dinner and always encouraged me. I have been working on Taradale since we met. I can only think that it is a good sign that my current project is tentatively entitled 'a history of leisure and pleasure'.

Caroline Daley
February 1999

CHAPTER 1

Introduction: Gender and the Taradale Community

In 1890 the board of Taradale School held a meeting to discuss the behaviour of the boys and girls under their charge. They were concerned about the lack of control the teachers had over the children, and how some of the young people were interacting. The solution was obvious to the school board – they decided to build a 'dividing fence' in the playground. The boys would have one side, the girls the other.[1] Within a few months the school committee reported that 'the improvements made to the playgrounds and fences had greatly added to the comfort and discipline of the children'.[2]

A couple of years later the school board was able to purchase another acre of land, adjacent to the girls' playground. At first the committee saw this as a way to extend the girls' playground.[3] But then, without any discussion, the board decided to swap over the playgrounds. The boys got the newly enlarged play area. No one seems to have considered that both the girls and the boys could have benefited from the extra space.[4]

For the most part the children stayed within their respective playgrounds. Although there was an opening in the dividing fence, there is no indication that it was used often. Occasionally boys and girls crossed the gendered boundary for a furtive liaison or 'dare' but generally they preferred to stick to their own turf. Girls considered the boys' area rough: boys knew the girls' playground was for sissies. This

1

understanding was not lost on their teachers. When William Cliff got nine out of ten spelling words wrong, his teacher, the infamous Miss Shugar, made the other boys carry him around the school shoulder high for breaking the record of the most words wrong. Then 'I had to play with the girls on the maypole . . . That's the biggest insult you can give to anybody.'[5] The maypole was in the girls' playground. William was humiliated by being forced to cross over into the girls' territory and join in their feminine games.

These school stories encapsulate what this book is about. This is a history of a local community through a gendered lens. It does not aim to be a total historical account of the area. Rather, it offers insights into the meanings of gender in the lives of the women and men, girls and boys who lived in the small, semi-rural community of Taradale, New Zealand, in the late nineteenth and early twentieth centuries. It does this through examining kin groups and interactions, the household economy and leisure. Of course, many other aspects of gender could be examined, such as sexuality, ethnicity and violence. However, they are not my focus here, partly because of the sources available.

Most of the historical studies of women and men in New Zealand have traced their separate lives. I am as interested in their joint activities as in their different histories. Boys and girls had separate playgrounds, but they went to the same school and spent many hours together. For much of their lives the people of Taradale did not live in so-called separate spheres.[6] Kin was central: people in Taradale lived in a community which revolved around family life and family ties. The first focus of the book is on these shared, often familial activities.

Yet within their shared spaces women and men, girls and boys often had different experiences. As the photograph of Taradale School indicates, boys and girls not only played in different areas; they also entered the school grounds through separate gates, and entered their classrooms through separate doors. Once inside, they sat in sex-segregated seats. Their gender was made to matter, and this continued into their adulthood. So the second focus of this book is on the different, gendered experiences the people of Taradale had within the shared world they inhabited, whether at home, at school, at work or in leisure.

My third focus is not so much on the events and experiences themselves, whether shared or separate. Rather it is with the meanings they were given. While William's female contemporaries had fond memories of playing on the maypole, for him this was a shameful, emasculating experience. For the most part, the way gender was understood in Taradale is explored through examining and comparing

GENDER AND THE TARADALE COMMUNITY

Taradale School. The dividing fence in the front playground is clearly visible, as are the separate doorways for boys and girls. WILSONS REAL PHOTOGRAPH POST CARD, PRIVATE COLLECTION

the oral histories of the men and women I interviewed. What they recalled about family life, the household economy and leisure, and how they recalled it, reveals much about the pervasiveness of gender ideas and ideals in this community. Their stories were gendered in both content and form.[7]

The playground fence was a physical reminder to the children that many aspects of their lives were circumscribed by gender. The idea of boundaries – whether they are as solid as an iron fence or as intangible as an emotion – is useful in thinking about gender relations. The geo-political parameters of Taradale were set when it acquired town district status in 1886. But within that area, gender relations were not fixed. This book is about how people negotiated and measured femininities and masculinities, how they challenged the iron fences, and at times were defeated by them, and how they defended their gendered territory.

Taking a gendered approach to New Zealand history is still something of a novelty. Over the last 20 or so years the history of women's lives has received increasing attention in New Zealand. Edited collections such as *Women in History* and *Women in History 2*, *Standing in the Sunshine* and *Women Together*, together with monographs and biographies such as *A Woman of Good Character* and *The Story of Suzanne Aubert*, have raised many issues about women's pasts. Some of these feature in this book too. The outpouring of feminist history, both here and overseas, has also encouraged a few historians to consider anew men's lives and masculinity. Jock Phillips's *A Man's Country?*, first published in 1987, encouraged others to think about masculinity as a social and historical construct. Without such provocative and important works, this book would not have been written.

Yet while New Zealand's historiography is now rich with work focusing on women's separate lives, and histories of men are growing apace, few studies have investigated the interactions and interconnectedness of women's and men's history. Claire Toynbee's recent history of work in the early twentieth century is one of the few published studies to look at both men's and women's history in concert.[8] This book is, therefore, something of an exception in New Zealand's historical writing, and should be read as a step in the direction of gendering New Zealand's history. It is not a definitive account. After all, my focus is on one small community, over a relatively restricted period. But I hope that it will encourage others to see, as the American historian Joan Scott has so powerfully argued, the potential of gender as a useful category for historical analysis.[9]

Joan Scott's work on gender has been both hugely influential and controversial. She and many of her followers have argued that taking a gendered approach to history is a useful way to analyse and understand the relationships between male and female experiences. At the heart of her analysis is the idea that power is articulated through gender. However, many feminists have taken issue with Scott's work. They do not dispute the analytical power of gender per se; but Scott's poststructuralist approach to gender leads her to focus on language and meaning, symbols and metaphors, rather than on the sort of empirically grounded evidence historians are often more comfortable with. There is an ongoing debate now among feminist scholars about whether taking a 'linguistic turn', and looking at meaning rather than actual events (indeed, disputing the idea that there are actual events to study) is the way to transform historical practice and understanding.[10] In many respects I regard this debate as an arcane academic exercise. But it has brought to the fore many interesting ideas about ways to use gender to study history, and these ideas have shaped this book.

Scott's central claim, that gender is a major way of signifying power, lies at the heart of my understanding and use of gender as a concept. The power and control men had over women must be considered. But it is also important to recognise that power is dispersed and differentiated. In one situation a woman might use her femininity as a form of power over a man; in another situation that same man might use his financial or physical strength to control her. In either case, it is clear that power is manifested through gender, and gender is about relationships. These relationships may be between men and women, or they may be among men or among women only. What is important is that gender is a relational concept. Masculinity is defined, in part, by what it is not – that is, by femininity.

The way I define and use gender in this book is centred on issues of power and relationships. Gender was of course not the only defining motif in the lives of the people of Taradale. Class, ethnicity, age, religious belief, and length of residence all helped to define them too. While I do not ignore these factors here, I view them through a gendered lens. As Gisela Bock writes, 'each one of the apparently gender-neutral relations between human beings is also conditioned by gender relations; gender is one constituent factor of all other relations'.[11]

I am less concerned with issues of social construction and biology. It has been common for feminist scholars to make a distinction between 'sex' and 'gender' on the grounds that biology was fixed, whereas the social construction of masculinity and femininity allowed for change over time and across societies. However, this seems less important to me. As Bock has demonstrated, biology itself is socially constructed.[12] So I have written here about men and women, as well as masculinities and femininities. Most people do not wake up in the morning and decide which gender they will be today; their biological sex determines this. But as Judith Butler has argued, how they perform masculinity or femininity in a particular situation or over time can change.[13] This book explores the performance of gender in Taradale between 1886 and 1930.

Butler's idea of gender as performance does not mean that it is easy to alter the script. Most of the citizens of Taradale knew at any given moment, in any situation, how a 'proper' woman or a 'real' man should act. There was no question about sexual orientation; 'normal' heterosexuality was assumed. But within this culture of hegemonic gender relations, of knowing how you should perform your femininity or masculinity, there was some room to manoeuvre.[14] How gender was performed depended on the context. A young woman could act out her femininity in ways different from those of her mother or grandmother. A man who played croquet rather than rugby could still reiterate his masculinity through sport.

The gendered script had no major rewrite in Taradale between 1886 and 1930. The idea of a crisis in gender relations, prevalent in historical and contemporary writings about masculinities, seems out of place in discussing Taradale's gender history.[15] No one stormed the playground's dividing fence. But challenges and changes can come about without a crisis. For many these were years of repositioning, a time when influences within and outside the community led them to question the relationships between men and women.

Like the rest of New Zealand, Taradale felt the changes of women's suffrage, improved access to secondary education, and six o'clock closing. Its people suffered through the Boer War and the Great War. They watched more and more young women leave their homes each day for paid employment. New forms of transport allowed them to move beyond the community more easily. New organisations sprang up to cater for their growing leisure demands. As all of these things happened around them and to them, their gender performance altered.

For the young women of Taradale, especially, new opportunities arose. Taradale was not the home of the notorious New Woman. A highly educated, politically active, single, smoking, bicycle-riding, bifurcated-skirt-wearing woman would have been run out of town by women and men alike. But there is evidence for a lower key, lower case, 'new woman' in Taradale. We need to turn to these young women if we are to understand some of the changes that took place within and between genders and generations. Chapters 4 and 7 show how these new women capitalised on changes in education and paid work for women, and bought themselves more leisure time and opportunities. These new women were the beneficiaries of the battles other women had fought and won. To some extent the changes they experienced in their lives became challenges to the lives of others. Gender is a relational concept, and gender relations are not always ones of solidarity. There were tensions between generations of women, as well as between femininities and masculinities. These need to be discussed, as do the ways that women and men pulled together at home, at work, and in leisure. Chapters 3 and 6 look at the household economies and communal leisure of the people of Taradale.

As there were tensions and changes among the females of Taradale, so the parameters of masculinities also shifted over the years. As society settled down, and more men married, a new family man emerged.[16] More involved with his family on a day-to-day basis than the patriarch of old, he was more of a presence in it, balancing rather than overshadowing the feminine influence of his wife. Margaret Marsh has coined the term 'masculine domesticity' to describe this 'manly' man about the home, and it is a useful concept for considering Taradale's married men.[17] Chapter 2 looks at men's changing relationship with their families through the rituals of birth, marriage and death. Chapters 5 and 8 focus on how these men interacted with their kin, especially their male kin, at work and in leisure. Whereas inter-generational change and tension marked femininities in Taradale, masculinities were far more inclusive. The men of Taradale were keen to involve their sons, nephews and grandsons in their lives. One of the results was that men's power was rarely threatened.

Because gender is about relations between people, it is an ideal concept for examining local communities – the people who live in a particular area and the relationships they are enmeshed in. New Zealand historiography may lack studies with a gendered focus, but it more than makes up for it with a wealth of local area studies. Many of these community histories are written by local enthusiasts. As Peter Gibbons argues, they tend to combine 'the rhetoric of the pioneer legend with about as many names as the district's telephone directory'.[18] Alongside these tales of worthy men and road building stand a range of more academically focused local studies. Readers can find out about how the western world intruded on the Taranaki township of Kaponga, how the skilled workers of Caversham built themselves a new world, what the Nova Scotian Scots did once they arrived in Waipu, and how the Wellington suburb of Johnsonville came into being.[19] They can also read a stinging critique of the assumption that community bonds existed in nineteenth-century Pakeha society.[20] Although this study of Taradale shares a similar time frame with several other community histories, it differs in its emphasis. This is the first explicitly gendered history of a local community. But before that gendered analysis can begin, the area must be introduced.

Taradale has not often been the subject of historical investigation.[21] This small, semi-rural Hawke's Bay community, eight kilometres south-west of Napier, flanked to the west by the Puketapu hills and bordered to the south by the Tutaekuri River, quickly earned a quiet reputation as a warm, sunny spot, with fertile soils that sustained quite intensive farming. Named by Henry Alley, the first Pakeha to buy the land, Taradale came into being in 1858.[22]

A couple of kilometres to the north-east of Taradale is Greenmeadows, created in the late 1850s by Henry Stokes Tiffen.[23] Although Greenmeadows did not formally become a part of the Taradale Town District until 1941, from the beginning it was seen as an extension of Taradale rather than as a separate community. Greenmeadows is therefore included in this study.

To the south-east of Taradale is the settlement of Meanee.[24] Like Taradale and Greenmeadows, Meanee was known as a fertile area, and was the scene of much dairying. It was also known to be frequently flooded by the Tutaekuri River, a problem largely solved by the middle of the twentieth century. Meanee had more of a sense of being a separate community than Greenmeadows, but it too has been included in this study, largely because it was the site of the only Roman Catholic church in the district, and housed the convent school. It was also home to the Roman Catholic seminary until 1911; due to constant flooding, the seminary was then moved to nearby Greenmeadows.

These three localities make up what I refer to as the Taradale area. History 'takes place'.[25] The geographical boundaries and landscape features of this place have shaped its history. The inner harbour, hills and rivers that bordered the area helped to define what the people did and how they interacted. They also go some way toward explaining why the people of the area saw themselves as belonging to a separate community.

This study begins in 1886, the year Taradale achieved separate town district status. The area had a long history before that. Otatara Pa, just outside Taradale, was built prior to the sixteenth century.[26] From the late 1850s Pakeha began moving into the area, living in close physical proximity to their Ngati Kahungunu neighbours, but seemingly having little to do with them. Within a decade of Alley's and Tiffen's purchases, land was subdivided and sold to men whose families were to remain in the area for generations: John Hammond, William Harpham, George Rymer, and Isaac Jeffares, among others.[27] Rymer was a coach owner, and set up a coach route linking Taradale and Napier via Meanee and Awatoto. A swamp and the inner harbour hampered access from Greenmeadows to Napier.[28] The building of Taradale Road in the early 1870s, linking Taradale, Greenmeadows and Napier, ensured that the area had a future.[29]

With the road complete and many of the urban sections sold, Taradale became a bustling area with its own social life and identity. By establishing its own organisations and economy, it maintained its separateness from nearby Napier. In 1867 its first artesian wells were dug and a post office and general store opened. Two years later Taradale's first hotel, the Duke of Edinburgh, opened its doors. A second hotel followed within three years. The first church in the area, the Roman Catholic church in Meanee, heard Mass from 1863. Within a few years the Presbyterians built a church and from the early 1870s Anglican services were held. All Saints Anglican church was consecrated in 1875. By 1888 Methodists were also holding services within their own church. As these developments took place, Henry Stokes Tiffen decided to sell more of his land. In December 1876 he held a sale at which men such as Richard Neagle and Robert Guppy bought land.[30] When the government conducted a return of freeholders in 1882, 93 people owned land in the area, including nine women.[31] Land sales and population grew in the 1880s. In 1884 the Meanee Mission offered 64 properties for sale, ranging from one acre to 21 acres.[32] Purchasers included the Murphy brothers, Thomas Peddie and Francis Collinge. The next year, Tiffen sold more Greenmeadows sections. Among the buyers were Mark Jarvis and the Reverend Charles Tuke.[33]

As more land was sold and families established themselves in the area, they called for greater control over their lives. Taradale wanted to be a self-governing area, a town district, controlled by elected town commissioners. In August 1886, Taradale's householders petitioned the Governor to proclaim the Taradale Ward of the Meanee Road District in Hawke's Bay a Town District. The petition, signed by 94 of the 113 households, was successful. On 2 December 1886, Taradale was gazetted as a Town District. By the end of the month the householders had elected their first town board commissioners, and at 6 p.m. on Thursday 30 December the duly elected commissioners met for the first time at the Mechanics' Institute in Taradale.[34]

In 1886 the Taradale area had about 1300 people in it. As in the New Zealand population as a whole, there were slightly more males than females. By the 1926 census, over 2800 people lived in the district. With the exception of a few Chinese market gardeners and a handful of Maori, Taradale was a white community of mainly British settlers and their descendants. The census showed only 17 Maori living in the Town District.[35] Most Maori lived at the nearby Waiohiki pa, to the south of Taradale. The people who lived in Taradale were not always 'settlers' in a literal sense of the word. Many people moved into the area, stayed a few years, and moved on again. They were as geographically mobile as those in other New Zealand areas at the time.[36] However, a core group of families, many of whom are named above, remained for generations and provided a stable centre for the area. Those who did move in were quickly incorporated into community life. It was not necessary to be a long-term resident to be considered part of this community.

Taradale was to remain a separate political entity for the next 80 years. This book does not cover all of that period. I decided to use two events to frame my study. The first is administrative: Taradale achieving town district status. The second is more traumatic: the earthquake that devastated Hawke's Bay in February 1931. Between these two dates I have used a variety of sources to reconstruct everyday life in the area. While birth, death and marriage records for over 4000 people formed the basis of my research, I was able to add to this with information from church records, school logs, newspapers, police and court records, friendly society material, electoral rolls, almanacs and street directories, probates, published and unpublished local histories, charitable aid requests, town board minutes, valuation rolls, and official publications. By the end of the research my database contained some information on over 9000 people.

Alongside these written sources I taped interviews with over 30 women and men who lived in the Taradale area before 1930. The earthquake that rocked the area in early 1931 was a very useful marker in the interviews. People in Hawke's Bay often divide their lives into before and after the earthquake. Many of my oral informants were born in the area; some never left it. The oral histories have been invaluable in providing information on matters not covered by the written sources, fleshing out the official records, and sometimes forcing me to question and re-examine the written orthodoxy. This is not to say that the oral accounts have been accepted uncritically. The tensions between oral and written accounts and the contradictions within and between individual oral testimonies needed to be carefully examined.

A major part of examining oral sources has to do with the gendered nature of oral history. As I mentioned in discussing William Cliff's story about the maypole, the content and form of oral accounts show much about the operation and meaning of gender in this community. It is not surprising that the women I interviewed had more to say, and seemed to know more about the lives of their sex, than the men did. Separate, gendered experiences gave rise to very different memories. But the forms of men and women's oral accounts are also gendered. By this I mean that the female and male narrators constructed themselves and their histories within a dominant gendered ideology. Implicitly, and sometimes explicitly, the stories they told and the themes they returned to were gendered. As will become clear in the following chapters, the women told stories about home and family, religion and community, and presented themselves as home-loving, law-abiding, religious and tolerant citizens. The men were much more likely to talk in long bursts. They saw themselves as the natural storytellers of the community, and tended to place themselves as the heroes of the tale. They were more forthcoming about crime and disorder, alcohol and fighting, than about chores around the house or familial relationships. Their past was full of adventure and bravado, a larrikin world where men were firmly in control.

I do not want to 'essentialise' women and men here.[37] There is no single female voice to be heard. But the voices of the women share a great deal in common, as do the voices of the men. What is interesting is the degree to which women's and men's texts seem to conform among themselves, despite sometimes quite disparate histories. Whether these women were home-loving or not, whether the men were personally involved in any bravado or not, this is the way they present their past. In this way memories and self-perceptions, and thus oral history, take a gendered form.

The end result of all of this is a microhistory, a local study that uses a sharp focus on particular details to examine wider questions about the past.[38] I am not trying to claim that gender relations in New Zealand between 1886 and 1930 were those of Taradale writ large. But the parameters of this book are not limited by events within Taradale. Whether looking at the relationship between gender and family ties (chapter 2), the household and local economy (chapters 3–5), or leisure (chapters 6–8), this book explores the different meanings and manifestations of femininities and masculinities. It is a contribution to the on-going project of understanding New Zealand's gendered past.

CHAPTER 2

Family and Community

In May 1866 Henry Alley began to sell off sections within what was to be Taradale township. One of the buyers attracted to this 'favourable opportunity for judicious speculation', as Alley put it in his advertisement, was Isaac Jeffares.[1] Isaac soon married Mary Jane Villers, and within a few years they had five children. Their daughter Charlotte married John Egan and gave birth to four children in Taradale; their son Charles married Eileen Higgins and they had two daughters; daughter Fanny married William Halpin and gave birth to nine children between 1904 and 1922; son Isaac junior married Jessie Taylor in 1910 and had two sons, while his brother Clarence married Rose Russell and fathered two boys. All these grandchildren were born in the Taradale area. Isaac and Mary Jane were surrounded by their children, grandchildren, and by other members of their extended family. Isaac's brothers Joseph, Richard, Robert, Thomas and William also moved to the Taradale area. William died young and single, and Richard's past is hard to discern from extant records, but Joseph, Robert and Thomas married in the area and added to the Jeffares clan. Thomas, for example, married Hannah Smith, and had nine children, several of whom went on to marry in Taradale and bring even more Jeffares into the area. At least one Jeffares was born in Taradale each year between 1886 and 1930. In most years several were added to the kin group.[2]

As part of his attack on the idea that nineteenth-century Pakeha society was organised around cohesive local communities, Miles

Fairburn has argued that it 'would be crass to assume' that examples like the Jeffares family 'are typical and that the organisation of any local area was based on the interweaving of its households through marriage and blood'.[3] Fairburn has a point. We cannot assume that all the inhabitants of Taradale were part of a complex web of family relationships. Yet the work of others who have studied familial ties within a particular area, such as Raewyn Dalziel's examination of kinship in 1840s New Plymouth, and Maureen Molloy's study of Waipu, 1854–1920, indicates that when family ties are studied in depth, the ties that bind were very strong indeed.[4] One of the aims of this chapter is to explore the extent of family ties in Taradale. Were the Jeffares atypical? Rather than uncritically assume the existence and importance of family ties, or deny them, we need to trace and quantify familial relationships.

However, this cannot be a detailed demographic chapter. The time frame of the study is not long enough to demonstrate major demographic shifts. The destruction of census manuscripts in New Zealand means that it is very difficult to reconstruct households and thus trace all the people in the area. Other sources such as street directories and electoral rolls are not much help either. Apart from the fact that they record only heads of households and enrolled voters, they do not give precise information on where people lived. Ironically, the street directories listed people as living in Taradale or Greenmeadows; no actual streets, let alone households, were noted. By 1928 the electoral rolls sometimes mentioned the street a voter lived in, but never the house number. It was still common for people's place of residence to be given as Meanee or Taradale.

Given these problems, this chapter is based on the birth, marriage and death records for the area. Between 1886 and 1930, 2200 children were either born in the Taradale area or had their births registered there; 587 couples – at least one of whom either usually or currently lived in the area – got married; and 773 people from the area died.[5] Rather than follow through the family ties of each of these 4000 plus individuals, I have traced the kinship patterns of those who were born, married or died in 1886, 1890, and then at five-yearly intervals until 1930. Amounting to just over a fifth of all births, a quarter of the marriages and a quarter of all adult deaths, this sample forms the basis for the following discussion, along with other sources, notably oral histories.[6] Even so, the lack of detailed information for each individual means that the figures I arrive at are conservative. Only when the information is complete enough do I claim that an individual's parents, siblings, spouse, offspring or other relations also lived locally.

In many cases a lack of information, rather than a lack of local kin, leads to an underestimation of the extent of family in the area.

Clearly the lack of census manuscripts hampers this type of family reconstitution work. Perhaps it explains why so few studies in New Zealand history offer detailed family analysis. But at least it means that we are not confined to studying snapshots of families on census night, nor do we fall into the trap of assuming that family ties were static between each census. While the Jeffares family had a strong hold in Taradale throughout the period, many other families drifted in and out of the area. The familial relationships of the geographically mobile, as well as the settlers, are covered in this chapter. The focus is not on the long-term picture of family, but on the extent and nature of family ties when a baby was born into the area, a couple married, or a person died.

The second aim of this chapter is to explore the meaning of family in the lives of Taradale's inhabitants. In the introduction I argued that family was the cornerstone of this community, but that people's understanding and experience of family was often gendered. Later chapters explore this idea through examining work and leisure. But for now, the focus is on the ways three quintessential family rituals – birth, marriage and death – brought men and women together, as well as their separate experiences of these moments, and the different meanings and memories held of them.

On 17 January 1886 Mary Ann Pritchard, the first Taradale baby of the year, was born. Her proud parents, Alfred and Elizabeth, celebrated the birth of their first child with Mary Ann's maternal great-grandmother, Ann Hammond, who registered her birth, and various members of Elizabeth's family. Elizabeth's parents, Henry and Eliza Harrison, lived in Taradale, as did her brothers Edward and Thomas and her sisters Mary, Jane, Ethel and Alice. Although Mary Ann had no paternal aunts or uncles, cousins or grandparents in the area, within a few years she had a dozen cousins to play with. She grew up in Taradale surrounded by family. Her parents soon had other children, ten in all. Mary Ann went on to marry in Taradale, tying the knot with Harry Edser in 1906. Her sister Alice married Harry's brother in 1910.

Assessing the quality of the relationships Mary Ann had with her nuclear and extended family is difficult. Establishing the quantity of those ties is easier. Like half of those born in Taradale between 1886 and 1930, Mary Ann was greeted by grandparents, aunts, uncles and cousins – that is, by immediate extended family who lived in the area.[7]

While some of these people may have lived in the same household, the analysis is based on extended family living in the same community. Some of the newborn also had other relatives (great aunts and uncles, second cousins, cousins once removed, and so on) in the area, but I have not attempted to untangle such genealogical knots here.

The overall figure of half the babies being born into local immediate extended families stayed fairly constant throughout the five-yearly sample group. There was not an absence of kin at the beginning, followed by a great increase by the 1920s.[8] When James Rundle was born in 1886, his birth was celebrated not just by his parents but also by both his grandfathers, John Rundle and George Lucas. His grandmothers were dead, but his maternal step-grandmother, Hannah Lucas, lived in the area. James's aunts, Emma and Mary Ann Rundle, also seem to have been living locally, since they both married in Taradale, in 1890 and 1896. His uncle, Henry Lucas, also married in the area, in 1897. James Rundle hardly experienced a dearth of kin ties. Neither did Noel Robert Tong, born in 1930. All his grandparents lived in the area at the time of his birth. His maternal uncle, Edward Howard, had recently married a local woman, Violet McCutcheon, and they had had two children.

These new Taradale residents were born into extended families on both the maternal and paternal sides. Overall, this was so for just over a third of those born into extended families. However, it was more likely that a child would be greeted by extended family on the mother's side than on the father's. The women of the area who gave birth had slightly stronger kinship ties within the locality than their husbands did, especially in the earlier period. Where extended family could be traced, then it could be found on the maternal side in three-quarters of the cases, and on the paternal side in two-thirds. Over time it became more likely that the father's kin could be traced, from six out of every ten births where kin was found for 1886–1905, to seven out of ten births for 1910–30.[9]

For Taradale's illegitimate babies, too, extended family was not unknown.[10] While some women came into the area only to have their child, and left soon after, others were locals who relied on their families at such times. When Edith Cattanach gave birth to her daughter Phoebe in January 1895, she turned to her mother, Phoebe senior, who was present at the birth and registered her new granddaughter. Three years before Edith had given birth to Annie; that birth was registered by her grandfather, John. Annie died a couple of months later, but Phoebe junior became part of the extended Cattanach family. There was uncle Charles, a storeman; uncle William, the blacksmith;

uncle John, the milkman; and aunts Agnes and Grace. Grace married soon after Phoebe's birth, and within a few years Phoebe had cousins to play with. There is no hint as to who fathered Annie or Phoebe, so it is impossible to say if the girls knew extended family on that side. In some cases, of course, the parents of an illegitimate child married after their baby was born. Ena Nelson's parents, Alfred Nelson and Lavinia Grinham, appear to have done so soon after Ena's birth in 1920. She was born at the McHardy Home in Napier, rather than Bethany, the Salvation Army Home on Napier hill, where many unmarried mothers went to have their children. Her birth was registered by both parents. Alfred and Lavinia were certainly married by the time of Ena's accidental death from burns in 1926.

No extended family can be traced for Ena; she may have had cousins or aunts in the area, but there is too little information to confirm this. For every Ena, however, there was a Phoebe. The figure of half of all newborns having local immediate extended family must be seen as conservative.

What did it mean to have family in the area? While it is much more difficult to understand the meaning of family in Mary Ann Pritchard's life than it is simply to trace her kin network, there are various ways of seeing how extended family came to the fore when a new baby was born. One of the most obvious ways in which family helped out was by being present at the birth, as Phoebe's grandmother was. We cannot know exactly how many of the local births were assisted by family. What is clear is that most births took place either in the mother's home or in a small, unlicensed home run by a local maternity nurse. By the 1920s more of the births were taking place in McHardy or Bethany, but a significant number were still 'home' births, often attended by local midwives, such as Nurse Wallace.[11] Even as the move to hospitalised care was taking place, the evidence suggests that female kin were still heavily involved in helping with both birthing and post-natal care.

The birth records give no indication that male kin were present at the births, but oral narrators occasionally mentioned how their mother was 'caught short' and gave birth at home with only her husband to help. This was to be avoided if at all possible. Women wanted their mothers, sisters or aunts around them, and in many cases their wish was granted. The shared experience of becoming a parent was not to be confused with the gender-specific event of giving birth. Not only was birth often a separate, female experience; the ways birth was recalled also reflect gendered histories. Women retained stories about birth, including their own, in a way that men did not. Women were

FAMILY AND COMMUNITY

more likely to have asked their mothers about their own births and remembered the response than men were.

Men were reluctant to remember or talk about birth; it was a feminine process, not a part of their masculine worlds. When Matthew Silk was asked 'Can you remember what would happen when [your mother] was pregnant and about to give birth? Would someone come and look after you?' he paused before replying:

> Um, oh well, it was usually one of her sisters, I think, you know. She had one, two, three or four sisters, you see, so it could have been one of those there. And there was a Nurse Wallace, she'd be around a lot too, that was one of the old midwifery nurses. But oh, I don't remember just so much about that.[12]

His sister, Emily Jones, on the other hand, brought up the subject when family in general was being discussed:

> . . . It was a close knit family, very much so, really. And of course when Mum was at the home with all us kids it was the sisters that came to light and helped out with the younger ones, Mum's sisters.[13]

She was certain that her mother's younger sisters, Dolly and Mary, were the ones who helped.

Other women could also say who helped their mothers when they were about to give birth. Alice Parke knew that her paternal grandmother, a maternity nurse in Dunedin, had come up for her birth. Ann Pearce recalled that her maternal grandmother had looked after her as a baby, after her mother had a very difficult labour, while Grace Miner said her maternal grandmother brought her into the world. Like Theresa Pond, quoted below, these women retained memories of childbirth and freely discussed them:

> *Would they [family] come and help out in times of need?*
> Oh yes. Grandma, Dad's mother, came and helped, kept house once or twice when Mum was having one of the children or something like that. When Mum was in the home once she came and kept house.
> *When your mother had David and William, did she have them at home?*
> She had David at home and I helped there. Not with the delivery but I had to help Dad. My auntie came down, Mrs Sarah Rogers, she was my Dad's sister, and she used to help. In those days auntie used to come down and David was born in the daytime.
> *Did your auntie deliver the baby?*

No auntie didn't deliver the baby. They had a nurse there, a paid nurse. I can't think of her name now. We did have Nurse Wallace and Jones, Mrs Jones. She lived by us, in Peddie Street, next door in fact. She was a midwife. But Florence was born at home and they didn't have a doctor. It was a terrible night and there was no phones then and it was a bad night so Mum said to the Nurse, 'Oh well'. Course I don't remember that . . .[14]

Theresa may not have remembered that – after all, her sister Florence was only a year younger than her. But she recalled the story 75 years later. No male narrator did the same.

Even preparing for birth was feminised. Theresa Pond recalled how she and her sister Florence were allowed to help their mother prepare for the impending birth of their brother. They herringbone stitched around his flannel nappies. But when their male cousin came to visit, and Florence showed him what they were doing, their mother 'nearly had a fit'.[15] There were certain things that males were not to be involved in. Caring for the new mother and her babe also fell to female kin, regardless of which side of the family they were from. Even in old age, these men did not see birth as something a real bloke talked about.

Oral evidence also suggests that family ties drew women back to the area to have their children. All of Martha Edwards's grandparents lived locally, but for a period of her early childhood Martha's nuclear family lived in Mokotuku, in Hawke's Bay. When it came time for Martha's mother to have her babies, she returned to her mother: 'We used to go home, go down, come down when we were in Mokotuku, come down to Granny's when Mum had another baby.'[16] After a few years the family returned to the Taradale area, where Martha still lives.

The actual birth remained a female experience throughout the period. Even when women went into a male-owned hospital to have their baby, they relied on their female support networks to look after their other children, or to help them when they returned home. Other practicalities, though, crossed gender boundaries. Men were more likely to register the baby's birth than women. Indeed, it became increasingly common for the new father to do this. Every so often a maternal grandfather or older brother would also make his new relation official. Yet it was more common for a female relation from either side of the family, such as Mary Ann's great grandmother or Phoebe's grandmother, to act on behalf of the parents, than it was for male kin to do so.[17]

Registering the birth could just have coincided with a visit to town, but the name of the child lived with it forever. When it came to naming the newborn, the importance of family is clear (as Molloy found in Waipu).[18] Throughout the period it was common for children's first names to be the names of their parents and grandparents. There was also a trend for children's middle names to be identifiable family names. This was especially so for boys. In the late nineteenth century many boys, such as Hugh Radford Gray, born in 1894, and Charles Villers Jeffares, born in 1895, were given their mother's original surname as their middle name. In a few families this applied to both boys and girls. In the Lowe family, George, born in 1893, and his older sisters, Catherine, born in 1887, and Mabel, born in 1890, were all given their mother's maiden surname of Wakeling as their middle name. But there was also a growing trend to use the father's middle name, which was usually *his* mother's maiden name, as the newborn's middle name. When local clergyman Alfred Pickering Clarke and his wife Blanche named their sons, Alfred's familial middle name was chosen as the middle name for them all: Eric Pickering Clarke (1896), Keith Pickering Clarke (1899), and Leathley Pickering Clarke (1900). The Clarkes were a middle-class family, but Charles Villers Jeffares's father was a carpenter. From 1910 onwards it was almost as common for middle names to be from the paternal as the maternal side of the family, for both boys and girls. Dorothy and Joan Wood, born in 1908 and 1911, shared their father's middle name of Razell, as did their brother John, born in 1915. Duncan Le Quesne Badley had it both ways: born in 1922, he took his first name from his mother's maiden surname and had the same middle name as his father.[19]

Illegitimate children were also often named after family members, as Phoebe Cattanach was. But not all families were as understanding as the Cattanachs. In such a close-knit society it was difficult to hide illicit sexual activity. Gossip, or the fear of gossip, often acted as an effective means of social and sexual control. For those who defied the gossips, the consequences varied, partly according to the degree to which the family's life was disrupted. If the woman got pregnant but a wedding could be arranged in time, then little shame seems to have hung in the air.[20] From 1913 it is possible to determine from birth certificates whether a child was the first born to its parents. Since the date of their marriage was also noted, it is easy to see how many of Taradale's newborn were the result of pre-nuptial conceptions. Overall, a quarter were conceived before their parents had sworn to love, honour and obey.[21] While some of these marriages were no doubt hastily arranged shot-gun weddings, others were probably between already betrothed people who viewed sexual activity as permissible once their engagement had been announced.

It was when young women became pregnant and carried the child to term without the promise of marriage, or the possibility of securing a wedding, that the sexual double standard came to the fore. For these women, life in Taradale could be very unpleasant.[22] Several recalled girls who mysteriously left the district, often returning after several months away. Some were sent to relations in other places, others were said to have gone to Australia. All came back alone. At times the whole family would permanently leave the area.

Only one person talked about illegitimacy in her family. Kathleen Thomson's sister had an illegitimate child in the 1920s. When she was found to be pregnant she was sent to Bethany until her child was born. Kathleen and her mother visited her regularly:

> *How long would they go into the Home for?*
> Well as soon as they'd find out. Straight away because it was a shame for a young girl to go around big and to hide it. Some people used to send their children right away. But she was put in the Salvation Army and my God they made them work too. Betty, that's the one, the second one, next to me, it was her and we went up there one day to see her and there she was, cleaning the stove.
> *They used to do a lot of laundry work, didn't they?*
> Laundry work. Scrubbing, everything was scrubbed and had to be as white as snow. They were, they had to work hard because there was a girl from the Puketapu Hotel up there, a girl Murphy, her father had the hotel and she was up there with Betty and she was never used to work. She soon did. And my sister, she was doing the stove when she was in labour. She had a little girl, dear little soul she was too.
> *And your mother brought her up?*
> And mother brought her up, yes. They didn't adopt her but they brought her up and she's up in Auckland with her mother, her mother's up there, Betty . . . We sort of had to keep up a sort of a reputation, I don't know what it was. If there was a disgrace, God it was disgrace. I know when Betty fell we were very distressed about it but we got over it. As Dad and Mum said, well the only thing is to stick by her and that's what we did. We don't turn our back on one another . . .[23]

Few of Taradale's illegitimate children were officially adopted. There is no indication in the birth registrations of any illegitimate children being adopted out before 1913, and only eight cases of adoption were recorded between 1913 and 1930, five of them in the 1920s.[24] Before then, if the children continued to live in the area they tended to be brought up by their mother's relations, as Kathleen Thomson's mother did for her illegitimate grandchild. When Rose Boland gave birth to Gladys Lilian Boland in 1905, she did not name the father. Gladys's grandmother, Margaret Boland, registered the birth. When Gladys married Arthur Lord in 1925, she named her grandmother and her late grandfather, James Boland, as her parents. They had brought her up along with their own children, James (who also married in Taradale in 1925), Johanna and Eliza. Gladys was part of the community; she married into a long-established and well-known family, and over the next five years gave birth to three daughters and one son in Taradale. Being illegitimate did not necessarily exclude you from your family or the community.

When it came to talking about weddings, it also tended to be the women who had tales to tell. The shared experience of getting married seems to have resulted in gendered memories. One of the few men who had anything to say about his own wedding was Henry Nolan, and then it was a very dismissive: 'Things were different in them days. Things wasn't as elaborate as what they are today, you know. We got married and we come home. We come home to boxes. Never had the money to go away then. Nobody much did.'[25] Although Henry and the other men interviewed had little to say about the actual wedding, none of them expressed any doubts about getting married. Yet while the women recounted far more details about their weddings than the men, they also expressed hesitation about getting married. Marriage meant hard work, and spoilt the fun and freedom of single life.[26] Women seem to have enjoyed the romance of courtship and the leisure opportunities it offered. Bridget Tweed recalled all the shows she used to see while she was courting: 'and we then got engaged and I wasn't very keen, no, because we were enjoying ourselves and I knew then that they'd bought this place up at Eskdale, Waipunga'.[27] Foreseeing the work she would have to do at the new home, and the loss of her leisure time, Bridget was understandably not keen to marry just yet. Hannah Field also felt pressured into marriage: 'I'd sometimes think I couldn't get rid of him, you know. But anyhow that's how we ended up. [At first] I just took him as a matter of course, you know.'[28]

Hannah's hesitation was soon replaced by concerns about the big day. Like the other female narrators who married before 1930, she was very clear on the preparations for her wedding. Who made the dress was an important memory for most of these women. Again, female kin played a large part in this family ritual. Louisa Plumb's mother made her dress and catered for the wedding breakfast. Charlotte Rose turned to her sister to make her dress, and Grace Miner's sister-in-law was her dressmaker. Although Kathleen Thomson employed a professional dressmaker to make up the satin she had bought, her sister made her veil. Hannah Field's mother-in-law made her dress, an experience that was not without tension. Her fiancé's mother was a strict Presbyterian:

> I was sort of scared of her I think, really. To me she was always narrow minded, but we got on all right. Actually she ended up making the wedding dress for me. She was a lovely sewer, she had three sisters, they were all lovely sewers. But when I was getting it, trying it on she said to me, 'You're not pregnant, are you?' I said, 'No'. I wondered what she was talking about.[29]

Why do the male narrators not have any similar stories to tell? It could be that they have forgotten such events, or chose not to recount them. Perhaps they were never as involved in the organisation of their wedding as their bride-to-be. Yet men and their kin were also involved in planning the big day. Marriage records provide more opportunity than birth records to ascertain local kin ties, since both the bride's and groom's parents' names are recorded on the marriage certificate.

Where the immediate extended family of both bride and groom was traced – their parents, siblings, siblings' partners and children – then in the vast majority of cases, at least one side of the bridal party had kin living in the Taradale area at the time of their wedding.[30] Of the 150 marriages studied, some extended family of the newly created nuclear family was found in four out of every five weddings. Only in 1886 was kin not traced in half of the weddings. Again, it must be remembered that these figures underestimate familial ties. The parents of both parties could be searched for, but the siblings of the bride and groom are underestimated: only if they were born, married or died in the area was their parentage recorded. Nor have aunts, uncles and cousins been searched for. Even so, the evidence suggests that kinlessness was by no means the norm among those who married in the Taradale area, regardless of how long they lived locally, either before or after their wedding. As with the statistics on kinship and birth, the evidence on kin ties and marriage shows a consistent pattern rather than a changing one. Three-quarters of the couples who married 1886–1905 had some extended family in the area, and four out of every five who married 1910–30 had kin living locally. So there was not a great increase in the extent of kin over time.

On 26 November 1890 David Hastie and Eliza Howard were married by the Reverend Tuke at All Saints Anglican Church, Taradale.

Their marriage was typical in that both of Eliza's parents lived in the area, as did several of her siblings, some of whom also married locally, whereas none of David's extended family could be traced. As for births, the marriage data indicates that the brides had more kin living locally than their grooms did. If local kin were found for only one side of the bridal party, as was the case in over half the weddings studied, then it was over twice as likely that they would be the bride's relations. The number of marriages where kin on both sides could be traced did increase slightly over time, but the grooms never came close to having as many local kin as their brides had.[31]

Eliza Howard may have had kin in the area, but we cannot assume that they were part of her life. Again, we have to look for evidence of active kin relationships. One way to do this for weddings is to see who the official witnesses were. At Eliza and David's wedding, Eliza's father, Henry, and her teacher sister, Marion, signed the register. The Hastie–Howard wedding was typical in this respect. Not only was it more likely for the bride to have kin in the area, it was also more common for her kin to act as witnesses. In only a quarter of all marriages could no kin be positively identified among the witnesses who signed the marriage certificate.[32] Parents, brothers, sisters, aunts, uncles and cousins all witnessed their kinfolk's marriages. In almost two-thirds of the weddings where kin can be identified among the wedding witnesses, that kin was on the bride's side alone. Only in a very small number of cases could the groom's kin only be identified. In about one in five weddings, kin from both sides of the bridal party were witnesses. So overall, the groom's kin acted as witnesses in about a third of the weddings, while the bride's did so in over four out of five.[33]

Eliza called on both her male and female kin to act as her witnesses. While there was a slight tendency for brides to call on their female kin to act as witnesses between 1886 and 1890, overall brides were as likely to have male as female family members sign the register. However, grooms tended to call on their male kin, and this tendency increased over time. When Fred James and Josephine Johnson married in 1924, Fred's brother Lawrence acted as his witness. Lawrence also witnessed his brother William's marriage to Josephine's sister, Marjorie, the next year.[34] (The practice of siblings in one family marrying siblings in another was not as common in Taradale as in Waipu, but it did occur.)[35]

Over time, men increasingly acted as official witnesses at their kinfolk's marriages, and also had their kin to witness at their own weddings. Even if their family was not local, the likelihood was growing that they would travel to attend the wedding. About one in five witnesses at Taradale's weddings did not live in either Taradale or Napier. The figure was slightly smaller at the beginning of the period, no doubt because of poorer means of communication in the nineteenth century. Half of those out-of-town witnesses can be positively identified as members of either the bride's or the groom's extended family.

Two patterns are discernible from examining this group of people. First, two-thirds of the out-of-town kin were male. This reflects a variety of factors, such as higher transience rates among single men and larger male incomes allowing for more travel. But it also indicates that even when distance separated kin, men did not forget, and were not forgotten by, their family. Men travelled the length and breadth of New Zealand, and in a couple of cases across the Tasman, to witness their sister's, brother's or cousin's wedding.

The second emerging pattern is that at the beginning of the period, it was more likely for the bride's relations to travel to her wedding and be official witnesses. But after 1910, it was more common for the out-of-town witness to be the groom's kin, and to be male.[36] More men were calling on and responding to their extended families. In May 1916 Norman Fussell and Elsie Harvey were married at All Saints, Taradale. Elsie's sister, Isabel Rymer, and her brother, a clerk in Taradale, acted as witnesses, along with Lieutenant F. N. Fussell, from Palmerston North.

Another indication that kinship was an active social relationship can be seen by looking at the family ties of those people who married in the area, but never themselves lived locally. The fact that they chose to marry in Taradale seems to have had a lot to do with the presence of their extended families. Among these cases it was three times as likely that the bride had kin in Taradale than the groom. No doubt this related to the tradition of the bride's parents putting on the wedding. Even if women like Cecily Hindmarsh, who married Vivian Walter Cox in 1920, did not continue to live among their extended family once married, family ties and obligations were important enough to determine *where* they got married. Vivian had no traceable family in the area, but Cecily's parents, John and Charlotte Hindmarsh, were both locals, as were her sister, Nora, who had recently married Arthur Heale, and her brother, Adrian.[37]

So it seems that the oral recollections of weddings that began this section are deceptive. While women talked more freely about marriage and the rituals surrounding it, we cannot assume from this that men were not involved in planning their big day. What they wore may not have preoccupied them in the same way, but having their family present and involved in the ceremony was important both to them and to their kin.

For the very young, the first year of life was precarious, especially in the nineteenth century. Like other babies around New Zealand, about one in ten of Taradale's newborn in the 1880s and 1890s did not live to see their first birthday. That figure had halved by the 1920s.[38] This dramatic decline in infant mortality preceded the impact of Plunket in Taradale: the local Plunket rooms were not opened until after 1930. From 1919 a Plunket nurse did visit the area each week, but many mothers did not subscribe to Truby King's ideology.[39] Charlotte Rose took her baby to the Plunket nurse in the 1920s only because she was visiting her sister-in-law, who was a Plunket mother. As Charlotte told it:

> When she [the Plunket nurse] saw Peggy . . . she made such a fuss of Peggy. She said, 'Oh, what a beautiful baby.' And then she said, 'I suppose you're very strict with her feeding.' And when I said 'Glaxo' she almost dropped Peggy on the floor. Handed her back to me and nothing more was ever said. They hated Glaxo, they liked their own mixture you see.[40]

While Plunket was gaining wider local acceptance by the 1920s, the figures on child mortality clearly indicate that as, Philippa Mein Smith has argued, Truby King cannot take the credit for the decrease in child deaths before then.[41] Obviously this decline in the rate of infant mortality had an impact on family life.

Although infancy became less precarious over time, illegitimate babies in Taradale, as elsewhere in New Zealand, continued to experience a higher than average infant mortality rate.[42] Many of both the legitimate and the illegitimate young children who died were victims of summer diarrhoea, a complaint that declined as drainage and sewerage improved. In the 1880s half of the babies who died did so as a result of summer diarrhoea and related illnesses. None of the infant deaths in the 1920s were attributed to this cause.[43] But among the illegitimate children who died, other causes took their toll. One such child died in 1899 due to hereditary syphilis; another died at ten weeks of suffocation in 1902, the result of being 'accidentally overlaid'. That certainly could have been a case of infanticide, yet no police action was taken. However, in 1920 an illegitimate child was asphyxiated due to being left in the pan of the earth closet. The mother was 26-year-old dairymaid Phoebe Cattanach, mentioned above, herself illegitimate. After an inquest, she appeared in court and was charged with the murder of her new-born son. She was committed for a Supreme Court trial, where the Grand Jury unanimously decided to reduce the charge to manslaughter. Although acquitted on the manslaughter charge, she was found guilty of concealment of birth, and sentenced to three months in the Napier gaol.[44] The judge was reported to have uttered an unfortunately worded comment: 'it was his intention to impress upon her, and upon all women that the law regarding the concealment of the birth of children was not a dead letter'.[45] Even so, the unanimous decision to reduce the charge from murder to manslaughter, and her acquittal on that charge, indicates a degree of public tolerance and understanding for the plight of women like Phoebe.

For those who died under the age of 21, it is very difficult to ascertain familial relationships in the area. They were too young to be on the electoral roll, unlikely to have started their own family, and less likely to have siblings who had married and had children. For these reasons, the following discussion focuses on only 125 of the 530 adults who died in the area.[46] When their spouses, children, grandchildren, parents, siblings, and siblings' offspring were searched for, in the majority of cases the deceased person turned out to be not a kinless atom, but a member of either a nuclear or an extended family. In fact it was more likely that the person left behind a grieving extended family than just a nuclear one.[47] There was a slight increase over time in the proportion who left kin behind. But overall, three out of four of those who died in the Taradale area between 1886 and 1930 left local kin behind them.

Charlotte Hatton's death, in February 1890, was fairly typical. Charlotte had been married to Arthur, a local butcher, for ten years, but they had no children. They had married in England, just before joining Charlotte's parents, Edwin and Mary Jane Pointon, in the migration to New Zealand. Mary Jane had died in Taradale in 1888, but Edwin, who was also a butcher, continued to live in the area until his death in 1925. Charlotte also had three brothers living locally, two of whom had married. So Charlotte left behind both nuclear and extended family. This was more common among the women of the area who died. For the early period, 1886–1905, just over a quarter of the women and men who died left only nuclear family, whereas almost half left both nuclear and extended family. However, this was more likely for women than for men.[48]

By the second half of the period, 1910–30, the proportion of those dying who left some kin increased only slightly. A third of women and men left only nuclear families; the proportion leaving both nuclear and extended families was the same as in the earlier period. The consistency of the data does mask a degree of change. Slightly fewer women were leaving both nuclear and extended families, while the men were more likely to be leaving kin than in the earlier period.[49] Women still had more locally living kin than men, but the differences between men and women in extent of local family ties were decreasing.

Within the five-yearly sample, only two single adult women died in the area. This makes it difficult to come to any conclusions about the effect of women's marital status on their kin ties. However, a third of the adult men who died in the area were unmarried, and they were far more likely not to have any known kin living in Taradale than any other group. In only a third of the cases could some local kin be traced for the single men who died.[50] Married men and married women left kin in over four out of five cases, with married women being more likely to leave both nuclear and extended family members than married men. Marital status clearly played a part, as well as gender, in the extent to which the deceased had family living locally.

As in birth and marriage, so in death; even from beyond the grave, family ties continued to determine people's actions. The wills of people who died in the area indicate not only the extent of local kin connections, but also the importance placed on them by the deceased. Most of these wills were written less than five years before the testator's death, so it seems safe to assume that they reflected the current attitudes of the deceased. The wills reveal that almost three quarters of their beneficiaries lived solely in the Taradale area. In four out of every five wills, only members of the nuclear family were beneficiaries of the deceased's estate.[51] It was in fact more likely that a man who died in the area would leave his estate to his family than that a woman would do so. In nine out of ten male wills, nuclear and extended family inherited all the man's estate, whereas this was true for just three-quarters of female wills. At the beginning of the period women left everything to their nuclear family. But as time moved on they tended to leave some of their property to non-family members too, such as friends or clergymen.[52]

On 26 March 1894 Francis Collinge, a farmer, signed his last will and testament leaving everything to his immediate family, who lived locally. Within a month Francis was dead. While this family commitment in men's wills remained strong throughout the period, there were changes in the married men's wills. Men continued to leave their estates to their families, but placed different conditions on the administration of their property. Between 1886 and 1930 few men left their estates to their widows absolutely; that is, few men allowed their spouses to do as they wished with their property. But the proportion who did so increased over time. More men left their widows in complete control of their estates, and fewer left their property to their wives only as long as those wives remained widows. The proviso that the widow enjoyed the estate only while she was alive, that is, she acted as a trustee of the property for the couple's children rather than as an independent owner, also decreased, as did the number of cases where the widow had to share the property with her children.[53] Although Francis Collinge had left his estate to his nuclear family, he left his property to his wife Ann only 'for the time of her widowhood'. If Ann remarried, 'all my property shall go to my children'.[54] By the 1920s it was more common for men to leave everything to their wives, as Patrick O'Reilly did on his death in 1925. Patrick left his estate of over £3000 to 'my dear wife Ellen Margaret O'Reilly for her own use absolutely'.[55]

Among women, the few extant wills from the nineteenth century all leave the entire estate to their nuclear family. In her 1896 will, administered on her death in September 1897, Annie Goddard left everything to her 'beloved husband Charles Goddard, absolutely'.[56] By the twentieth century women were also leaving money and property to non-family members. Mary Neagle, a widow who died in 1928, left most of her £3000 estate to her children, but set aside £30 for the local Roman Catholic priest to say 'masses for my soul'.[57] In most cases, though, women continued to leave everything to their family.

The strength of kin ties, even if the family did not live locally, can also be seen in the Taradale wills. Most beneficiaries were local kin; yet about a quarter of all wills included non-local people among the beneficiaries, most of them family members. George Condie, an unmarried sheep farmer, left most of his estate to his brother David, who also lived in Taradale. But he also left £400 to his brother Thomas, who lived in Maraekakaho, in Hawke's Bay, and £600 to his two sisters, Annie and Margaret, who lived in Kinross Shire, in Scotland.[58]

George Condie never married, yet like the majority of those who were born, married or died in Taradale between 1886 and 1930, he had family in the area, and those familial ties meant something to him. In Condie's case they dictated to whom he left his estate. Condie died in 1890, at the tail end of the period Miles Fairburn has characterised as a time of atomisation in Pakeha society. Fairburn's argument that the process of immigration led to a dearth of kinship ties in nineteenth-century New Zealand, and thus an absence of community, does not hold for nineteenth-century Taradale, just as it does not hold for New Plymouth or Waipu.[59] The majority of people who were born, married or died in the Taradale area did not do so as kinless atoms. This held true for the twentieth century too. No great increase in the extent of familial ties took place in Taradale as the nineteenth century gave way to the twentieth. The majority of the new-born, newly wed and dead were members of local, extended families throughout the period of this study.

I have spent some time establishing the extent of kinship ties in Taradale because numbers do matter. To argue that kin was the cornerstone of this community requires solid evidence. But quantitative evidence is not enough. How these familial ties were made to matter is also important. The rituals of births, marriages and deaths reveal how such ties played out in Taradale. The new-born were named after family members; siblings, cousins and parents acted as witnesses at local weddings, even if they had to travel to do so; most of the deceased left their estates to locally residing kin. These qualitative examples should be read as the first installment of the evidence that family ties mattered in Taradale. Later chapters explore many other ways in which these ties bound people together.

The rituals of birth, marriage and death brought women and men together. In some respects they were gender-neutral. While the women of the area had slightly more kin in the district than the men, both men and women were involved in these family moments. Yet this is not to say that their experiences or memories were the same. As Joan Scott argues, gender is in part 'constructed through kinship'.[60] In Taradale, women family members made the wedding dresses and cooked the bridal breakfasts. They sewed the baby's layette, assisted at the birth and looked after the new mother. They also laid out the dead. These were feminine tasks, ways in which the women and girls of the area reiterated their femininity. Years later, the women I interviewed were still part of this gendered culture. They, rather than the men, had stories to tell about these family rituals, even if sometimes they were painful or ambiguous memories.

But it would be shortsighted to argue that familial rituals were solely feminine. Kinship in Taradale was not 'largely the domain of women', as Claire Toynbee has argued for this period.[61] The male narrators may not have recalled stories of weddings or births, but they never questioned the desire to marry and establish their own families. Perhaps they were taking the lead from their fathers. While the early twentieth century did not see a great increase in kin ties within Taradale, men's understanding of their obligations to their families underwent some changes. New fathers were more likely to register their child's birth and be more involved in naming the baby; grooms were asking their brothers and male cousins to be witnesses at their weddings; husbands were entrusting their estates to their wives. A new type of family man was emerging, an involved father, who took an interest in the day-to-day affairs of the family. This was Taradale's version of masculine domesticity: a husband and father who was more involved with his family, but within certain boundaries.[62] He cared about who the witnesses at his wedding were, but did not recall who made his wife's dress. This concept of masculine domesticity helps to explain some of the tension between the written sources and men's recollections. When asked about family rituals, the men I interviewed presented a uniformly masculine picture. Births and marriages, especially, were women's business, and men were not supposed to recall details about them. Yet other evidence points to increasing male involvement in familial rituals. The gendered boundary moved a little, but only a little. Any movement, though, had repercussions for men's and women's lives.

This chapter has focused on kin relationships as they were experienced in birth, marriage and death – the family-centred rituals par excellence. Clearly not everyone in Taradale married, gave birth or died between 1886 and 1930. However, these were not the only occasions when kin were called upon, nor were they the only times that Taradale's gendered boundaries were challenged. The next two sections of this book continue to explore the role of the family, and the ways in which femininities and masculinities were negotiated, by focusing on the household economy and leisure.

CHAPTER 3

The Household and Local Economy

Margaret and Thomas, the parents of Grace Miner and Patrick Stevenson, married in Taradale in 1893. Thomas described himself as a gardener and storeman; Margaret gave her occupation on the marriage certificate as 'domestic duties'. Within a year the first of their children was born, a son who was to die in the Great War. A couple of years later son Tom was born. He grew up to be a carpenter, and on his marriage his parents gave him some of their land, so that he and his family lived next door. After Tom came John, but pneumonia killed him when he was ten months old. Margaret and Thomas's first daughter was born in 1900. Like Tom, she married in the area. Her younger sister Delcie died soon after her first birthday, but within a couple of years Margaret had another son, then gave birth to Grace in 1905. Four years later she completed her family with the birth of Patrick.

By the time Patrick was born his parents were well established economically. They owned just over four acres of land, where they had built a home and work buildings. They soon purchased another acre.[1] At times they also rented land to graze their cows on, besides making full use of the 'long paddock' – the grass verge along the side of the road. Letting cows graze there was a breach of the by-law, and Thomas had been convicted and fined for this back in the 1890s. But old habits died hard, and the family kept on doing it throughout Grace and Patrick's childhoods. Both children were in charge of minding the cows on the long paddock, although Grace often became too engrossed in her knitting, and then had to tear about, rounding up the straying animals.

The Stevenson household gives interesting insights into how people made a living in Taradale. For many years Thomas worked as a storeman in Port Ahuriri, some miles from home. He would cycle to work each day, leaving behind his wife and growing family. Like most of the married women in Taradale, and in New Zealand, Margaret was never in paid employment after she married, but this does not mean that she did not work. Apart from raising the children and doing the cooking, cleaning, mending, washing and preserving, she also played a vital role in the household's productive economy. She was the one who milked the cows each day, separated the milk so that the children could take the surplus milk and cream to her customers, and churned the butter. With the children's help she fed the fowls and ducks, and sold eggs and non-laying fowls. For many years Margaret and Thomas entered their fowls and ducks at local shows, but as Patrick put it:

> They showed their poultry for so long we had, my mother and father had, just about every breed of fowl at one time that you could get and quite a lot of breeds of ducks. But by the time I got old enough to take any notice of them they had more or less finished showing them and reverted to more or less the eggs. More money in eggs than there was in showing poultry, because you got sweet Fanny Adams for showing them out there. I still can remember the number of cards for first prize or second prize that you got at the show, a thick bundle tied around with string, all the different prizes that Pop had had and my mother. She always, nearly always took the prize for dressed poultry out there as well but the show in those days, well, that was a real event in their lives.[2]

Although competing in the show did not earn them anything, in other respects the show grounds were lucrative for this family. Thomas had a sideline selling show schedules – booklets listing all the events and competitions. He also sold race books at the local course. When Patrick was underemployed in the late 1920s, his father said 'You can come out with me and sell race books and pay for your keep.'[3] So he did.

Everyone in the Stevenson household contributed to the family economy. All the children had chores to do around the home, many of which helped to bring in cash. They shelled the maize for the fowls and ducks, fed the pig with scraps and skim milk, delivered the surplus produce to neighbouring customers, and helped in the extensive vegetable garden their father had created. First there were the tomatoes:

> He [father] bought a section next door that had a glasshouse of tomatoes, he bought that from the man that lived in there and we had to water those every day, either two or three minutes each row. I don't know whether it might have been five minutes each row that had to be watered. And we all got a turn at that. That was a chore.[4]

Then there were melons:

> . . . my father used to grow rockmelons and watermelons in the section next door to us, he bought it off an old chap and he would try to get those plants going early and he'd have half a benzine tin or kerosene tin, cut in half and a sheet of glass, we also had a big glass house but these melons, you put that glass on as soon as the evening started to get cool and you had to go round hundreds of them, not dozens, hundreds of them and take that off if it was a nice day the next day. If it was cold, a southerly or something like that, they were left on but normally they went on in the evening and came off in the morning.[5]

In their spare time the boys would go fishing and hunting, providing flounder or duck for dinner. Once they were old enough to leave school and earn a living, they were expected to hand their wages over to their mother, and she gave them spending money. It was not until they married and left home that they could break free from the household economy. Even then, Tom and his family lived on the adjoining property, and still lent a hand when required. In return, his mother provided him with milk, cream and butter. The household economy spilled over the fence.

This chapter is about how the people of Taradale worked for their living. Little has been written about the economies of specific historical communities in New Zealand. The men, women and children in Claire Toynbee's study of work came from different areas. Erik Olssen's work on Caversham offers valuable insights into the lives of skilled urban workers, but such a community had little in common with semi-rural Taradale. Perhaps Rollo Arnold's study of Kaponga, a dairying town in Taranaki, comes closest to Taradale's experiences. But Arnold has little to say about the household economies in Kaponga. Instead he focuses on the public economy, especially the development of dairying in the area.[6]

The focus here is different. Understanding the economy of Taradale means understanding how households and families worked together to survive. Some prospered. There were a few large landowners in the area, and some people ran profitable businesses employing many.

Others failed miserably. Through bad luck, bad management, or both, some ended up living on Friendly Society sick pay entitlements, charitable aid, or the proceeds of crime. But most, like the Stevenson family, made do by hard work and seizing opportunities as they came up. Whether you were male or female played some part in the work you did, and the next two chapters examine women's and men's gendered experience of work. But here the spotlight is on the familial and local economy everyone worked within, and the ways they worked together.

Although the men of the area often saw themselves, and were seen by others, as the head of their household, there was more mutuality in men's and women's work than has often been acknowledged. Recognition of this mutuality has been clouded by two ideologies, present both at the time and in subsequent historical accounts. First, as Wally Seccombe has argued, by the time of the Great War an ideology of the male breadwinner wage had developed in the western world. This was the idea that a man should earn enough to support himself, his wife and his children.[7] Yet most men in Taradale throughout the period of this study did not earn enough money to do this. They relied on the labour of their wives and children. All members of the household contributed to its financial well-being. Nevertheless, the *ideal* of the male breadwinner economy held sway. Men's work was assumed to be more important and valuable than women's work or children's work. The tensions between the perceptions of men's primary economic contribution and the reality of the familial economy need to be kept in mind as we look at the area's economy.

The second ideology that has helped to hide the degree of mutuality in men's and women's work is the concept of women as men's helpmeets. This idea gained currency within the New Zealand literature on work with the publication of Raewyn Dalziel's article, 'The Colonial Helpmeet'. Dalziel's argument is that women's domestic work and contribution to the household economy was acknowledged in nineteenth-century New Zealand. She argues that women gained the vote in large part as a reward for their domestic role.[8] To some extent the idea of women as men's helpmeets is consistent with the idea of mutuality: she helped him with his work. But the idea and ideal of the female helpmeet ignores the other working relationships women were enmeshed in. Although few married women in Taradale were in paid employment, the women of the area worked hard, as wives, mothers, daughters, sisters, nieces, friends and neighbours. They were involved in many households' economies. The same was true of the men of the area. Moreover, men sometimes helped out the women in their lives –

their mothers, wives, sisters or neighbours. Both the male breadwinner wage ideal and the female helpmeet idea help to explain why women's work was regarded as less valuable than men's work, and why men were assumed to be the head of the household. Yet as the Stevenson family and many other such families reveal, survival depended on the labour of all the household members.

The official picture of the area's economy had little to do with household and familial economies. The 1908 *Cyclopaedia of New Zealand* described Greenmeadows as having 'several orchards and vineries in the vicinity, and the wine made there is sold all over the colony'. Taradale's 'chief industries' were listed as 'dairying, market gardening, and fruit farming', while Meanee was noted for its vine culture and wine-making and its fertile grazing lands. 'Dairy farming, market gardening, and fruit growing are the chief industries.'[9] Although Greenmeadows was referred to as being 'largely composed of suburban residences of people engaged in business in Napier', and Taradale was described as 'almost a suburb of Napier', it is clear that the local economy was more semi-rural than urban.[10] Thomas Stevenson may have gone into Napier each day to work, but he also worked his land in Taradale, with the assistance of his wife and children. The Stevenson household was not the only one to practice a mixed economy.

Examining these mixed economies is not a simple task. One of the many fires caused by the 1931 Hawke's Bay earthquake destroyed the area's land records. Census material on occupations, apart from being notoriously unreliable, is of no use to us since the area was always incorporated into the Napier or Hawke's Bay figures. Even the electoral rolls, useful for men, have their limits for women. From the outset, many women were listed by their marital status, or defined by vague terms such as 'domestic duties'. Within these limitations, though, some knowledge about how people made a living can be gathered.

Although the land records have not survived, valuation records from 1905 have. Along with the 1882 Freeholders Roll, these give us some indication of who owned land and what they did on it. Most of the landowners in the Taradale area did not have substantial holdings. Almost half of the men and women who owned land held plots of less than an acre. Almost as many had holdings of between one and nine acres. Only one land holder in ten boasted a site of over ten acres, although about a quarter of the men who owned land owned more than one plot, whereas few of the landed women did. While a man was more likely to own land than a woman, and more likely to own more than one piece of land, men and women used their land in very similar ways.[11]

The most common use was as a site for the family's home. In almost half of all cases the land had a dwelling on it and was fenced.[12] With a homestead and clearly marked boundaries, the scene was set for a mixed family economy. If the land was owned by a woman, chances were that she was married or a widow. Few single women owned land, but quite a number of single men did. Many of these single men involved members of their families in working and living off their land.[13] So a family economy should not be assumed to be a nuclear family economy.

The *Cyclopaedia* was right about the fertility of Taradale's land. In the warm, sunny climate of Hawke's Bay, with a usually reliable average rainfall and enough frosts to kill many orchard pests, even those with smallholdings could grow an amazing variety of fruit and vegetables. Grapes, lemons, persimmons, strawberries, apples, gooseberries, cherries, raspberries and stone fruit were grown, as well as all manner of vegetables. Keeping poultry was the norm, and many families had their own milking cows. It was not uncommon to have a pigsty, and smallholdings of sheep were also familiar sights. But given that the vast majority of holdings were less than ten acres, many households relied on outside income to supplement their homegrown produce. Although they could often sell surplus milk or eggs, they needed more cash than these commodities could raise.

Despite the fact that there was a move away from men working on the land, even after the Great War almost half the men of the area still identified themselves as being primarily employed in the rural sector.[14] Some of these men were self-employed, like gardener William Waterhouse, who worked his eight and a half acres of land in Taradale intensively. He had nearly 4000 square feet under glass, where, with the help of his four sons, he grew tomatoes and grapes. His grapes supplied local markets, and also found buyers in Taranaki and Wellington.[15]

One of the largest landholdings in the area, and a major employer of men and children, was the 77-acre Greenmeadows Fruit Farm. Henry Stokes Tiffen established the farm in 1891. In that year 16 acres of vines were planted. Tiffen employed Sidney Anderson as his manager, and sent Anderson over to Australia in 1894 to learn about the wine-making industry. Anderson later became the Government Viticulturist.[16] Amelia Randall inherited the property from her uncle in 1896, and the following year her farm boasted sales of 10,000 gallons of wine.[17] By the turn of the century she had 30 acres in vines and the rest in fruit trees. Apricot, apple, pear, persimmon, peach, fig and plum trees filled the orchard. The land also housed a press house, a brick cellar, and a homestead.[18]

Amelia Randall was described by Alice Parke, who worked for her as a general servant in the 1920s, as having a 'brilliant brain'. But she relied on Anderson and later Flewellen King to manage her estate. This did not mean she had no say in how the property was run. In the early twentieth century she had all the vines uprooted and ceased wine production. Whether this was due to her religious beliefs or a conviction that prohibition was soon to be introduced is unclear. What is clear is that economically she was one of the most powerful people in the area. She had a core staff who ran the farm and household. At harvest time she employed dozens of people to pick and sort fruit. When she died in 1930 seven members of her staff acted as her pallbearers.[19]

Although Amelia Randall ceased wine production soon after inheriting the Fruit Farm, others in the area did not share her religious beliefs or fear of prohibition. Since the Marist Brothers came to Meanee in the 1850s, wine had been produced in the area. In the 1870s, with the arrival of Brother Cyprian, the son of a Loire valley vigneron, their wine growing took a step forward.[20] Even so, Mission production was aimed at internal consumption, and as late as 1895 the estate sold only 703 gallons of wine.[21]

More commercially oriented was a former Brother at the Mission, Bartholomew Steinmetz. By 1908, he was advertising madeira, port, sherry and burgundy from the Church Road vineyard for sale.[22] Steinmetz later sold his business to an employee, Edward McLean. Like the Mission, that vineyard continues to this day to produce award-winning wine.

Alongside the vineyards, orchards and market gardens dotting the countryside were sheep and dairy farms. Sheep flocks in the area ranged in size from Mr Jeffares's four, in 1886, up to almost 25,000 sheep on the Dolbel brothers' property in 1891. The average flock size ranged from 4269 sheep in 1891 to 431 sheep in 1921. Most flocks contained between 500 and 2000 sheep.[23] The presence of such a large number of sheep in the area led to local slaughtering houses, such as J. Nicol's Meanee property, and fellmongery firms, such as Mr Beatson's.[24] George Davies' father and uncle worked at J. F. Miller's wool scouring plant on Tannery Road. Since George and his cousin used to go along to the plant in the evenings if their fathers were working late, George could describe the process of washing the wool, putting it in 'the hydro' to extract water from it, then loading the wool

The Butcher Brothers' Fellmongery and Woolwash in the 1920s. The business was owned and managed by Henry Fairburn Butcher until his death in 1923. The wool is drying on huge sheets, as George Davies described, before being pressed. COLLECTION OF HAWKE'S BAY CULTURAL TRUST–HAWKE'S BAY MUSEUM, NAPIER, NEW ZEALAND, 6966

into carts to take it outside where it was placed on sheets to dry. Later the drying wool was turned; once it was dry it was rolled up inside the sheets it was drying on, and carried inside to the upstairs press, where it was baled. The Tannery Road plant also processed hides and sheep pelts and sent them away by the barrel load. Other industries developed to process the area's produce. In 1889 a tomato sauce factory began operation in Taradale, and its onion-flavoured condiment took a medal at the Indian and Colonial Exhibition. By 1892 it was preparing to begin regular exports to Glasgow.[25] In the late 1890s a dairy factory was established as a co-operative venture in Meanee.

Men who were not involved in primary production or local processing industries were employed in the service sector. Men made up the bulk of the local shopkeepers, and professionals such as government officials and clergy. Many other men were self-employed, as skilled artisans, blacksmiths, saddlers and the like, or worked for others in small enterprises. Then there was the large group of men who gave their occupation as 'labourer' – men like Thomas Johnson, who worked for many years as a surfaceman for the Taradale Town Board.

THE HOUSEHOLD AND LOCAL ECONOMY

Picking grapes at Mount St Mary's, the Roman Catholic station in Meanee, before 1908. While the little boy looks on, the men bring in the harvest. Schoolboys were often involved in grape picking, a practice the school committee frowned upon, since it took place during the school term. COLLECTION OF HAWKE'S BAY CULTURAL TRUST–HAWKE'S BAY MUSEUM, NAPIER, NEW ZEALAND, 7329

Johnson had a long career with the board. As a young married man with a growing family, he was employed in 1888 to work as a labourer, creating footpaths.[26] By the time he had five children, he had permanent employment as a surfaceman, earning 7 shillings a day.[27] Within a few years he was winning contracts with his relation J. Johnson.[28] Perhaps Thomas preferred being employed to the competitive world of contract work. By the time his family of ten was complete he was back working as a surfaceman, slowly working his way up to being the foreman.[29] His new position paid 1s 10d an hour, including his 3d an hour bonus for being foreman, although this was reduced to award level after an arbitration court decision in 1922.[30] As the Town Board cut back on spending, Thomas was reduced from being foreman to surfaceman, and with the other surfaceman was to work week about during slack times.[31] All his years of service did not add up to much. But like many men in paid work, Thomas also worked his land. He, his wife Margaret, and their large family made sure that their six acres of land provided for them when the Town Board could not.

Margaret Johnson's contribution to the family's economy is much harder to trace than Thomas's. Like most married women in the area, there is no indication that she worked outside the home for money. But as for other women, her contribution was crucial to the family's well-being. There certainly is evidence that a strong sexual division of labour operated in Taradale. How this manifested itself is the subject of the next two chapters. But we need to be careful that we do not overstate the case. It should not be assumed that the family economy was male defined, or that women's role was only a supporting one. Harriet Bradley has argued that the practice of 'incorporating' women into their husbands' work maintains sex-segregated work. If women provide back-up support, they are prevented from developing their own independent work life.[32] But viewing women's work in this way, as men's helpmeets, subordinates women's work to men's work, seeing it only in relation to what men did. As John Mack Faragher has argued, women's work needs to be seen as part of a wider household economy.[33]

Although Sophie Richardson's mother enjoyed the outdoor life, she never did any of the actual harvesting on the family's farm. Instead, she sewed the sacks to store the stock's feed, and provided the food to maintain the harvesters:

> He [father] did quite a lot of harvesting and I can remember my mother for the harvesting because we made these big sacks to feed the stock in the winter and I can remember in the harvesting times mother would make these huge batches of what we called rock cakes. They were really very nice, with lots of sultanas in them and lots of scones and sandwiches, she would cut sandwiches and take these enormous quantities of food up to the harvesters and shearers.[34]

Sophie's parents' work was intimately related, and from a young age Sophie herself played an important part in the household's economy. To view Sophie and her mother as mere supporting players to her father's main act is to take a very masculinist view.

A symbiotic or mutual relationship characterised the household economy. Take Emma Needle's parents, who made some money from their poultry. Her mother plucked the fowls, and her father took them into Napier to the Masonic Hotel, where they ended up as dinner. Many other women cooked and cleaned for boarders who were employed to work in the family's enterprise. Men and women continued to have separate tasks within these combined efforts, but women were doing a lot more than 'helping out' in the male economy.

This symbiosis is also evident in the wills, probate records and testamentary registers of Taradale. Not surprisingly, men left behind larger estates than women.[35] But both men's and women's wills reflect

THE HOUSEHOLD AND LOCAL ECONOMY

the important contribution of all family members to the household's economy. Primogeniture was rare in Taradale. Instead, as shown in the previous chapter, the estate was fairly evenly divided among the surviving local family members. Julia Tracy died in 1898. She left her estate 'for all my children in equal shares'.[36] Like many parents, Julia stipulated that her sons were to inherit when they were 21, whereas her daughters could inherit before reaching that age, if they married someone approved of by their father.[37] Sometimes those who had had a special involvement in the family's economy were singled out. When widower William Waterhouse died in 1919, he left money to his two daughters. But the four sons who had worked the land with him were left equal shares in it, as tenants in common.[38] When it came to writing wills, both mothers and fathers acknowledged their children's participation in the family's economy.

It would be misleading, though, to suggest that everyone in Taradale was part of a successful familial economy. Not every household could balance its budget; not everyone lived within a familial situation. What happened to the families where the mother died or the father deserted his wife and young children, where crops failed or fire devastated a home, where illness prevented work or work was hard to come by?

Taradale had its fair share of economic failures, its bankrupts and charity cases. Not surprisingly, all those known to have been bankrupted were men. For the most part these were married men, such as Henry Gilberd, a nurseryman. He was declared bankrupt in 1895, owing money to Henry Stokes Tiffen and Amelia Randall, among others, and he reappeared in the bankruptcy courts in 1898. Ill health, lack of regular employment or floods tended to be the scapegoats when men declared bankruptcy. James James, a Meanee labourer, found it impossible to support his wife and eight children when he could find only irregular employment at 7 shillings a day.[39] Cornelius Collins, another labourer, fared even worse. The father of seven children under the age of 13, he was unemployed, lost £80 through a recent flood, and then had his home destroyed by fire. He added to his problems by turning to drink and being convicted of being drunk in a public place. Eventually a prohibition order was taken out against him.[40]

There were several avenues open to men such as James James and Cornelius Collins. Families often came to the aid of members in distress. The newspaper report of Collins's bankruptcy case stated that: 'His wife had always got money from his brothers when she wanted it.'[41] When Charles O'Donnell Bourke, a local farmer, appeared in the

41

courts on bankruptcy charges, it was revealed that his wife's brother had lent Charles £50 'to help him along'. His brother-in-law had in turn borrowed the £50 from his father.[42] It was extreme to end up bankrupted. But many went through lean periods when sickness or old age prevented them from earning a living. If their extended family could not or would not help out in such circumstances, sometimes an application was made for charitable aid.

The fact that so few local people applied to the Hawke's Bay Charitable Aid Board indicates that they understood the system was one of last resort. The men and women whose applications were successful tended to be the 'deserving' poor, the ones whom fate had dealt a savage blow.[43] Elizabeth Hunt was 'deserving'. She applied for, and was granted, four rations per diem for three months in 1893.[44] Her husband John had recently died of consumption, leaving her with eight children ranging in age from 15 to newborn. Mary Robinson was also 'deserving'. Her husband Edward had deserted her, leaving her with their three children, aged five, two and one years. Mary was given two rations for three months on two separate occasions, and was to get housing when it became available.[45]

In several cases the illness of the father and husband drove the family to resort to aid. Although John Bryon was in hospital for only four days to have his duodenal ulcer seen to, he could not resume work as a labourer for some time.[46] Two months after his operation, in October 1909, the Anglican clergyman, Reverend Clarke, was asking the Charitable Aid Board for assistance for the family. Adding weight to the claim, the local constable, O'Halloran, also reported on the case. With support like that, the Bryon family of John, Charlotte and their children received the 'usual assistance'.[47] In 1911 John was ill again, and again his family received aid.[48] John died in June 1914. Within a month Charlotte was in hospital for 20 days, suffering from pneumonia.[49] Perhaps her six children who had already left school looked after her seven younger children, including the twins, born in 1912, and baby Rose, born three weeks before her father's death. If Charlotte's life had been hard before, it suddenly got a lot harder.

The Bryons do not appear to have had any other family in the area. But they were deserving: married, hard-working, honest. Few 'undeserving' poor received any aid. Taradale shoemaker William Cantelin applied for aid in 1890, but was refused. The Board took the view that he could have worked and earned £3–£4 a week, but instead chose not to. Cantelin then took to stealing letters containing money, encouraging his daughter Eliza to do the same. He was soon found out and imprisoned, leaving his wife and four dependent children destitute. Mrs Cantelin was seven months pregnant, so was not able to go out to work; her two daughters in service were paid their board but no wages, and her 21-year-old son had disappeared. She had no other family to turn to when the rent was due, and had already pawned the furniture. Even the Charitable Aid Board took some pity on her then, and voted her 4 shillings a week and rations for one month.[50]

William Cantelin resorted to crime to make ends meet. In this he was unusual. While there were many petty property offences in Taradale, few people seem to have seen crime as a way of life. Most of the economic crime in the area had to do with impounded stock being 'released' by its outraged owners, or boys stealing fruit from local orchards. Rather than crime, or even the Charitable Aid Board, locals relied on their friends and family, or on contributory schemes, in times of hardship. Here gender seems to have mattered. While family helped out men and women, if the community rallied behind someone down on their luck, that someone tended to be a worthy woman. It was common for local fund-raisers to be held in support of women recently widowed, especially when those women had young children. Such fund-raising efforts were usually organised by married women. In August 1898 the people of Taradale held a social and dance in aid of the recently widowed Mary Farrelly. Her husband of 23 years, James, had suicided, leaving Mary with three sons under the age of ten. A general fund was also set up and it was reported that individuals, such as a 'Lady Friend', gave donations. A concert was held too, raising £38 for the Widow Farrelly Fund.[51] Women's networks of female friends and neighbours leapt to their aid in such times, but women like Mary Farrelly did not retreat into a female world. Her community of family and friends ran across as well as along gender lines.[52]

In times of need it was more common for men to turn to their friendly societies and receive not aid, but their dues. Lodge Meanee of the Manchester Unity Independent Order of Odd Fellows was formed in Taradale in 1871, while Court Redclyffe of the Ancient Order of Foresters began in 1886. Between 1910 and 1916, Catholic men of the area could attend the St Patrick's branch of the Hibernian Australasian Catholic Benefit Society.[53] It is common to see lodge membership as a form of insurance against sickness.[54] In a society where a visit to the doctor or hospital led to a sizeable bill, and being too ill to work meant going without wages, having a doctor provided by your Lodge, and being able to claim sick pay and funeral expenses, was economically reassuring. As David Thomson has shown in his recent work, during this period friendly society spending 'remained relatively substantial'.[55]

Almost half of the Taradale men who paid their weekly lodge subscriptions received sick pay at some point during their lodge membership.[56] Men could claim sick pay either through a debilitating sickness or an accident. They were usually paid 20 shillings a week, although this amount was reduced the longer they remained on the sick-pay roll. The Hunt family relied on lodge payments in 1892, as John lay ill. For six weeks the Foresters paid him. The following year John's illness became worse. From New Year until his death in March, John and his family of wife Elizabeth and eight young children received a total of £13 16s 8d. When he eventually died of consumption, Elizabeth was helped with the funeral costs by the friendly society's funeral allowance. No doubt other members of the Hunt family helped out in their time of crisis, but providing for yourself and your family was an important ethos for many of the men of Taradale. John left his estate to his wife and children 'in equal shares for all their own use and benefit absolutely and for ever'.[57]

It was not just the dying who turned to their lodge. William Howard was hospitalised in November 1913 for 22 days. No doubt he and his family were glad of the £3 13s 4d that the Manchester Unity paid out. Other men joined lodges after they had been hospitalised, perhaps spurred into action by the cost of their recent illness. Soon after Frank Bennett, a joiner, severed his wrist, an accident which resulted in his hand being amputated, he joined the Foresters. Bennett could no longer work as a joiner. Now he gave his occupation as clerk.

Men preferred to receive their dues rather than charity when they could not work, as the local Town Board realised. When times were tough and work was hard to come by, the board provided some assistance to men. During the Great War it decided to take positive action and employ some of the men 'who are unemployed and in distress through the influence of the war'.[58] When the depression of the late 1920s was taking hold, the board decided

> That for the purpose of providing relief works for unemployed residents of the town District, the Taradale Town Board hereby authorises the raising of a loan of two hundred and fifty pounds (£250) for a term of ten years, such loan to be expended on the construction of concrete water channels and general labour.[59]

By residents the board meant men. It employed both single and married men, but paid them at different rates. Married men received 14 shillings for an eight-hour day, while single men 'without dependants' were paid 10 shillings. It was left to the overseer to use his discretion to employ the men in most need. The Town Board worked within the tradition of viewing only men as providers, but it acknowledged that single men could also have dependants, be they elderly parents, or younger siblings in need of support. The board did not propose any similar scheme for women who worked in paid employment.

The Town Board did not have enough money to employ many men, or to keep them on the payroll full-time. Many of the men they hired worked in a mixed economy, doing some paid labour while also working their own land, just as Thomas Johnson and Patrick and Grace's father did. Understanding the local economy means looking at both the paid and the household work done by the people of Taradale. Few households in the area had enough land to allow them to live off their own holding. But whether the focus is on working the land or on paid employment, to see this as a male breadwinner economy is to miss the complexity of local coping strategies. Men and women, boys and girls, all contributed to the economic well-being of their household. Some could focus on the family farm or business; most worked the land and supplemented their income with some paid labour. Few married women were involved in this non-domestic employment. But that should not blind us to the important contribution all household members made to the local economy. Everyone had a role to play.

However, the roles they played were different. I argued above that we should not view married women merely as men's helpmeets, as supporting players in the male breadwinner economy. Feeding shearers, plucking poultry, and looking after boarders could be seen as propping up their husband's work, or it could be viewed as working within a family economy. Within this family or household economy the work women and men did was often gender-specific. How the gendered division of labour operated within Taradale, and what this meant for the construction and maintenance of ideas about femininities and masculinities, is the subject of the next two chapters.

CHAPTER 4

Women's Work

When Sophie Richardson's mother sewed the sacks to store the stock's feed, made hay covers from flour bags, and fed the shearers, she was fulfilling the role of helpmeet to her husband: her work complemented his. But Sophie's mother was more than a helpmeet. She was also a mother, who reared her five children, sewed all their clothes and cooked their meals. She was a daughter, who lived next door to her parents, helped her mother out with chores and was helped by her mother. She was also a sister and niece. As a young girl she stayed with her aunts when they went into labour, and looked after their homes and families as they convalesced after giving birth. When it was her turn to have a family, her aunts and sisters came to her side. Sophie's mother had all her children in a private maternity hospital, but when she returned home her female kin were always there, ready to take over for as long as necessary.

She was a friend and neighbour, too. A stalwart of All Saints church, she ran the produce stall at church garden parties and was an active member of numerous sewing bees. With other local women, she raised money for the church while enjoying the company of her friends and neighbours.[1] Like many married women in Taradale, Sophie's mother did not work only at men's bidding, or for men's benefit. She worked within a complex web of familial and community ties and obligations. Her work was not subordinate to men's, and should not be seen solely in relation to men's work.

Sophie's mother, grandmother and aunts were fully enmeshed in this world. Their working lives, like those of women in American and British society, revolved around home, family and community.[2]

WOMEN'S WORK

Through their domestic and reproductive work they reiterated a type of femininity. Their understanding of proper womanhood involved being a good wife and mother, keeping the pantry full and the floors swept. They earned respectability by their domestic labours. For the women of Sophie's generation, though, other options were emerging. These new women were going on to high school and technical college, and many were eschewing the domestic work their mothers did. They operated within different boundaries. They did not always share their mothers' understanding of femininity.

This chapter is about women's gender-specific work. It explores not only what women did, but also the meanings associated with it. Through their housework, their productive and reproductive labour, their paid work inside and outside the home, women's work and women's memories of it tell us much about prevailing ideas of femininity in Taradale.

The day-to-day running of the home was the main occupation for married women in Taradale. It was a job they were well trained for. As girls they had been their mother's part-time assistants. In adolescence they were expected to graduate to full-time apprentices, so that once they married and had families of their own, they were well versed in the art of domestic management. Such important work is often downplayed in historical accounts. It is only in recent years that people have taken the history of housework at all seriously.[3] There are few extant written records from Taradale detailing what women did within their homes, but the oral evidence is very clear – they worked long and hard, and their work often made the difference between the family surviving and prospering or going under.

Oral accounts indicate that parents allocated childhood tasks along gendered lines. Some jobs, such as feeding the fowls and collecting the eggs, were not gender-specific; but for the most part demarcation lines were adhered to wherever possible. In households where there were no sons, girls were expected to cross the boundaries, but they were reminded that they were doing so. Sisters Florence Rifle, Theresa Pond and Jane McNight only had very young brothers, so they had to help their father outside with the milking and harvesting, while their other sister assisted their mother inside the house. As Jane remembers, their father boasted of his daughters' abilities:

> As a matter of fact Dad used to say that we were better than boys. He used to go to the Hotel occasionally, father did, and skite about us girls, down

there. He wouldn't have sons. 'You can have your sons' he used to say, 'my daughters can do' and he'd skite, 'my daughters can do every bit as good as your sons can'. So we were quite proud.[4]

While girls had to become *de facto* sons, there was no similar crossing of gender lines for boys born into daughterless families. Thomas Raven was one of a family of six boys, and he voluntarily took on the role of the daughter: 'I was the only girl in the family, I think! Well, I could see that if I didn't do it none of the others had any intention of doing it'.[5] Even so, the 'it' he refers to was gardening rather than cooking or cleaning, and vegetable gardening at that. While girls were expected to fill the 'gap' of boys, only in rare and temporary circumstances, such as their mother being ill, were boys expected to take on feminine chores.

If family circumstances allowed, and most families had both boys and girls, then girls seem to have been expected to do more and spend more time around the home than their brothers. Their tasks tended to be inside the house, helping their mother. From an early age girls were washing dishes, preparing vegetables, helping with the preserving and jam-making, minding younger siblings, sewing, baking, making butter, cleaning and scrubbing. At school, too, they spent some time preparing for their future as wives and mothers. In his annual report of 1895, the Inspector of Schools in Hawke's Bay, Henry Hill, lamented that:

> The regulation permitting the exemption of girls in geometrical drawing has been claimed by most teachers. Personally I am sorry for this, but the teachers say the boys take geometrical drawing whilst the girls are sewing, and the latter is looked upon as an equivalent for the girls.[6]

The situation for girls did not alter much over the years. As the headmaster of Taradale School noted in his logbook in 1924, the infant mistress taught senior girls 'Sewing, Home Science and Moral Instruction'. The three were assumed to be natural allies. What had changed was the boys' curriculum. Rather than teaching them geometrical drawing while their sisters learnt acceptable feminine skills, the headmaster was now taking them for drill.[7]

Some of the women narrators were aware of how separate and different their chores were from those of their brothers. Martha Edwards raised the issue of disposing of human waste in the days before night carts. She was asked who buried this before a regular night-soil service was begun:

> Oh Dad, that was Dad's Saturday morning job [laugh]. Saturday morning,

yes. And, well I suppose you added some disinfectant, I don't really remember. I mean it's one of those things that us girls anyway were kept away from. We weren't allowed to go out and watch. You see my brother – us girls we weren't allowed – my brother who was about two and a half years older than I was, he was allowed out and about and doing those sorts of things or watching Dad or helping Dad or whatever but us girls were never allowed to . . . There were lots of things that he was, were going to do and Mum would say you can't go out there now, without really saying why. We just knew why, we knew what was going on. That's why she'd say, 'Don't go outside just now, just leave it a while' . . . there was the business about the cow when the cow came into heat and it was time to get it into calf again. Well of course you took the cow, I don't know where, down the road somewhere to somebody or other who had a bull. Now Robert was allowed to go there but us girls never were. We were never allowed to do anything like that. We weren't even suppose to know what was going on. It was classified as taking the cow for a walk [laugh].[8]

The women who were interviewed spent their childhoods helping in the home. Not surprisingly, they knew a lot more about their mothers' routines than their male counterparts did. The men had little to offer when it came to discussing domestic work; they had never taken part in it, and had spent most of their lives away from the home, at school, at play or at work. The only thing they all seemed to remember was 'I know that the house was scrubbed out every day, especially the kitchen. Everywhere was the same.'[9] No doubt young boys who ran inside onto freshly scrubbed floors were severely reprimanded.

Women, too, remembered the endless scrubbing, and much more besides. Hannah Field, recalling her mother's work, said:

She used to do all the beds and everything, all the front of the house but I had to keep the kitchen done, and that was a big kitchen, I can tell you. We had a great big table that we cooked on and another smaller one and that had to be scrubbed every day, it was just white. And the big bench, the scrub bench went right round the, oh, from the stove right round to the back door, it was a fair way and that had to be done every day. The tea tin had to be polished, Brasso. Oh, Mum was very fussy . . . we weren't allowed to go near the beds once they were made. They had to be all, you know, how they had them, all starched pillow shams and everything and we weren't allowed to go near the beds after they were made. Of course I can see now, we used to think she was being fussy but I can see now it must have been hard work, you know, because there was no washing machines or anything like that, no fridges.[10]

Hannah never had to blacken the stove; her mother did that. Wood-fired stoves were commonplace in Taradale throughout the period and were labour intensive; they required about one hour's labour a day to maintain.[11]

Washing and ironing featured predominantly in women's memories of their mother's domestic work:

> Wash day was Monday. Well you heated up the copper and bailed some water into the top to wash the clothes in and in the meantime and then you had one of those, either, well we had a wooden one to start with, the wooden ones and then we had a glass one and you washed everything and everything was sort of washed or scrubbed violently and then into the copper and boiled up. And then back into the tub again with cold water to rinse them and then into the next tub, which had blue in it and then out onto the line.
>
> *Did you have a wringer?*
>
> Just a hand wringer. Just a hand wringer that sat on the outside edge of the tub. And then everything was carted out and put up on the line . . . Tuesday was ironing.
>
> *With a Mrs Pott's iron?*
>
> Yes, with a Mrs Pott's iron. And of course in those days everything was ironed and you starched a lot of stuff. A lot of things were starched which of course meant damping down . . .[12]

It is little wonder that women rested on Sunday, in anticipation of wash day on Monday. It has been estimated that the process of washing by copper and scrubbing board was as exhausting as swimming five miles of energetic breaststroke.[13] Although electricity was switched on in Taradale in 1924, few women had electrical appliances by 1930. Like most homes around New Zealand, those connected to the local grid used the power for lighting, rather than for washing machines or electric stoves.[14]

While scrubbing and washing and ironing undoubtedly took up a great deal of women's time, it is interesting that these chores take pride of place in women's memories of their mother's work. Other people saw the results of these activities. They saw whether a woman had scrubbed her verandah white, and whether her family was dressed in clean and well-pressed clothes. Such domestic work was a way that a woman could maintain or increase the status of her family, a public declaration that they were respectable, rather than rough, and that she was a good wife and mother.

The women oral narrators were sometimes aware of the importance of this to women's lives. Kathleen Thomson recalled the wrath of her aunt when she 'tramped' on a wet, freshly scrubbed verandah:

> Well as I say. My sister and I got into trouble one time. We come up from the orchard, the toilet was right down the orchard but we come back and she was scrubbing the verandah and we got on, we tramped on it, we crossed over it to go inside and God she gave us a spanking and marched us down to the toilet, right down at the end of the orchard and locked us up in there, in the toilet. Well we got out, they had a little trap door and we were able to get out. One false move and we would have gone down the hole. I'll never forget that.[15]

Nor is it any wonder that Ellen Store's grandmother expressed her anger at her daughter not being in when she went to visit, by defiling her daughter's scrubbed verandah:

> I remember once Grandma had been to see her daughter three times and she was out, so the fourth time she went, the verandah went right round the front, oh it was beautiful, scrubbed and cleaned, you know, very proud of it, and Grandma wrote in a chalky sort of, a burnt stick, and wrote right across 'Always out' [laugh]. My aunt did not appreciate it [laugh].[16]

Ellen remembered the story, just as Louisa Plumb remembered her mother's reaction to the doctor's advice. Dr Swansegar told Louisa's mother that by ironing her baby's clothes she was removing all the goodness from the sunshine right out of them. Some men may have been trying to make women's domestic work more 'scientific' and therefore appealing to women, but it appears such efforts were wasted on the women of Taradale.[17] Louisa's mother was not having her baby seen in crumpled clothing; she continued to iron every garment.

The other area of their mothers' work that women recalled in detail, and with great knowledge, was their productive domestic work. Again, men had little to offer when asked about this. They were aware that their mothers preserved fruit, made jam, sewed clothes and churned butter, but they were generally ignorant of these work processes because men took no part in the domestic work place. That was a female domain, where women sewed, knitted, crocheted and made a range of foodstuffs. Apart from everyday cooking, they baked bread, preserved fruit, made jams, preserved meat, churned out pounds of butter and collected dozens of eggs. They were also involved in the production of household goods such as candles and soap. This was true for both the beginning of the period, 1886, and the end, 1930.

Contrary to recent assertions, women retained their productive functions well past the 1860s.[18]

These types of production took two main forms: as use value for the family, and as part of a cash or exchange economy. Many women produced solely for their family. This meant fewer cash purchases were needed, but at the same time it did not earn the household any money. Sometimes they produced at their husband's request. Ellen Store's mother baked bread for a while, even though the baker had a delivery round. Ellen believed that 'she used to do it in preference. Dad preferred it so she did it.'[19]

One of the ways that women could save the household money was to make soap. Since everywhere was scrubbed so often, each home went through a lot of soap. Everyone had a shelf in their laundry dedicated to curing soap. The dripping from endless roast dinners was saved in a kerosene tin, and when there was enough fat, soap would be made:

> You save the fat and then you clarify it . . . by heating it up and putting water over it and letting it set and taking the fat off the top and you keep on doing that until you've got every bit of salt out of it. Then you put it in the copper with some resin and some water and some borax and caustic soda – you have to be very careful that you didn't have very much firing underneath when you put the caustic soda in because it would foam it up and if it boiled over the top you were likely to have a fire, so you had to be jolly careful – and you let it cook for so long and then we used to leave it in the copper to set and then used to use a long butcher's knife and cut it into slices and into slabs and put it on the top of the copper and let it dry out.[20]

Harriet's mother used this soap for scrubbing her steps and verandah white, and for washing clothes.

Preserving fruit and making jams was another way women used freely available produce in a way that saved the household money. Most people in the Taradale area had fruit trees in their gardens. And most women spent long, hot days in the middle of summer boiling up vast quantities of peaches and plums and berries so that their families could have puddings and jams throughout the year. They also made their own jam jars:

> . . . most of our jam jars were chopped off beer bottles . . . you just collected these jars and bottles and things from around . . . and you downed the top, you wound a piece of wool around them, dipped in kerosene, lit the kerosene and when it flared up plunged the top of the bottle into cold

water, which took the top off the bottle. Mind you, it was pretty dangerous jam jars because it had this terribly sharp edge. And jam was sealed in those jars with a piece of, well either several layers of newspaper or a piece of cloth, dipped in flour and water paste and slapped over the top. It dried hard and stiff and sealed your jam perfectly but most of our jam jars in those days were broken off bottles.[21]

Women were also involved in preserving meat. After Louisa Plumb's father had killed a pig it was up to her mother to make sure that nothing was wasted:

My mother used to cure the bacon, and these big sides of bacon hanging up there and one day she'd have to do saltpetre all over it and the other day it was brown sugar and cured the whole of the ham, the pig, for bacon.[22]

The pig was hung in the outside wash house. Another woman recalled that when meat was freshly slaughtered her mother hung it in flour sacks in nearby trees. She put pepper on the sacks to keep the flies away. The meat would last a week.[23] Men often slaughtered an animal with their brother or father or next door neighbour. It was then up to their wives to work together to preserve and divide the beast, as Sophie Richardson's mother and grandmother did after her grandfather had 'stuck' a pig.

Another way that women made a productive contribution to the household by saving rather than generating cash was through sewing clothes for themselves and their children. The women who were interviewed were usually taught to sew by their mothers, as well as at school, and so could remember details of their mother's sewing. Jane McNight, for instance, recalled how her mother used to 'line the boys' trousers with flour bags, you know.'[24] Sewing afforded women a rare opportunity to transform their work into leisure. While cooking and cleaning and washing tended to be done by women alone, perhaps with the help of a young daughter, sewing allowed women to work collectively. Taradale's women never seem to have been involved in quilting bees, but they did gather together to sew items for fund-raisers. When Sophie Richardson was asked about her mother's leisure activities, she replied:

They had very little leisure time because they would be knitting, they would be sewing, especially for bees, the garden parties. There would be sewing bees in different people's homes. A lot of that sewing, in the early stages was done with little hand sewing machines and then, of course, the Singer

treadle machine came in and that was a marvellous help to women which made sewing very much easier because you had both hands to steer your sewing where [before] you had to do it with one hand and turn the handle of the sewing machine with the other one.
How many women?
About a dozen. [They talked about] just the local gossip I think . . . they just talked about what was happening in the district, who was getting married . . .[25]

Sewing may have been a communal activity, but it could also be a competitive one. From school days on, girls entered their sewing into competitions. At the annual school picnic the best sewers in each class would be rewarded for their skills.[26] As adults their sewing skills were judged when their family turned out in home-made garments. Some women also continued to enter competitions, notably at the Agricultural and Pastoral Show.

The work women did that had use value for their households was generally carried out independent of men. It was an important contribution to the overall household economy, but it did not bring cash into the home. The second form of women's domestic production did. The butter women churned and then sold, and the eggs they collected and sold, were important because they could visibly generate cash. Through producing surplus products, women entered into either the cash or the exchange economy. Butter production and egg collection were seen as acceptable ways for married women to do this. They were not unsexing, non-feminine tasks. Marilyn Lake found the same pattern among women in rural Australian families, 1870–1930:

It was far more ideologically acceptable . . . for women to work with poultry or cows than to plough a paddock or sow a crop. The cow and poultry yards were a permitted extension of women's domestic sphere justified in the case of dairying by the desirability of milkers being of a soft and gentle – 'feminine' – disposition.[27]

Many married women in Taradale did not do the actual milking, but Lake's point remains. Married women's sphere of work could be extended, but only in certain ways. It was very rare indeed for women in Taradale to work on the land, even if their husbands were ill or had had an accident. This was true whether men worked on land around their own house or further afield. On such occasions, men's kin, friends and work mates took over, just as when women were ill or

WOMEN'S WORK

incapacitated their female network stepped into the breach. Women and men relied on their gender-specific networks to lend a hand at such times.

Making butter was a labour-intensive process. Few men made butter, although quite a few boys seem to have helped with the churning. When the price for a gallon of cream fell, Theresa Pond's mother decided to increase the family's revenues by adding value to the cream. She began making butter, with Theresa's help:

> Mum decided, she decided that what she'd do, she'd churn it and my uncle had made a big churn about, it might have been my great uncle for all I know, a big churn, a wooden one, it was all wood except it had steel for the handle . . . So we had this churn and Mum used to churn this butter and it was very difficult you see. Well in the winter it was very hard to get the jolly cream to break, you see, because it was very cold. So what we used to do was, a couple of us used to sit on top of the churn and Mum used to churn it.
> *Why would you sit on top of it?*
> So that Mum could churn it so that the cream would break. Anyway Mum used to make the butter . . .
> *How long did it take you to make the butter?*
> Well if it was really cold, oh it could take anything from 20 minutes to half an hour to get it to break you see and then it could take more than that. If it was very cold it was dynamite. You'd churn and churn and churn and then after that you see, once you'd got that you'd keep on churning so that it would come. They threw water into it you see and they'd keep churning and it would come together then you see. After it broke it was, that was the hardest part, well it wasn't the hardest part. But it would come together and then Mum would take it out of the churn and she had a big board on the kitchen table and she had butter pats and that . . . she used to put salt on her hands. She'd wash her hands with cold water and the butter never stuck to her hands, they were so well done, and she used to do the same with the butter pats, and then to start with we used to put it in ordinary white paper and I don't know if we ever just took it in a big lump to the grocer, I can't remember that, but there was a time when it went to the grocer in a big lump and the grocer did it in the shop. But we were using, Mum used to cut the paper you see, just ordinary white paper, and so then they gradually went on and you had to have your name on it and you could write your name on it yourself you see, so you had to have your name on this paper and then afterwards, later, they made it so that you had to have it done at the printers, so you had it like that. She did it for quite a long time really, I don't know how long it was.[28]

Like many women, Theresa's mother made butter to aid her family's financial survival. It was a skill she passed on to her daughters, as Ann Pearce's mother did:

> After I was married I still kept on some of the things that my mother did. For instance, we kept a cow and I used to make Devonshire Cream. At the Nook we had what they used to call a dairy and it was a building that was outside the house. It was a long building with a shelf inside it running down one side. Sometimes you might have a shelf on the other side, a narrow shelf, on the other side. But a wide shelf running down one side. And you milked the cow at night and the milk would be put into a pan and the pan would be put on the shelf and you'd always have two or three pans sitting on the shelf at the same time because you'd have the night milk in and you'd have the morning milk. Well then, after your milk had been sitting there all night you took the pan, it had handles usually on both ends of it, you took that in and put it on the stove and slowly brought it to the boil but you didn't boil it. And then you left it there for a little while at that temperature and then you took it back and put it back into the dairy and you left it all day and that night or the following morning you could take the cream off it and make butter with it or use it for cream. We always scalded it and our butter kept better because it had been scalded. And in fact my mother had customers in Napier that, she used to go into Napier with two or three pounds of butter that was ordered by people and any other produce that she had. So she had one or two customers that she supplied. Sometimes they didn't want salt in the butter, they definitely didn't want preservatives in the butter.[29]

Poultry keeping was another area where female labour generated cash for the household economy. Once the family's own need for eggs was met, any surplus would be sold. Before the 1926 census it is not possible to determine how widespread poultry keeping was in the Taradale area, since poultry figures were not broken down into town districts. But in 1926 the Taradale town district was home to just under 5000 fowls, duck, geese and turkeys. Almost three-quarters of the households in the area kept poultry.[30]

Some women had specific customers for their butter and eggs, and their produce might be taken into Napier. After the Great War, butter fetched anything from a shilling to 18d a pound. But often women exchanged their surplus production with the local grocer. The grocer would come around to people's houses and take their orders. He would also take any butter or eggs they had, and then deduct an amount from their grocery bill. From the oral evidence this was common in 1920s Taradale, but it also appears to have been the practice in the earlier period.

'The Account Book of Mr George Ridley's Wife' details the way one woman paid for her groceries through her domestic production.[31] Sarah Jane Harpham was born in 1861. She married George Ridley, a 39-year-old farmer, at All Saints Church, Taradale, in 1889. Sarah's account book covers the period from 1904 to 1919. It shows how, month after month, she financed the family's groceries through providing eggs, and sometimes butter, to either Mr Glenny's or Mr Goddard's grocery store. In December 1904 Sarah bought 10s 5d worth of goods from Mr Goddard's store. Apart from the staples of coal, wheat, tea, candles and blacking, she was also doing her Christmas baking, so she bought currants, sultanas and lemon peel. Despite her preparations for the festive season she still managed to collect twelve and a half dozen eggs, earning 11s 1d. So her domestic production paid for the family's basic supplies. In 1905 Sarah paid for her groceries through butter production rather than egg collection. She also switched to Mr Glenny's store. In May of that year she sold butter to Mr Glenny on four occasions, each time selling either six or seven pounds of butter at 8d a pound. Her churning earned 17s 6d. On five occasions that month she bought groceries from Mr Glenny – candles, sugar, soda, tartar, paper, matches, seed, coconut, tea, currants, salt and oatmeal. She spent just under 16s. The pattern is repeated month after month. Whether she produced surplus eggs or butter, she always made a small cash surplus, even though her purchases became more elaborate over time. By August 1919 she was buying shop-made biscuits, Creamota, coffee and tinned salmon, as well as the usual staples. But even so, her supply of 63 dozen eggs meant that at the end of the month she came out of the deal with 13s 8d.

While Sarah may have felt pleased with the contribution she made to her family's budget, the way the local economy was organised isolated her and many other women. Not only did the grocer pick up orders and deliver; the baker visited, the butcher had a round, even the iceman called. Women's work could physically confine them to the home.

Women also contributed to the household budget by producing services, in exchange for either work or cash. Two of the main services married women provided were taking in boarders and doing sewing for other households. Like the other aspects of their productive domestic work, it is impossible to quantify these services. Joan Jensen had the same problem when considering the household production of American women.[32] As Jensen points out, census takers were instructed

Arthur Hatton's butcher's cart, in the late nineteenth century. Like other local storekeepers, Hatton travelled Taradale's dusty roads, plying his wares. While this saved women time, it also meant they had fewer excuses to leave their homes.
PRIVATE COLLECTION

not to count women involved in such production as gainfully employed.[33] Yet the provision of these services did entail extra work for women, and brought valuable cash resources into the household. John Modell and Tamara K. Hareven estimate that in late-nineteenth- and early-twentieth-century urban America, about 15 to 20 percent of households took in lodgers at any particular point in time.[34] It is impossible, given the available material, to place any figure on the situation in Taradale. From the oral evidence it would appear that taking in boarders was commonplace. Often these were young men, given lodgings as part of their wages. Florence Rifle's father employed a boy to help around the property, particularly with the milking. As part of his wages he was provided with board and lodgings. In other households boarders were taken in solely on a cash basis. Ernest Edward's mother earned money through taking in lodgers. Louisa Plumb's mother, on the other hand, brought money into the household by taking in sewing, as did Harriet South's mother. All these married women were using their domestic skills to provide services that either had exchange value or generated cash.

Women's domestic work was a crucial part of the local economy. It was also a distinctively feminine part. Men's involvement in these activities was as end-user or purchaser; they took no part in women's work places or work processes. Women relied on other women to teach them how to perform these tasks and to support them in their work. If they were ill they relied on female kin or neighbours to lend a hand, just as when they were pregnant they relied on their female support networks.

A major part of married women's work was reproductive, and a major way that wives reiterated their femininity was through being good mothers. The work of motherhood – giving birth, helping family or friends who were having children, raising children – was central to the way many women defined themselves and were defined by others. In New Zealand as a whole, a woman who married in 1880 had, on average, 6.5 live births. Those who married in 1923 averaged 2.4 live births. Even though the average completed family size decreased markedly during the period, child bearing and rearing took up a sizeable proportion of many married women's lives.[35] Take William and Mary Ormond, who were married in Taradale in July 1886. Within six months their first daughter, Mary, was born. Three days later she was dead from convulsions. But in February 1888 Patrick was born, followed by James in 1891, Jessie in 1895, William in 1897 and Eileen in 1901. From 1886 to 1901 Mary spent 54 months being pregnant. Between the ages of 22 and 37 she was repeatedly pregnant, so that she was 58 before her youngest daughter came of age. By the 1920s the situation had changed. Kathleen Thomson married in 1924. She gave birth to a son in 1926, a daughter in 1928 and had a stillborn child in 1930. She had no more children. Kathleen spent just over two years of her life being pregnant, and was 46 when her youngest child turned 21. Married women like Kathleen had the time and energy to join the Women's Institute and other such organisations in a way that their predecessors did not.

When women were pregnant and about to give birth, they turned to their female networks for support. As Chapter 2 showed, this often meant relying on mothers, grandmothers, sisters and cousins. But women beyond the family, including midwives and maternity nurses, were also crucial. Bridget Tweed still had fond memories of the nursing sister who, in the 1920s, kept her in the private maternity home for longer than was necessary:

> She kept me in there for three weeks, she wouldn't, because I was living, while they were getting Waipunga, the house built, and they had to fence

> off around the house and do all the things, anyway I lived with my husband's mother for a year. Well, I was waiting for the house to be built and all the trees put in before we went up and took over. And Mum was a pretty grim old girl, you see and I had to work hard, you know, housekeeping with this old mother-in-law and I wasn't very keen on it. So, instead of being there on a seven day label, she kept me for three weeks and my old mother-in-law kept saying, 'Isn't it time she came home?' and Sister, she was lovely, she said, 'No, Mrs Tweed had a very bad time, and no, she's not going home just yet, she's not in a fit state to go home just yet.' I hadn't had a bad time, it was bad enough, it was quite bad enough. But I was quite eager to go home but she [the mother-in-law] had her mother and her sister staying at her place, see, and I'd be quite good help, to go and help, and Sister, she knew this and she said 'If you go now you'll only be a maid for these people and you're not well enough for it'. And of course they wanted to have Bridget and the baby home. And so she kept me there for over three weeks and of course, I was as fit as a fiddle and they had me out in the sun and it was really funny.[36]

Not all female kin were as supportive as some thought they should be.

It was not just adult women who helped new mothers. Older children, especially older daughters, were also expected to share in this aspect of women's work. Girls were not always happy with the tasks they were given to do, but very few tended to rebel against the role assigned to them. To this day Emma Needle feels embarrassed about the time she tipped her younger brother out of the pram:

> I didn't even know that Mum was going to have Jenny and you see you went round there [to the nursing home] you called round there to see her and of course you're told, another little, and you really, you're so pleased about it and that . . . but, you'll think I'm awful . . . but that's how I come to give the pram a bit of a shove, because I was going home with these two kiddies to get them fed and get them to bed and I thought 'Ow, another one to look after'. [laugh] I've never ever told Jenny that and I've never told Richard either. I was going along with this high pram and I thought, 'Ow, another one' [laugh] and yet you loved them and that. I suppose you felt a bit of a Jack of all trades or a bit of a flunkey, that's the way it was. I mean we didn't have a hard life but you never got bored . . . I mean you'd go for picnics and things like that, if you went as a family or Dad used to take a load in the express, with the horse, but you made your own fun.[37]

Emma's recollections reveal two important trends in the women's oral accounts. First, her 'rebellion' was private and short term. Secondly, she suggested that her chores were fairly insignificant – even though she was standing in for her mother.

Births, like weddings and funerals, were female rituals, a time when women worked together.[38] These were irregular but important occasions when women turned to their female networks for help. On a more regular basis, women relied on their female kin and friends for help with raising their children. Fathers were important when it came to disciplining their offspring, and spent time at play with their children – especially their sons. But it was the mothers who had the day-to-day responsibility for raising Taradale's youngsters.

Mothers were the main caregivers when members of the family were ill. Harriet South's mother nursed her through measles, chickenpox and other childhood illnesses, and then had to contend with Harriet's 18-month-old sister's bronchitis attacks: 'Mother didn't have her clothes off for a fortnight. She had open fires going and Kate was in a pram.' A steaming kettle and perseverance kept Kate alive.[39] It was rare that a father tended the sick or dying, although this did happen. Such involvement was often mediated by other factors. Widowers or men whose families all came down with an illness, as they did in the 1918 flu, had to take the lead role. There was no chemist in Taradale until 1911, and no doctor until Percy Carter Boddington Swansegar began a practice around the time of the Great War. Given Swansegar's German origins, this led to some animosity, but his services were in demand, and he remained in the area until his death in 1927. Before that, medical advice had to be sought in Napier. Going into hospital also meant a trip to Napier.

If the mother of the family became ill, her female neighbours or kin would look after the children, and perhaps prepare a meal for the family. Other women would simply take over the child-care sometimes to relieve a harassed mother. Often a woman's mother did this. Several of the oral informants spent time at their grandmothers' houses, frequently being fed there. Brother and sister Matthew Silk and Emily Jones both fondly recalled visiting their grandmother's house most afternoons. Their grandmother baked bread, so they ate afternoon tea with her and took loaves of bread home with them. Others had female relations who lived in the same house and often took on much of the child minding. Ann Pearce, for example, was virtually brought up by her grandmother, who lived with her family. Reproduction and child raising took up much of women's time, not just when they themselves were giving birth or had young children, but throughout their adult lives. It was a major way that women could and did help other women in their work.

Most women in Taradale married, and most had children, hence the focus on their household and reproductive labour.[40] Even though women were having fewer children by the 1920s, and some were benefiting from new household technology, there was continuity in women's lives and in their understanding of what it meant to be feminine. Throughout the period they were learning domestic crafts at school, and applying them at home. They expected to have children, and were expected to raise them as good citizens. But in another respect there was a growing discontinuity in women's working lives. When it came to paid work outside the home, an important inter-generational shift was occurring. Daughters were increasingly preferring to be an apprentice in a factory rather than mother's little helper at home.

An important stimulus to this change came from increasing access to education. By the turn of the century, school attendance requirements at Taradale's primary school were being enforced. Parents were being prosecuted if they failed to comply with the regulations. While some boys' attendance remained haphazard, girls were now instructed in the three Rs with little interruption.[41] Some girls were even able to continue their education past the proficiency examination, taken at the end of primary school.

It is impossible to know how many of Taradale's young women went on to secondary or tertiary education. Given the elite nature of the country's university colleges then, it is unlikely that even a handful of Taradale's young women studied at that level. Those who went to secondary school had to travel to Napier Girls' High School (NGHS), which began teaching the young women of Hawke's Bay in 1884. From the outset it was attended by girls from the Taradale area, such as sisters Lizzie and Ella Rymer. But the school remained quite small until the government brought in a free place scheme in 1903.[42] Under this scheme, all pupils who had passed the proficiency exam were given two free years at secondary school. From that time on, the roll at Napier Girls' began to grow, mostly with girls on scholarships and free places.[43]

Several girls from Taradale attended NGHS in the early years of the twentieth century. John and Charlotte Hindmarsh's daughters journeyed to Napier for their secondary schooling. Barbara, Dorothy, Cecily and Annie (also known as Madeline) Hindmarsh were all pupils, as was Bessie Peacock. Some Taradale girls went on to become head prefect or dux. In 1916 Charlotte Lily Halliwell held both honours, and so did Clarice Mary Williamson in 1917. Irene Rhodes, who had passed her proficiency at Taradale School in 1916, was head librarian at Napier Girls' in 1920, and five years later Taradale-born Jeannie Cattanach became dux.[44] Among the women interviewed,

Sophie Richardson and Sarah Stevenson went to NGHS and Alice Parke and Ellen Store attended secondary schools outside Hawke's Bay. Some girls, notably those who had attended the Meanee Convent primary school, went on to attend the convent secondary school in Napier.[45]

Between 1915 and 1924, the number of pupils receiving some form of secondary education in New Zealand doubled.[46] Part of this increase was due to the development of technical colleges, with their practical rather than academic focus. 'Napier Tech' opened in 1899, and by 1908 was operating as a day school.[47] It provided Taradale's young women with more opportunities for secondary education.[48] Martha Edwards, Emily Jones, Harriet South and Kathleen Thomson all recalled attending Napier Tech, and Ann Pearce went to Wellington Tech. Having some form of secondary education was far more common in the 1920s than it had been in the 1880s.

Education was beginning to mark young women off from their mothers and grandmothers. The NGHS curriculum prepared its pupils for university study. 'Tech' may have been less academically oriented, but it still opened up new opportunities. The young women who went to the technical schools increasingly spurned domestic courses in favour of professional or commercial ones. In 1919 there were four girls doing professional or commercial courses for every one doing a domestic course.[49] Martha Edwards was one of the few doing a domestic course, but as her recollections make clear, 'Tarzan' (the headmaster) was struggling to maintain numbers in this increasingly unpopular stream:

> *Why did you choose to do home science at tech?*
> I really don't know. I think for some reason or other my mother decided I was slightly more domestically inclined than my next sister who took a professional course, a commercial course, took a commercial course with typing and she ended up in an office. You see I was one of those children who was excruciatingly shy and probably trailed along with whatever idea that one's parents said. And then there were not very many, there were not very many in the home science course and I dare say Mr McLaren, he was the headmaster, known as Tarzan, he probably talked mum into it and suggested the home science course because he was keen to get enough in it to keep it viable. But other than that I really haven't any ideas about it, I can only think that that was probably how it was and sort of, I trailed along with the suggestion.[50]

The older generation saw the benefit of such an education, but when Martha's sister left 'tech' she expected to work in an office. Her mother may have spent her life at home, but she had no intention of repeating that pattern.

It would be a mistake to assume that all the young women who enjoyed improved access to education suddenly threw off the shackles of domestic work. Many continued to be classified as dependants or domestic workers.[51] On leaving school they worked within the domestic world, at home, in the home of a member of their extended family, or as paid help in someone else's home. Their lives mirrored the lives of their mothers. Several of the women interviewed spent some or all of the time between leaving school and marrying in helping their mothers. Grace Miner helped at home for a while, and also worked for a time at the local post office. Hannah Field worked with her mother, cooking food for the tea gardens they owned, until she married. This daily contact strengthened daughters' ties with their mothers and with other female kin who visited. Some women also worked as domestics for other members of their families. When Emma Needle's brother Edward McLean took over a local vineyard, Emma became his housekeeper. Kin was important in determining women's work.

Interestingly, the women who did domestic work on leaving school were reluctant to discuss it. They were happy to talk about their mothers' domestic work, and how they helped out when they were children; but when it became their own full-time job, they had very little to say. This was especially so if they worked for family members. Even those who worked in the homes of others, for a regular wage, were not forthcoming about the domestic work they did. However, they did make it clear that even though they were 'just' a domestic, the money they earned gave them some bargaining power. When Theresa Pond's mother broke her leg, Theresa's father wanted his eldest daughter to leave her job as a domestic servant and return home to run the household. On that occasion Theresa refused. On another occasion, when Theresa was working as a domestic down in Central Hawke's Bay, she negotiated with her father:

> Anyway, I said to Dad, 'Oh well, if you're so keen for me to come home well you've got to pay me Dad, you'll have to pay me' I said, 'I'm not just going to come home and get handouts all the time' I said, 'I'm not going to spend all the money I've got in the bank just to come home. You'll have to pay me'. So he paid me.
> *How much did he give you?*
> Oh he gave me about £1 a week, that wasn't bad money then. The first time I went into Public Hospital [to work] we only got 18 shillings a week and our keep.[52]

The Theresas of Taradale may have mirrored their mothers' work, but they were keen to be seen in a more independent light.

The women who had escaped the moral economy of domestic service were far more eager to discuss their working history.[53] These were young women who worked outside the home, often in the company of other young women. They were paid more than domestic servants, and usually worked shorter hours. Paid work outside the home meant that these women had a legitimate right to be in the public sphere. Whereas their mothers' work confined them to the home, they had to travel to and from work, either walking to the local shops or taking the bus ride into Napier. Some had to run errands as part of their jobs. Alice Parke, who worked for Mrs Randall, the owner of the Greenmeadows Fruit Farm, learned how to drive a car so that she could chauffeur her employer around. Louisa Plumb had to pick up grocery orders as part of her job at the Greenmeadows general store:

> Most people had accounts that you got the grocery orders from. I used to have to pedal around on my bike two days a week in Taradale and two days a week in Greenmeadows, go back to the store and make up the orders and Mr Badley would deliver them in the afternoon and sent out the accounts and when they paid their accounts they got a bag of boiled lollies. That was a highlight for the children, a bag of lollies . . .[54]

Children with bicycles tended to be male, so usually such chores were done by boys. Many young women acquired their own means of transport in adolescence. But the mobility of work was not always pleasant. Harriet South worked at the local post office during the Great War. As a 15-year-old she had to deliver telegrams informing families of the death or injury of their sons and fathers:

> It wasn't easy because I knew a lot of the boys who were killed. We weren't supposed to say anything but when I went I would give the parents or whoever came to the door a warning. I used to say, 'I'm sorry, it isn't good news'. Or if they were wounded 'It isn't the best but it could be a lot worse'. You know, something like that. Give them some sort of warning.[55]

Sex-segregated work outside the home also offered young women the opportunity to establish their own, female, work cultures – especially if they worked in larger establishments. Among their fellow workers normally taboo subjects, such as sex and sexuality, could be discussed. When talking about contraception, Theresa Pond mentioned that she had never seen a condom until after she was married, but that she knew they existed:

> *How did you know there were such things?*
> Well I'd heard it. I first heard a lot of things when I worked at Harris's factory.
> *From other women?*
> Well they didn't talk a lot about it at Harris's. Of course there was always a lot of things in *Truth* which we weren't supposed to read, I mean we didn't, Mum used to get the *Truth* but she never used to leave it so that we could look at it like that, you know. But at Harris's some of the girls, like one of the girls there, she was quite a cobber of mine really, she didn't have a mother, she was a bit older than me but she always used to get the *Truth* and bring it in there and read the features out of the *Truth* and that. I used to go to her place.[56]

Factories and offices, rather than small shops and domestic service, gave young women workers opportunities to share information and misinformation.

Kin remained important in women's non-domestic paid work. Sisters and other female relatives often found work for their younger kin. Theresa arranged a job at Harris's hat factory for her sister Florence. Kathleen Thomson found her own job as a shop assistant in Napier, but her aunt managed to get her a position at the department store she worked in:

> And Aunt Em, she got me a job at Blythe's, she was manageress in the tearooms there, when they had the tearooms, and I was working at McGruer's and she wanted me to go into Blythe's and I remember I had to go in me school gear to Blythe's to the interview with her because she reckoned I looked so nice in me school uniform and me boater hat, damn boater hat. And I had to go with an interview with Mr Conn was the manager, for an interview for a job in the shop and I was quite happy at McGruer's but she wanted me in Blythe's so I went into Blythe's and they put me in the underclothing department, the corset department. Started off as an apprentice sort of junior and then there was the manageress and then the first saleswoman. Well I suppose I got to the second saleswoman. I couldn't do any serving until the manageress and the first saleswoman, if they were serving then I could serve. That's how they worked it.[57]

Kathleen's memory of her experience in paid work has much in common with other women's recollections. They clearly remembered names of the women they worked with, and the names of their bosses – or, in Kathleen's case, the name of the man who interviewed her – and recalled the whole experience fondly. Young women often formed strong bonds with their work mates. Emily Jones's ties with her employers were so strong that they 'gave' her her wedding. Mr and Mrs Richards, who owned the drapery store Emily worked in, provided the cake and wine for her wedding breakfast. These sorts of ties also separated young women's experiences from their mother's lives.

But the most important aspect of young women's paid work was the fact that they now earned their money. This marked them off not only from other girls who were denied the chance to earn, but also from their mothers. While many married women were active contributors to the household economy, the money they earned from selling butter or eggs was not theirs so much as the household's. Even though the young women did not earn very much, and often handed over the bulk of their wages as board, most still had more economic independence than they had ever experienced before, or, in many cases, would ever experience again.

In the 1880s a young woman employed as a pupil teacher might earn as little as £10 per annum, as Annie Harpham did in 1886. By 1892, her last year at Taradale School, Annie was earning £38 a year.[58] By the early 1920s a first-year female probationer teacher was still earning only £83 a year, whereas the female head of the infant school, Miss Burness, was paid £283 per annum.[59] This was considerably less than similarly qualified male teachers, but in general teaching was among the better paid occupations women could take on. Apart from official positions like teaching, it is difficult to determine how much women were paid. Among those interviewed, Harriet South, a post office worker, seems to have been the highest paid. She recalled her annual salary just before the Depression as being £150.

Once they were contributing to the family economy through paying board, few of these women were expected to do very much around the home.[60] Their mothers did their washing, had their dinner ready for them when they returned from their day's work, and generally took on the tasks their daughters had previously done, or else passed them on to their younger daughters. A young woman's status within the family improved as she began to pay her way.[61] Her earning capacity gave her a degree of independence she had not enjoyed as a child. Now she had both leisure time and discretionary spending power, she could enter the consumer culture.

The new women who worked in shops, offices and factories had a different experience of work from their mothers, and a different understanding of femininity. For their mothers, femininity was about propping up the twin institutions of home and family. Being a proper wife and good mother gave them status and purpose. For the new women, paid work was the exciting phase between school and marriage, an interlude of relative independence. They knew that ultimately the domestic world of family awaited them, but in the meantime they could redefine themselves. In many respects, the redefinition was slight. Most women worked in low-paid, sex-specific jobs. But the fact that they were no longer confined to the home, worked with other women, and received a regular wage, was central to how they saw themselves and wanted others to see them. Little wonder, then, that the single women who continued to be dependants and domestics were reluctant to discuss this phase of their lives.

For most of the new women, paid work was the adventure before they married and had their own family. But women who did not marry until later in life or never married, women who became widowed, divorced or separated, and women whose husbands either could not or would not provide for them, also had to find paid work.[62] Their jobs were often determined by their marital status. A woman who never married could continue with her career as a school teacher or nurse, remain as a live-in domestic for a family member or stranger, or run one of the shops along Taradale's Main Road. All of the female school teachers, clerks, telephonists, typists and shop assistants in Taradale were single.

Widows and divorcees found work as nurses, domestic servants, shopkeepers, dressmakers, postmistresses and music teachers.[63] Like the younger single women discussed above, these women were more mobile and public than their married counterparts. But their relative freedom was a double-edged sword; women's wages were rarely sufficient to allow them to establish or maintain their own households. The women who managed to succeed economically usually inherited a business or other assets. These women operated within a very limited economic sphere. They ran shops selling confectionery rather than fruit and vegetables. They sewed for local people rather than for the growing department store sector. They did not create a separate economy relying instead on male customers. Ideas about what a 'proper' woman did curtailed their employment opportunities.

For women who were still married but needed to bring some money into the household economy, this feminine imperative was even stronger. Married women generally moved into the non-household world of paid work only when the sexual division of labour began to break down. If their husband was ill, if he was unemployed or underemployed, if he drank all of his earnings, or if he simply refused to support his wife and children, then married women had to find some way to make ends meet. Their options were limited. In almost all cases, married women ended up replicating the types of work they did within their own homes. School and church cleaning was an acceptable employment avenue for married women. Once they had cleaned their own homes, they could go out and clean up after other people. Some held such jobs for many years. Taradale School first employed Mrs Phoebe Cattanach as its cleaner in 1889. At that time she was paid £1.9.0 a month. The Cattanach household was not well off. Phoebe's husband John, a storeman, hardly earned enough to support their seven children. When daughter Edith had an illegitimate child in 1892, and another in 1895, the family's budget was stretched to the limit. In 1899 Phoebe asked for an increase in her salary, to compensate for building additions to the school. The Board agreed to an increase of £1.6.0 a month. Phoebe continued cleaning the school until 1906, when she was 62 years old.[64] She died the following year.

Women who cleaned for others were not paid very much. Although Phoebe Cattanach had been paid £3 per month by the time she left, when Henrietta Strachan took up cleaning the school in 1909, she was paid only £2.5.0. No doubt she was pleased to get the job. Henrietta was the mother of ten children and her labourer husband, Alexander, was a drinker. In 1909 and 1910 Henrietta requested that prohibition orders be taken out against him and in 1910 she requested a separation from him and £1 a week maintenance. Clearly she needed the money from cleaning, even though the job was arduous. In 1910 the school committee informed her 'that it will be necessary to have the school scrubbed, back offices [toilets] washed and sides of urinal attended to during the holidays'. No extra money was forthcoming. It was not until 1915 that Henrietta's earnings reached £3 per month. In 1918 she resigned from the job, but by 1920 she was back cleaning, this time at the Presbyterian church. By 1924 she was earning the princely sum of £13 per annum.[65]

Not all of the married women who worked in the public economy did so because their husbands drank a large proportion of their wages. The Taradale Town Board employed Lena Larson's husband, Berhardt, in 1914 as its clerk and librarian. In 1915 Berhardt was taken ill, so Lena took over his job. The Town Board conveyed 'its thanks to Mrs Larson for the able manner in which she had managed the Board's business during Mr Larson's illness.' Lena Larson was paid the librarian's salary in 1915 and 1916.[66] In other words, in emergencies women could sometimes step into their husbands' shoes, although usually this was much more of a short-term measure than in the Larson case. (Lena Larson's actions could be seen as supporting her husband and thus suitably feminine. Library work could also be constructed as feminine; 'it was genteel, it was "cultural", and it gave opportunities for women to serve others'.)[67] There is no evidence that Taradale women did this when it came to harvesting or working on the land. Although Claire Toynbee believes that New Zealand women often did men's manual work, and Nancy Grey Osterud argues the same for rural American couples, their evidence is slight.[68] There is also little indication that men returned the favour. Instead, women turned to their female kin and neighbours and men to their masculine network.

There were, of course, other women in Taradale who defied this unwritten feminine code. Elsie Baylis pulled a gun on her husband Frank during a particularly fraught Christmas in 1929. The mother of two young sons, she served two years' probation and divorced Frank in 1934. Years earlier, in 1901, Bridget Jeffares overstepped the mark when she called neighbour Hannah Moreland a 'bloody cow'. Bridget had a lot to cope with. Her husband Robert had a drinking problem, her baby son James had recently died, and she had four other young children. Ironically, Bridget and Hannah were later to become relatives, when Bridget's oldest daughter married into Hannah's family. For some women the strain of being a good wife and mother was too much. Sarah Pointon, mother of two young daughters, was declared a lunatic at large and committed to care in 1892. Jane Lauchlan was committed to Porirua mental hospital in 1920. Married in 1913, she had given birth to five children in seven years. Her youngest daughter, Ada, died on 20 March 1920. On 25 March Jane smashed Bartholomew Steinmetz's window, and on 28 March she was sent to Porirua.

Sarah and Jane tried to live up to society's expectations of what a proper wife and mother should do, but failed. Others were more resistant of these norms. Alice Rising had an illegitimate daughter in 1908. By 1912 May Rising was an inmate of the Wellington Receiving Home and Alice was in court, charged with failing to provide for her child. Nora Wells sometimes worked as a domestic, and sometimes as a prostitute. She also fenced stolen goods and was arrested for receiving in 1918. Mary Walsh served three month for being idle and disorderly in 1926. But these women who flouted the gender code were very much in the minority in Taradale. Few women, married or

WOMEN'S WORK

single, rejected outright notions of what women's work and proper role were.

Although most married and single women worked within the acceptable boundaries of what was considered to be women's work, there is some indication that their understanding of this changed over time. For married women, the expectation of being a good wife and mother remained. Status and respectability was earned as women married, had children, raised them as good, clean citizens, and kept their homes spotless. The scrubbed verandah and well-pressed clothes spoke volumes. All the while they had to be more than their husbands' helpmeets. Their work, whether productive or reproductive, linked them into a complex web of familial and community relations, and ideological expectations. Women's domestic work, motherhood, and ideas about true womanhood were intricately linked. As true women, they embraced both the responsibilities and the power that came from having a clearly demarcated domestic sphere and role.[69]

For other women, though, the link between work and the meaning of femininity was less stable. Occasionally women such as Jane Lauchlan tried to live up to society's expectations, but failed, and women such as Nora Wells refused to play by the rules. But the most sustained challenge to the understanding of women's work came from Taradale's new women, the young women who came of age after the Great War, and were part of the modernising society of interwar New Zealand.[70] In small but important ways, these women had a different understanding of femininity from their mothers. They saw that a secondary education could free women from housework and allow them to participate in a non-domestic work culture, where they could make their own friends, independent from the world their mother lived in, and above all earn their own money. The new women defined themselves by their paid work and new friends. They gained status and respectability through the clothes they bought and the places they went. Even the young women who stayed within a domestic work culture were part of this redefinition. They did not recount stories of the domestic work they did once they had left school. This was not central to their self-identification, as it had been for their mothers, aunts and grandmothers. As Chapter 7 shows, before these women married they defined themselves through their leisure.

The challenge to hegemonic femininity through the paid and unpaid work of Taradale's new women, and the few women who could not or would not abide by the rules, may seem paltry when compared to recent changes and challenges. But it is important not to project current expectations back onto women in the past. There was no watershed in Taradale's gender relations. But the small repositionings that took place were important, especially when compared with the much more static and much more inter-generationally inclusive experiences which typified men's work and their understandings of masculinity.

These last two chapters argue that Taradale's economy was not based on the male breadwinner, and question the idea that women were merely men's helpmeets. Yet the fact that men were not the sole breadwinners in many households does not imply that they recognised the importance of the work done by other household members. Although a degree of mutuality may have characterised the actual work people did, it does not follow that everyone understood this to mean that power was shared in the family. Indeed, the evidence suggests otherwise, as the next chapter shows.

CHAPTER 5

Men's Work

How men earned a living, and the values they associated with their labours, were central to defining masculinity. In certain respects men's work shared characteristics with women's work. Whether they worked paid or unpaid, inside or outside the home, both men and women set much store by contributing to the household, working with family, and being seen to be getting by. But men's work differed from women's work in several important ways. These differences help to explain why men continued to be seen as head of the household and head of the household's economy.

In studying masculinity, argues Caroline Ramzanoglu, it is crucial to look at the sources of men's power and how these are maintained and reproduced as the structures of masculinity shift.[1] Understanding how men's work was viewed and understood by men and by women is critical to understanding how the men of Taradale retained power and control over their families and the community. Why were men considered to be economically superior to women? The obvious answer is that on average, men owned more land and resources and earned higher wages than women did. In a limited sense, the ideal of the male breadwinner was a reality. This economic power bought men power over other aspects of their family's lives.

But other aspects of men's work are also important in understanding how men's labour continued to be seen as superior to women's. This chapter considers the public location of men's work, the generational inclusivity of men's work places and processes, the collective nature of much male employment, the visible ways men's work allowed them to prove their provider status, the physical strength required by so much of the work men did in Taradale, and the fact that many men in the area were able to control their work so as to leave room for leisure. By contrast, women's work – especially married women's work – was private, and was increasingly defined by where they were in the life cycle. It tended to be performed alone, often did not celebrate women's productive contributions to the household, downplayed women's physical strength, and allowed little time for leisure. Given these differences, it is little wonder that men's work was viewed by so many as superior to women's work.

Men's paid work is much easier to 'count' than women's work. Men were listed under more than a hundred occupations on the electoral rolls. Taradale was home to a banker and a billiard marker, a cowboy and a chimney sweep, a musician and a miner. These occupations have been grouped into six major categories.[2] Figure 5.1 shows how many men came into each category throughout the period. (Appendix B further explains each category.) The percentage of men in each category did not vary greatly over time, even if the nature of the work did.[3] For example, among those employed as skilled workers, blacksmiths were replaced by motor mechanics, but the percentage of men listed as skilled was fairly consistent.

FIGURE 5.1: MEN'S OCCUPATIONS BY CATEGORIES, 1887–1928

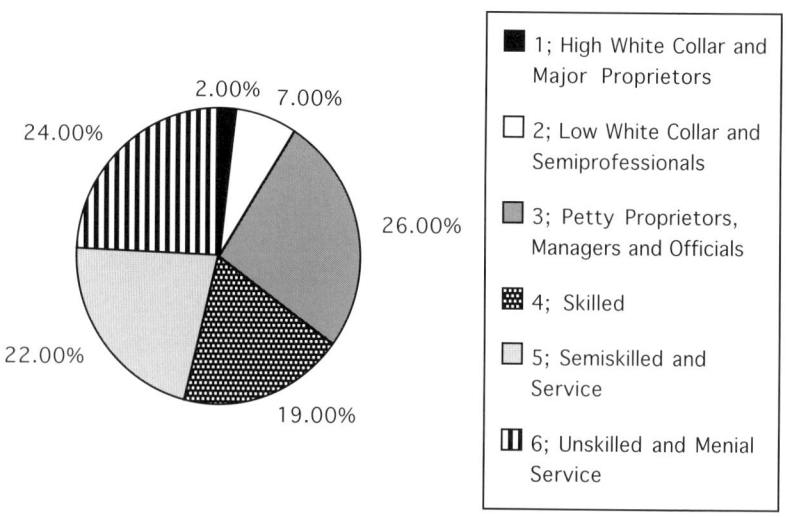

Counting occupations, of course, tells us little about the work men actually did or the meanings associated with those labours. What characterised men's work in Taradale? Whether we look at a farmer working his own land, a labourer who divided his time between paid and unpaid work, or a man who left home each morning for the office, shop or factory, men's work places tended to be masculine spaces. For the farmers, dairymen, market gardeners, orchardists and nurserymen, the scrubbed verandah around the family home marked one boundary of their territory. Although women might be allowed into the dairy or poultry yards, the land was men's domain. Their paddocks and gardens confined the home, but they were also constrained by the close physical proximity of their wives and families. However, these men made frequent trips away from home, to sell produce, buy stock, and so on.

The public world of commerce was a strongly masculine environment. Taradale's main road was a man's road. The hotel and billiard saloon stood at one end and the vast majority of shops were owned and run by men. Women were not even encouraged to go to town to do their shopping. The baker and butcher would call regularly on the surrounding homes, and the grocer would both pick up and deliver orders. The mobility of men's work meant that their work places covered a wide area, thus increasing their hold on the public world. However, over time this hold began to be threatened, as more women moved into these public spaces. The single and widowed women who took up paid employment encroached on what had previously been male territory. Men's work-a-day world was slowly changing.

While some women started infiltrating the public world that men had made their own, for the most part they were not working alongside men. As the previous chapter showed, women ran the post office and sold confectionery. Most men continued to work in predominantly masculine environments. At Golding the bootmaker's, or Bradley the saddler's, you knew that either Mr Golding or Mr Bradley or one of their sons would serve you. Family ties in general, and intergenerational ties in particular, were important bonds in men's work.

Boys in Taradale grew up with strong expectations that they would follow in their father's footsteps. Just as young girls were their mother's helpers, so many boys were officially or unofficially apprenticed to their fathers. During the school holidays, if Ernest Edwards was not droving with his grandfather, he was helping his builder father. On leaving school he joined his father full-time. Matthew Silk helped his father in the family's painting and decorating firm after school and in the holidays. His father, uncle and oldest brother already worked

Butchers standing outside a butcher shop in Taradale's main road, before 1910. Edwin Pointon's sons Edward and Ebenezer joined him in the business. They may be the men on the left. COLLECTION OF HAWKE'S BAY CULTURAL TRUST–HAWKE'S BAY MUSEUM, NAPIER, NEW ZEALAND, 7597

together, and at his father's bidding, Matthew joined them once he had finished his course at 'tech'. Thomas Raven joined his father in the family's blacksmith business at the age of 12: 'People used to think I was second sight, we'd be working and doing a job and he'd just look at the tools and I'd pick two up that he wanted. I just got used to it.'[4] William Cliff's father was a plumber who also worked 12 acres of land. When asked how his father managed both jobs, William replied, 'Well, he had me.' Together they not only worked on plumbing jobs – William went on to be a plumber too – but bred pedigree Jersey cows, grew lucerne to make hay, raised between 500 and 1000 fowls at a time, and grew flowers to sell at the market.[5]

These men were all growing up in the 1920s. By then their sisters were increasingly rejecting the domestic work around which their mother's lives revolved. The intergenerational work bonds between men underwent no such upheaval. Not only do their oral recollections indicate this, but at a more general level, comparing the occupations of men who married in the area with the work their fathers did showed that fathers and sons often worked in the same or similar jobs. As David Pearson found in his study of Johnsonville, most men 'inherited their father's "class" background'.[6]

An examination of almost 600 marriage certificates revealed that in just over a quarter of the marriages, the groom and his father were listed as having exactly the same occupation. This finding was fairly consistent throughout the period.[7] Patrick O'Dowd, a shepherd, married Louisa Gebbie in June 1890. Patrick's father, Charles, was a farmer, as was Louisa's father. While many of these men were farmers, a sizeable minority were labourers.[8] There were also numerous cases where fathers and sons had similar or related jobs. Arthur Lord, who married Gladys Boland in July 1925, was a jockey. No doubt his father, Arthur senior, a horse trainer, had stimulated his career. In other instances fathers and sons had related jobs, but their work appeared to be different due to changes in technology. Albert Rowe, who married Mabel Irvine in November 1915, was a motor mechanic – the modern equivalent of his father's job as a blacksmith.

Once they had learnt the job, men who followed in their father's footsteps were unlikely to walk away to start up their own businesses. Intergenerational family firms were important in Taradale. Fathers and sons, brothers and cousins often worked together, as many of the shops on the main road bore witness. Martin's butcher shop was a local institution where father and sons worked together. Orchardist William Waterhouse worked with his four sons. After managing the Greenmeadows Fruit Farm, Sidney Anderson established his own nursery business, where he worked alongside his son, Francis.

Family firms were also intragenerational. Some single sisters joined together to establish dressmaking businesses, as the Misses Hawkins did in the 1890s. These sisters ran a small establishment until they both married. While noted for their sewing, they gained wider fame as the originals for the Misses Harris, the dressmakers in Kitty O'Sullivan's Taradale-based novel, *The Curse of the Greenstone Tiki*.[9] Kin were important in women's paid and unpaid work, but family firms usually entailed male members of the family entering into business together. The most famous fraternal partnership in the area was the Dolbel brothers' sheep farm, although they later divided the property. Other brothers maintained family firms. Frank Powdrell and his brothers Harry and Herbert were the first in the area to introduce sheep crates for trucking livestock to the freezing works. They worked together for many years.[10]

The importance of kinship ties to men's work is also shown by the numbers of men who took over their fathers' businesses. Frank Lansdown, 'for many years . . . associated with his father in dairying', carried on the family milk supply business with his brothers after his father died.[11] When W. Lord took over the Greenmeadows Hotel in

1886, his son, W. Lord junior, took over his father's well sinking business.[12] When Mr Neagle, who had been a butcher in the area for 20 years, retired in May 1892, his son, R. J. Neagle, continued the family business.[13] To take over such firms, these men must have worked with their fathers previously, or worked in similar jobs for others. Either way, this indicates that they had strong ties with their father's work.

It is not surprising, then, to learn that Taradale's boys had a work ethic instilled in them from an early age. While their sisters helped inside the home, the boys of the area were set tasks to do outside. They learnt to collect and chop wood for the stove, and often set the fire for the copper before leaving for school on Monday mornings. They fed poultry, collected eggs, and cleaned the slaughtered chickens. If anyone helped with the vegetable garden, it was the young boys. They also picked the fruit for their mothers to preserve. Most of the male oral narrators said that they had helped in some way with the family's cows, by doing the milking, the separating, the churning or delivering milk and butter around the neighbourhood. As well as being outside, boys' jobs often involved moving around the neighbourhood on errands.[14] Men's and boys' work required greater mobility than the work performed by women and girls, as Patrick Stevenson recalled:

> *Who did you deliver the milk to?*
> Oh there was about one, two, three, four, about seven customers. Alf Burr and Harry Burr, when their cow was dry, otherwise they had their cow. There was Barnes, Brady's, Elborne's, Paul Russell, Jarvis, Clifton's, Cecil Burr and the Jones'. Then it was a case of going home, getting the cows and putting them out in the long paddock – that was the road – and I would have to mind those cows on the road until a quarter to nine, then tear home, get my – we had paddocks leased in Moeller Street and Elborne Street vicinity – tear home, get my school bag, run all the way to Taradale school from the Game Farm and if I was late I'd play the wag.[15]

Boys' work could lead to trouble. If Patrick's chores made him late he would play truant from school. When Henry Nolan ran errands for his neighbour he got an early taste for alcohol:

> As a kid I remember I'd run up to the pub, he [Jimmy, a neighbour] used to give me 7s 6d to get a bottle of whisky for him and I used to go up to poor old Mr Griffiths in the pub. I was only six or seven years old at the time. And I'd go up, 'A bottle of whisky, Mr Griffiths, for old Jimmy'. He took a risk givin' it to me. He shouldn't have done it but he knew who it was for and he knew me and that. Anyway, this particular day I took it back to

Jimmy and he gave me a drink of whisky see, oh quite a big thing in a dirty old pannikin it was, and I drank it and I got drunk on it, see. And I went home and I was staggering around everywhere. Poor old Mum and Dad, they didn't know what was wrong and I didn't tell them. Later on of course they found out. But they put me to bed and I woke up all right. I didn't know what the whisky was, I only knew that old Jimmy drunk it.[16]

Henry was not the only boy to get into trouble when running errands. In 1900 an 11-year-old pupil from Taradale School was convicted in court of theft. David White was delivering vegetables to one of his father's customers, Walter Smith, when he 'yielded to sudden temptation' and stole Smith's watch.[17] Then there was the case of Anderson Scullin, who went out blackberrying with his friend, Page. Page went home at 6 p.m., but Scullin was still picking berries. He did not return home that night, and fears were held for his safety, since he was subject to having fits. The next day, though, he turned up safe and well, with his bucket full of blackberries.[18] While Scullin's sisters helped their mother inside the house, Taradale's boys were already carving out a role for themselves in the public world.

Boys also tended to have fewer chores than their sisters had. Once the wood was chopped or the animals fed, and when their fathers did

Church Road, Taradale, c. 1920s. Boys and men on their bikes and in their vehicles still commanded most of the area's public space. COLLECTION OF HAWKE'S BAY CULTURAL TRUST–HAWKE'S BAY MUSEUM, NAPIER, NEW ZEALAND, 6868C

not need them, boys were often allowed to go out to play or earn some money. Sometimes they managed to combine the two. With his male cousins and friends, Richard Jackson turned earning some pocket money into fun. Like many of the young boys in Taradale, Richard learned how to use a gun at an early age. Once he had finished his jobs around the house, Richard would head out to shoot hawks and shags. After cutting off their bills and feet, he and his mates would take them into the Acclimatization Society, where they received 1s per hawk and 1s 6d for a shag:

> We used to put them in a paper bag . . . and [laugh] take them into the Acclimatization Society in Napier and by the time you got them in there they were pretty rotten, you know, smelly [laugh] and the girl behind the counter wouldn't count them, you see, so you'd always sneak a few extra . . . We used to get a whole lot sometimes. I bought my first suit through that.[19]

A suit with long trousers was a sure sign of manhood, as was the ability to earn money. Boys earned money through conventional jobs such as having a paper round or working in an orchard, but they also showed ingenuity. Ernest Edwards and his brother scythed prairie grass from local orchards, dried it on tarpaulins, beat the seed out with sticks, sifted it and then sold it to local seed merchants. After their success with prairie grass they turned to cocksfoot.

These were jobs and schemes carried out after school. But many boys played truant from school so that they could contribute to the family's economy, while also preparing themselves for the capitalist economy they were soon to enter full-time. Henry Hill, the Hawke's Bay school inspector, constantly lamented the poor attendance at Taradale School. In 1895 he calculated that Taradale's attendance of 68.5 per cent was the lowest of the five schools he averaged out for the December quarter over a five-year period. In 1904 he was still reporting that 'the worst cases of irregularity are met with at Taradale and Wairoa'.[20] Both boys and girls were irregular attendees. All children stayed away due to illness or bad weather, but if girls were absent it was often to help their mothers around the home. Boys stayed away to take part in the public culture of paid work.

It seems that boys were more likely to play truant than girls were. From the 1890s, Taradale School's headmaster made repeated comments in his daily log book about the poor attendance of his pupils. Often his comments were not gender-specific, but whenever they were, it was boys who were the culprits.[21] Several types of paid work distracted boys from their schoolwork. Sometimes boys took on paid work while still of school age. Mr Atkins's son 'was kept away frequently to go round with the butcher's cart'.[22] The headmaster saw a particular problem with this: 'When boys go away to work with men they do not return very well disposed to submit to the discipline of school.'[23] Other boys merely arrived late because of jobs before school. Alex Douglas was punished for playing truant. His morning paper round meant that he was often late for school.[24]

But most of the paid work that kept boys away from school involved their working with a group of their mates. In the 1880s several boys preferred picking potatoes to going to school: 'Many boys kept away [due to] picking potatoes during past fortnight'.[25] The local racecourse offered boys other sources of paid work, such as selling race cards. When the races were on, the senior boys at Taradale school were often absent. In June 1908 'several boys' in Standards 4 and 5 were away at the races.[26] The golf course also employed boys as caddies. A couple of months after the Standard 5 boys had been at the races, five of the 13 boys in the class were away at a golf match.[27]

Others were employed in local vineyards during the grape harvest. In 1898 the headmaster even recommended to the school committee that they change the midwinter holiday to the grape picking season, a suggestion the committee rejected. They did not want cheap child labour to deny unemployed men work.[28] Instead, they decided to prosecute the parents of absentee children. In late March 1898, after several boys had played truant from school to work on the grape harvest, the committee acted. The parents of Joseph White, Henry Walker, Arthur Gardiner, John Blackmore, Noel Sutton and Dillon Wilson were all charged with failure to comply with school attendance requirements. This was a new development. Previously, although the headmaster and school committee were not pleased with low attendance, especially as schools were financed through a capitation system based on average attendance, they took little direct action to force boys and their parents to conform to the school attendance legislation.[29] As Inspector Hill recognised in 1891: 'the enforcement of attendance is not popular with the committees generally, as it tends to arouse strong local jealousies in small communities, where every man deems himself as good as his neighbour.'[30] But from 1898 prosecutions were being laid against Taradale parents whose children failed to comply with the attendance requirements. They were usually fined 2s for every week the child did not attend school, as the Education Act required, as well as having to pay 7s court costs. Between 1898 and 1912, there were 40 truancy prosecutions in the area. Two out of three of these cases concerned boys.[31]

GIRLS AND WOMEN, MEN AND BOYS

By the outbreak of the Great War in 1914, truancy due to boys doing paid work was no longer a problem. Parents and the authorities were united in their desire to keep the boys at school.[32] But whether boys were working for money during school hours, after school, or in the holidays, the work they did and the work culture they were part of helped prepare them for the day when they left education and boyhood behind, and became real men.

Men's work obviously had a very practical purpose. Around the home or in paid employment, men were working to support their families. Sometimes this involved long hours. Harriet South's recollections of her father's work at the wool stores makes this clear:

> He'd be away early in the morning and home perhaps two, half past two in the morning and Mum would have a hot meal for him when he came in and then he'd have perhaps a couple of hours sleep, he'd get up and put the horse in the trap again, have his breakfast and go off. And there was many a time us children didn't see him once in a fortnight.[33]

The tone of Harriet's story is different from the way men remembered their father's work. They were less aware of how their mothers were involved in their fathers' employment, and less concerned about their fathers' absences from home, perhaps because they often accompanied their fathers to work.

Harriet's father worked long and hard so that he could bring a good wage into the house. But being a good provider was also important at another level. The breadwinner ethos, the idea of a man being the head of the household, even if not literally true, was an important aspect of how the men of Taradale defined themselves. The fact that Harriet's mother had inherited money and bought the house and land they lived on could be fudged if Mr South was seen as the main earner. Those men who failed to provide, who were bankrupted or relied on charity, were lesser men. Their masculinity was in question.

Providing took many guises. Given that so much of men's work in the area was concerned with primary production, the ability to be a good producer was important. George Davies's father took this to heart. He did not join lodges or clubs: 'His main interest was gardening, in his garden. He'd even be out there on moonlit nights, digging his garden by moonlight [laugh]'.[34] The growers of Taradale were not content with producing average crops: their yields had to be the biggest, their fruit the largest, their vegetables the heaviest. Time

MEN'S WORK

and again the local newspaper reported that men from the Taradale area had come to the office with news of their prowess as growers. Some even brought the evidence. Mr Waterhouse arrived with grapes the size of plums, Mr Snell showed off his ten-ounce onion, Mr Smith lugged in six potatoes weighing 20 pounds and Mr Harpham placed on show his 75-pound mangold wurzel (a type of cattle food).[35] In part these examples of vegetable gigantism were used to raise the profile of the area, and no doubt land prices as well. But it was also a way that the men could prove themselves as virile workers and providers. Like their land and their produce, they were seen as vigorous and strong.

Whereas William Waterhouse grew his plum-sized grapes for the market, many of Taradale's men worked a smallholding to provide for their families, while also engaging in some form of paid employment. This domestic labour was very important not only to the family's economy, but also to their definition of masculinity. Men's domestic work took place outside the home. The oral evidence indicates that very few men helped with domestic chores inside the house, even in emergencies. In such times, women called on their female kin and neighbours. Many of men's outside chores had a productive function. They often milked the household's cows, and most men seem to have had vegetable gardens. When Matthew Silk was asked about his mother's family, he replied that he used to see his maternal grandparents every day. He ate his grandmother's freshly baked bread, and sometimes he would help out in the garden:

> Oh yes, used to go down there and chop a bit of firewood you know, keep the stove burning and that type of thing. Do odds and ends. Sometimes get out and help her in the garden, just fork some of her prize bulbs [laugh]. Oh, she had a great garden in the front there but it was smothered with bulbs and everything you could think of, you know, one of the old type things. She had every type of flower. And she said, 'You can dig that piece' and I put the fork in and come up with a prize bulb, something like that [laugh]. In the end she'd say, 'Oh well, you'd better go round the back and help your grandfather' [laugh]. Oh yes, I remember that.
> *Was your grandfather in charge of the vegetables?*
> Grandfather, oh yes. Oh he had about seven acres there. He had a big patch of potatoes, things like that, carrots, big paddock of oats, lucerne. That used to keep him busy. Had a great orchard there, made sure they were well thinned out [laugh]. Oh yeah.[36]

Even men and women's gardens were separate and physically distinct.

If women gardened, they tended to the flowers at the front of the house. No women appeared to have had anything to do with vegetable gardens. They were masculine spaces.

It also seems to have been common for men to raise and slaughter a pig, for household consumption. Louisa Plumb and George Davies recalled their fathers spending most of their spare time gardening. Both fathers also regularly slaughtered pigs. George's father and uncle, who had worked in the freezing works, would kill the pig, sell part of it, and have the rest of it smoked for the family's consumption.[37] By spending their spare time doing such tasks, men saved their households from spending valuable cash resources. In the 1890s a labourer or gardener might earn only 7s a day, and lamb and pork was 5d a pound. So men's domestic chores were economically very important to the household budget.[38]

Like their wives, Taradale's men made valuable contributions to the family's economy through such chores. But unlike their wives, when men went to work, around the home or away from it, they often worked with others. A married woman might spend much of her day alone or in the company of small children, while her husband was probably working alongside boys and or other men. Even men who worked their own land rarely spent all their time alone. Dairymen often had a boy working with them, to help with the milking. Sarah Stevenson's father ran cows at Meanee, and had a milk round in Napier. He employed Bert Stansfield to help him:

> . . . he had a young chap who used to help with the milking in the afternoons. Well, he lived there of course, he had board and everything. He'd do the afternoon milking and then in the mornings he would milk for a while to get enough milk and then he would take off into town with that milk, just with a horse and cart, we didn't have a truck. . .[39]

Florence Rifle's father, a farmer, also often employed a boy to help. When it came to harvesting the hay, Florence recalled that the neighbours used to come to help: 'We'd always cook a hot dinner for all the men.'[40] Harvesters and shearers were often Maori, so it was not unusual for the Pakeha men of the area to spend some of their working time with Maori men.

The group nature of men's work was most evident among those who worked for large employers, such as the Greenmeadows Fruit Farm. The local authorities were also major employers, especially after the frequent floods the area suffered. Thomas Raven remembered seeing large groups of these men at the local hotel:

MEN'S WORK

Men working on the river bank after a flood. The collective, public nature of so much of men's work is obvious from this photograph. PRIVATE COLLECTION

> But when we used to have floods oh at least once every two or three years and they'd always be a big lot of people working on the river bed either in teams or on the shovel and all rode bikes and you'd see anything from 50 to 100 all biking down after work and they'd say they'd stop at Taradale Hotel and then they'd have a row with that publican and they'd all bike past him and go to Greenmeadows or Meanee.[41]

Even where men ostensibly worked by themselves, as in owner-operated shops, their work place still involved others – both customers and other shopkeepers:

> Taradale, in the olden days with the shops, talk about the Wild West was nothing to the shopkeepers, they – the local Chemist Mostyn Williams – of a cold morning he would be out on the other side of the road, talking to the bootmaker, Pat Golding and a couple of the others and if you went to go into his shop he used to lift his hand and say, 'Was there something you wanted?' 'Yes, a pack of aspirin' 'On the left hand side, over the thing there, 1s 6d.' And you put it down. He very seldom would bother to come over, he would direct you from the other side of the road.[42]

By working in gangs or as part of a close-knit network, men were able to further their hold on the community. There was strength in numbers.

Other types of strength and skill were also important masculine work traits. Since so few men in the area were employed purely for their mental prowess, intellectual ability was not highly regarded. But being able to conquer the land and control animals at work was a prime way to prove that you were a man. Henry Nolan left school the day he turned 14. A fortnight later he became a man by proving himself at work:

> Well there was a man named Mr Scagan and he had a team of horses and they were pulling down the banks and putting up banks down Riverbend Road . . . and one of the men got sick and he come and see me and said could I drive a couple of horses. Well, when I was about two years old, I could drive horses, we only had horses, you see, and riding horses. And I said, 'Yeah I can do it all right.' 'You sure?' he said, I said 'Yes'. Cor blimey days. I had done a bit before, see, not as a job but more for fun. For the first day he watched me do it and I got the horse out and being young I was a bit swollen headed like most people are when they're young, first job and that, I used to go along and the scoop had two handles on it and the horses in front of course, they had to be, and you was coming behind with it. And I used to have the reins in one hand and the scoop handle in the other hand and take a little bit at a time and when I had to tip it I had a knack of doing it, see, all I done was just lift it up slowly, not right over and the horses done most of the work, see. It tipped over. Anyway, he kept me on then, until they'd finished. They were pulling down the riverbanks along Riverbend Road. He paid me £3 a week, same as the men, good money . . .[43]

Fourteen-year-old Henry still felt like a boy, but to his employer he was a man and was paid men's wages. He proved himself through his skill with the horses and scoop, and was rewarded accordingly.

Thomas Raven became a 'man' when he was only 12 years old. When his blacksmith father's apprentice became ill, Thomas was brought in to replace him. He did not leave the smithy until he retired many years later. Edward McLean became a self-employed viticulturist while still in his teens:

> Then I left that and went to work for Mr Steinmetz at the vineyard and I seemed to have an affinity for that. He taught me the wine-maker's job and the grape grower's job and I worked for him for about five years and then

he thought he'd like to go home to see his people in Luxembourg and another young fellow was working with me there and he said, 'You fellas can run the business, you know enough about it to run it. I'll lease it to you.' So he did. I was 19 and the other fellow was older than me, he was 20. And that was 1927, just the start of the big Depression and it was a bit of a struggle for quite a while . . .[44]

But it was a struggle that Edward overcame. Edward's description of wine-making is an interesting example of men's work process in several ways. He is self-deprecating – making wine was 'a very elementary process' – yet he also conveys something of the skills involved, for example when he discusses how to clean out barrels. Size and quantity were important, as they were for fruit and vegetable growers, and so was the ability to survive under tough economic conditions:

Can you describe how you made the wine?
Well it was a very elementary process in those days. We had a wooden crusher, rollers, wooden rollers, and the grapes were picked and brought in in tubs and the wooden rollers were put over the top of 100 gallon carrier vats, the grapes were tipped into the hopper of the crusher and you turned the handle and crushed the grapes through the wooden rollers. They went into the vat and then you shifted the roller onto the next vat, you put the lid on the one you'd filled and the fermentation took place. Each vat had a tap at the bottom, a brass tap in those days, everything was brass or copper, and you used to run the wine through and ladle it over the top, all done by hand, there were no pumps in those days, it was done manually, done the way they did it in the early days, I suppose hundreds of years beforehand. Then the wine was put into casks to finish fermenting and settle to a degree, then run out, then that was clarified, we used Fuller's Earth to do that, and we then put that aside and matured it for three or four years, all in small barrels. We didn't have the large barrels, we had three 500's, two 800's and about three 300's and the rest were all 60's and 50's. There was a lot of hard work. The big barrels we only put clarified wine into but the small barrels we put the fresh wine into and when they were empty they had to be all washed out, which again is an easy job when you knew how to do it. We used a chain on the end of a bung, a fine chain, not very heavy, and you rattled the cask around and the chain rattled all the debris off the bottom of the cask that had settled. Once you got into the knack of doing it it was quite simple, but if you didn't have the knack it was difficult. After the wine had settled to a degree we then bottled off what had to be bottled off or sold it in two gallon lots, because in those days we could only sell two gallons at a time, we weren't allowed to sell a bottle at

a time and it was very difficult to sell it but we managed to survive. But the cash crop with the grapes, we sold a lot of grapes, table grapes and that pulled in the cash and helped to keep us going while we tried to sell the wine . . .

How many people worked for you?

I always had one permanent on the five and a half acres and two when we increased. You worked yourself too.

What time did you start each day?

Well, depending what you were doing. Spraying season you started very early in the morning and you'd work late at night . . .

In the 1920s when you were working on the vineyard, would you have a 12-hour day?

Oh no. In those days it was a 48-hour week, eight and a half hours, and four and a half hours on Saturday. When I was employing labour that's what we did too.[45]

Although at times Edward would work very long hours, in general men's working hours allowed them to plan leisure activities in a way that women's work did not, because men's work was more regulated.

The nature of men's work also meant that men could often mix work and leisure. Taradale's hairdresser and barber took this to the extreme. He alternated between work and pleasure:

Old Billy Barnes, he used to be a hairdresser and we always maintained that his hairdresser's shop wasn't far from the hotel because he [laugh] always had his bottle of whisky. He'd cut one head of hair and he'd put you in the chair when it was your turn and 'Oh, I won't be a minute' and he'd be off out the back, washing his hands as he called it [laugh], but he was at his bottle of whisky. He had a little whisky after each customer.[46]

Men had more time for leisure than women, and the collective nature of men's work meant that they could enjoy on-the-job leisure with their co-workers. Even if men worked alone, they were drawn into a network of men through their occupation. A dairyman, who spent most of his time with his cows, could look forward to his daily trip to the local dairy factory, where he could yarn with other men. Men also made leisure of their work. The Taradale and Hastings Ploughing Match Society held annual competitions and offered cash prizes and medals for the best ploughmen. Here was a chance for men to compete and show off their skills, all in the name of being a good provider. While the match had a competitive element, it also had a social purpose. It drew together men of all ages for the actual competition.

W. A. Colwill's Greenmeadows Store, c. 1910. Men could congregate here to discuss the price of grain while indulging in a soft drink. William Colwill worked alongside his brothers Edward, a carrier, John, a carter, and Charles, a grocer's assistant. The men and boys have positioned themselves by the shop's main entrance, while the two women in the photograph stand to the right. COLLECTION OF HAWKE'S BAY CULTURAL TRUST–HAWKE'S BAY MUSEUM, NAPIER, NEW ZEALAND, 4990

An Under 18 category meant that young men were involved too. There was also a dinner, where the prizes were distributed and speeches made. Women were not completely excluded from this ritual. In 1887 'ladies' were called upon to attend the ploughing competition: 'As there is a special prize for the best looking ploughman, it is to be hoped that some ladies will put in an appearance, so that they can act as judges.'[47] The ladies voted for Greenwood Willan, a single farmer, and he was rewarded, perhaps appropriately, with a perambulator.[48]

The men of the Taradale and Hastings Ploughing Match Society may have been having a wee laugh at Greenwood Willan's expense, but they were in a position to laugh. Men's work places and processes meant that they had power over the community. To understand masculinities in Taradale, we need to see how men gained and retained the sources of power in the area. Work was a prime source of masculine power. This was not only because men owned more land and resources than women did. Physically, even though much of women's work was demanding, men knew that they were superior. They also had control of the surrounding countryside. The paddocks and roads were men's domain. Young single women in paid employment were encroaching on some of that territory, but by 1930 this had not undermined men's position in the community. While they were part of a household economy, their work was physically set apart from women's. They kept their work places as men's spaces and kept their work processes masculine. Men were able to reproduce this situation by teaching their sons and nephews these values, and by working alongside their brothers, cousins and fathers. There was an inclusivity in masculine work that was no longer possible in feminine work. Through these bonds between and within generations, men's grip on the community remained firm.

More than women, the men of Taradale were defined by their work and their work defined them.[49] For some that definition was less than flattering. But although a man might not have been the main breadwinner in his household, few would have pointed this out to him. Just as there were women who failed or refused to live up to local expectations of women's work, so there were men who were not good providers, who were not physically capable of doing 'manly' work, or who did not want to or were not able to work with others, including their male kin. But the man who relied on friendly society dues when he was ill or injured was still a real man. The man who turned to crime was also a participant in a manly code. Only those men who turned to charity or went bankrupt were demasculinised, and such men were decidedly a minority in Taradale.

Work forged the basis for sociable interaction between men.[50] Men had more opportunities than women to combine work and leisure, but in general the honest burghers of Taradale all liked to kick up their heels every now and again. What they did in their spare time, and with whom, is the subject of the next three chapters.

CHAPTER 6

Communal Leisure

The Mikado Quadrille Club wound up their 1887 season with a fancy dress ball attended by over 40 couples. With Miss Barry dressed as the 'Welcome Cigarette' and Miss Gebbie as 'Vivandiere', they began at 9 p.m. and danced the night away. The *Hawke's Bay Herald* reported that 'the only damper [on the night] was a shower of rain about 4 o'clock in the morning, just as people were going home'.[1] Perhaps 17-year-old Louisa Gebbie danced with 19-year-old Patrick O'Dowd (dressed as a stockman), for within three years they were married, soon to be the parents of six children. Not that there would have been any unacceptable fraternising on the dance floor. Louisa and Patrick were dancing under the watchful eyes of Mrs Lord and Mrs Drummond, stalwarts of the community, and generous supper providers.

The Mikado Quadrille Club's fancy dress ball epitomises a certain type of leisure enjoyed by Taradale's citizens in the late nineteenth century. It was communal leisure, where young and old, men and women, gathered together in a non-commercial environment to have fun. The ball began late, because people's workdays were long. It did not finish until almost dawn, but there was no concern about this. Parents knew that their youngsters were in good hands. In his stockman's outfit, Patrick O'Dowd could almost have left the ball and gone straight to his job as a shepherd. Work and leisure were intimately linked.

Communal leisure was still very much a part of Taradale in the 1920s. Charlotte Rose was a member of the church choir then. She recalled that the 40 or so choristers often made their own fun:

> We used to have a lot of surprise parties, especially when we were in the choir. The whole choir would go to different people, you know, and they never knew that we were coming. But we took our eats and you never had drink in those days, you didn't even have soft drinks, we didn't . . .[2]

At these parties charades would be played, supper would be eaten at 10 p.m., and come midnight they would sing Auld Lang Syne and then go home. Charlotte's brothers did not bother going to bed as they had to begin milking the cows at 1 a.m.

Communal leisure, involving a wide range of people, was a constant in Taradale's social life. Whether it involved informal sociability, such as visiting friends and family or going on a family picnic, or more organised events such as the Agricultural and Pastoral Show or the horse races, men and women, boys and girls, were all drawn together. Yet their leisure, communal or otherwise, was not gender neutral. Just as all the members of the family contributed to the household economy in particular ways, so they all had roles when it came to leisure. This chapter explores the gendered boundaries of communal leisure, while the following two chapters concentrate on specifically feminine and masculine leisure. In all three, the continuity of community-based leisure is an important part of the story. But it is not the only part. Over the years more commercially oriented leisure activities began to compete for people's spare time and money. This change raises important questions about access to leisure and the values associated with it.

For most people in Taradale, communal leisure did not mean large scale, organised community festivals, with everyone participating.[3] In western societies at that time, few people had the time or energy to organise such events. Instead home-based sociability, drawing in family and friends, was the norm. In Sarah Stevenson's home, as in so many, this involved the piano. She recalled:

> But [my parents] used to have lots of little social evenings, with sing songs around the piano. And have friends to that and they used to be very enjoyable, I can remember as a youngster being allowed to stay up for that and have a sing song. Both Mum and Dad had nice voices.
> *Who would come to them?*
> Oh some of the neighbours or some friends who were musical. People who perhaps hadn't been here long but then they would be, perhaps get to know the other friends who were here, they would come along too. But none of them were here for any length of time.[4]

Sarah grew up in a nuclear family. Only for a short period did she have any other kin living in the area. But in a society with high levels of geographical mobility, it did not take long for people to make friends and invite others into their homes.

Sunday afternoon visiting was another vital part of communal leisure. Family, friends and neighbours made the rounds and caught up with the news. Often the whole family took part in this important ritual. But as Ted Ownby found in the rural south of the United States, such visiting would often see men talking to one another outside, while the women remained inside.[5] The children, too, divided off when they went out to play. Joseph Barnett, when asked about his childhood leisure, described playing football, swimming, bird nesting, and wandering over the hills with his brothers and mates. But when asked about girls and his sisters, he replied: '[t]hey'd be mucking about around the home, doing their thing, whatever.'[6] William Cliff similarly replied: 'I don't know what the girls played at . . .'. But he could describe in detail the games of tick tack he and his friends played in the boys' playground, the intricate rules of the marbles season, and how 'fly' – a game of progressive leap frog – was played once the marbles season 'closed'.[7] Girls had their own marbles competitions, games and activities. At school girls' and boys' play was physically separated by the iron fence dividing their playgrounds, but they also walked to and from school in single-sex groups and tended to play at home and in the neighbourhood in these groups too.

Parents and other adults had an important role in maintaining children's play as gender-specific. Throughout the western world at this time there was an increasing concern that mothers were having too much influence on their sons' lives, and that young boys would not grow into manly men if this feminine influence went unchecked. Fathers and other men were encouraged to take a more active role in child rearing to curb this feminisation.[8] Taradale's boys were not immune to this trend. As Chapter 8 will show, at school, at home and in the wider community, men in Taradale took an increasing interest in the leisure activities of boys and youths. This happened both at a formal level, organising groups such as Boy Scouts for boys to join, and also informally, during communal outings such as picnics.

Picnics seem to have been the most common leisure activity in the area. On a sunny afternoon men, women and children would load up the dray, or walk to the river or Shelly Beach, and settle down for a pleasant few hours. Such afternoons often saw extended family and friends join together. Take the Bartlett family of Meanee. One Saturday afternoon in late November 1889, after James Bartlett had finished work as a baker, he and his wife Jane and their three young children went down to Powdrell's Crossing on the Tutaekuri River. Jane's brother, William Gilmour, and his friend, Miss Alice Moore, joined them for the picnic. As so often happened on such occasions, the women were left to watch the children, prepare the food, and chat. The men went off to swim away from the women. But this picnic turned to tragedy: James Bartlett got into difficulties and drowned.[9] His death is why we have a record of the picnic. It indicates both how important kin were in leisure pursuits, and also the gendered roles played out at the ostensibly shared picnic site.

The oral accounts offer similar stories, without the tragic ending. Picnics often involved a wide family group. James Green remembered that:

> The whole family would go, pack up the car, perhaps two car loads of you. Other times we used to hire a dray, a long cart thing with forms in it and two horses in the front and we used to hire this. The whole family would go on, plus a few extras, pile everything into the back and off we would go.[10]

James was not alone in recalling picnics attended by extended family and non-family. Nor was he alone in remembering that once at the picnic site, men and women took on different roles and took over different spaces. James's father was a keen fisherman, so when they went on family picnics, James and his father would move away from his mother, sister and half sister, and go and catch snapper.

George Davies also recalled picnics with his extended family, and how such picnics were often made to serve a purpose other than the purely recreational. In season they would go out to Tongoio, where the blackberrying was best, and at other times they would make a picnic out of collecting firewood along the riverbank. Work and leisure blurred. On such occasions George and his father would use a two-man saw to cut up the river wood, while his sisters and mother prepared the picnic food. On other occasions the picnic became a shooting party for George's father:

> Sometimes when we were just out for a picnic, sometimes he'd [father] carry his, he used to have a double barrelled shotgun and he used to carry his gun with him and we'd be out and he'd see a rabbit sitting on the roadside he'd up his gun and he'd shoot it and take it home and make a rabbit pie with it [laugh].'[11]

COMMUNAL LEISURE

Left: A father fishes alone, while attending a family picnic. His son took the photograph. The female members of the family are nowhere to be seen.
Private Collection

Below: Bathing Beauties. Sisters and cousins pose for a photograph while at a Shelly Beach family picnic. In the bottom right hand corner a kettle is visible.
Private Collection

Just as with James Bartlett and William Gilmour 40 years earlier, there were clear boundaries at the picnic site.

Picnics sometimes developed into community festivals. The annual Sunday School picnic, for example, saw the children from Sunday School and the young people from Bible Class, along with many of the adults who attended church, gather together for a day of games, competitions and food. The erection of churches soon after the first settlers arrived was a crucial community building exercise, a sign that people saw themselves as belonging to a permanent area. But these buildings were more than symbols. They were important places for people to worship and socialise in and around.

It is often asserted that church-going is a predominantly female habit.[12] Certainly this was the impression gained from the people interviewed. Sophie Richardson was not the only woman who recounted that 'My granny, my mother and myself were all baptised in All Saints, all confirmed there and all married there.'[13] No men discussed such masculine loyalty to a religious institution. Indeed, it was far more likely for women than for men to talk at any length about churches and church-going, religion and Sunday observance. Church records on attendance backed this up. Of all those known to have been communicants at All Saints, attendees at the Roman Catholic Mission, or on the Methodist Members' Roll, two-thirds were female.[14]

However, it should not be assumed that married couples had no role in the church, or that only the female members of families were involved. A closer examination of the church congregations in Taradale reveals that although gender played a role in determining who went to church, so did marital status. It was not simply that more females than males attended church. Single females were the largest group attending, followed by married women, then married men, and finally single men. The difference between single and married women's attendance was about the same as the difference between married women's and married men's attendance. Although overall there was a female dominance of the congregation, breaking down the data suggests that married men and women attended church in much the same numbers, and that the overall figure for male attendance was brought down by the very low rate of church-going among single men.[15]

It was as common for a married woman to attend church with her husband as it was for her to attend without him; and it was more common for a married man to attend with his wife than without her.[16] This was recognised by the parishes. Church meeting minutes recorded their appreciation to individual married couples for the work they had carried out.[17] On the rare occasion that one member of the couple fell out with the church, their spouse usually defended their position. The Presbyterian church had to cope with such a dispute in 1911, when Mrs Carter was alleged to have verbally attacked the minister. He supposedly replied that the Carters were a 'disturbing element' in the church. Both Mr and Mrs Carter resigned from all positions in the church; Walter Carter had been a church manager and elder and Emily Carter had belonged to the Ladies' Guild and was the church organist. The dispute was settled in a matter of days by both parties apologising, although soon afterwards the Carters withdrew from St Columba.[18]

While Walter and Emily Carter attended church together, many of Taradale's church-goers attended Sunday services with members of their extended as well as nuclear families. When the Roman Catholic Mission was held in September 1894, most people who attended did so in family groups. Garret and Bridget Murnane were joined by their eldest daughter, Mary, and their sister-in-law, Johanna Murnane. Mary's future in-laws, the Clearys, were there, as were members of the Kilkenny and Halpin families, linked through marriage to the Murnanes. These sorts of family attendances were common. It was rare that no family connections could be traced among church-goers.

The family ties among the Sunday School teachers at All Saints were just as dense as the links among the Roman Catholic Mission adherents. The vicar and his wife taught classes, but few other men were listed as teachers. Instead young and single women, often sisters, led the children. From 1886 until 1898 Mrs Eliza Howard taught Taradale's Anglican children. In 1889 two of her daughters, Eliza and 15-year-old Marion, tried their hand at Sunday School teaching. Eliza did not continue, but Marion gave three years' service. Their brother, Samuel, later married another of the Sunday School teachers they worked with, Mary Charlotte Harpham. The Harpham family was very prominent in All Saints. Sisters Edith and Mary Corbin also taught Sunday School at that time, both ceasing when they married, Edith to Mark Wakelin, and Mary to Hiram Harris, a church leader.

Attending church and taking Sunday School classes were not the only ways that the social lives and leisure of Taradale's adults were shaped by the churches. Each parish offered many avenues for involvement beyond the Sunday services. Churches were the prime source of frequent socials, the holders of annual fund-raisers such as bazaars and garden parties, and the sites of many concerts. In May 1886 the *Daily Telegraph* reported that a concert in aid of the Meanee Mission School was held in a 'well filled' Odd Fellows Hall, and that 'among the audience could be seen a mixture of all denominations, which denotes a healthy feeling'.[19] Large crowds attended these concerts and socials, and many people were actively involved in them. Those who attended the opening social of the choir of All Saints, in May 1892, sat in a schoolroom 'tastefully decorated by a committee of ladies', and were entertained by 16 performers – single women such as the Misses Rymer, married men such as Mr Goulding, and one married woman, Mrs Spence.[20] Although single women and married men performed at such socials in much the same numbers, married women only occasionally took to the stage. Instead they provided the supper.

Many of the married couples who attended church together may have sat in the same pew, gone around the area as church canvassers together, or attended church socials as a couple. But for most of the years from 1886 to 1930, that was the extent to which they could act through church in a way that was not gender-specific. Rather than being gender neutral, the churches expected men to perform roles as administrators and managers, while women did the domestic chores and nurturing required in each parish.

Attendance at church and regular involvement in the parish was a minority experience. On a nationwide basis, between a quarter and a third of the population was recorded as being church-goers, and this was the case in Taradale too.[21] Most women and men were not regulars at church, although most of the young people attended Sunday School.[22] The churches recognised that it was often difficult for people to attend. As the Presbyterians noted in 1909: 'It was considered that parents in homes where there were very young children could not always be in attendance at communion.'[23] This is certainly the impression gained from the oral evidence. Martha Edwards' response was fairly typical among the women interviewed. They excused their mothers' non-attendance, but felt no need to offer any such explanation for their fathers:

> Of course, you see, nowadays you take your children to church. . . . But you see you didn't take your children, you didn't take babies to church. Going to church was pretty grim, you know, in the 1920s. It's not like going to church now. . . But we always went to Sunday School and occasionally went to the Morning Service at 11 o'clock before we came home, but if it was a Communion Service you only stayed for half of the Communion Service, until the end of the sermon, and then all you children always went out . . . . So of course you see there was a long time when Mum had all the babies that she never went to church because she couldn't. We all went to church and Sunday School and Bible Class and things but it wasn't until

years later. Well Mum would go, she would make an effort to go on a special occasion like when we were confirmed or something like that but I don't remember that she ever went any other times. . . . But then you see the service was at 11 o'clock in the morning and there was always this thing about cooking a hot meal midday Sunday, so I suppose she stayed home and cooked that . . . There were never any babies in church. We were all carted along and were baptised and we were all confirmed but there was never any, that was about it . . . .'[24]

Although most adults did not attend church regularly, the churches did have a wide impact. Adult men and women sometimes attended services, often went to socials and other church-run functions, and in most cases insisted that their children attended Sunday School. The influence of the church was also felt in other ways. As Martha mentioned, on Sunday the main meal of the day was held at midday. All the oral narrators had the same experience, regardless of whether they or their parents attended church and whether they were Protestant or Roman Catholic. The afternoon was devoted to letter writing, visiting and relaxing. Strict Sunday observance was rife in Taradale. Louisa Plumb gave a typical portrayal of Sunday and how it differed from other days of the week, even among non-church-going families:

My mother was always very organised. We didn't do anything on a Sunday, only the necessities. You didn't do any work on a Sunday. My mother would cook dinner at midday and that was about it. She didn't believe in doing anything on a Sunday. She'd generally write letters or sit and crochet. . . . Even today you would never think of doing your washing on a Sunday, or ironing or anything like that. Even today if I have to wash on a Sunday I say 'Sorry Mum'. It's sort of born in you, that you don't do those things.

While Louisa's mother wrote or crocheted, her father was outside digging the vegetable garden.

Like children all over New Zealand, each Sunday most of the school-aged children in the area went to Sunday School, church or both. Roman Catholic children were not only meant to attend the convent – rather than a 'Godless' school – and go to Mass each Sunday, they were also expected to attend monthly meetings of the Children of Mary.[25] Anglican children had Sunday School, the Band of Hope (formed in 1887) and the Sower's Union, a children's missionary group begun in the late 1890s. The Methodist Sunday School often had to close for want of enough teachers or a superintendent. This was hardly surprising, given the small adult congregation and the large number of children requiring instruction. In 1890, with only six adults in the congregation, the Sunday School had 25 scholars and four teachers.[26] By 1913 the school had 45 students and a Band of Hope with 89 children.[27] The Presbyterian Sunday School was also well attended, as was the Bible Class for older children.

All this Sunday activity drew the young people of Taradale together. But not all the Sunday School attendees saw these shared intrusions into their lives as leisure. The women, such as Emily Jones, had fonder memories than the men:

> *Did your mother want you to go or did you want to go?*
> We all wanted to go. You never had to force us to go, not to Sunday School.
> *Why was that?*
> Oh I don't know. Somewhere to go I suppose. But we were interested in the church, even at that early stage.[28]

On the other hand, Emily's brother, Matthew Silk, had this to say:

> *Did you go to Sunday School?*
> Oh yes, yes, I went to Sunday School. I suppose the earliest I remember. The oldest girls, you see, they had to go to Sunday School so naturally all of us ones had to follow suit. But as I was saying the other day the time didn't suit, didn't suit me so we used to always try to get away, to get up the river and have a swim, something like that. There was always something. [Sunday School was at 2 p.m.] But I used to get down to the Sunday School at about a quarter to two, see, I'd get a bit impatient so I'd get down there and I'd start tinkling the bell. I used to keep that going until 2 o'clock [laugh]. Oh dear.
> *How long would it last?*
> Sunday School? Oh I suppose it would be about an hour. About an hour, yes. And before the class, before the hour was up I used to sneak out and start tinkling that bell again [laugh], used to hurry things up a bit. And then away up to the river. It used to be annoying because my cobbers would be waiting for me somewhere [laugh] to get out. They were not Sunday School guys.
> *Did you have to go to Sunday School?*
> Oh yes, yes.
> *Were you allowed to stop when you got older?*
> Oh well, I suppose we sort of grew out of it. Yeah. I don't know if they, I think they had what they called a Bible Class going but I wasn't very keen on that either.[29]

For boys such as Matthew, Sunday School was an infringement on their leisure time. Or as Henry Nolan put it when asked about Sunday School:

> We went along until we were too big to give a hiding to, I think. I'd be about 12, I suppose, 12 or 13. Only sissy girls wanted to go there. We had to go to Sunday School.[30]

To make the most of having to go, boys made up rhymes about their Sunday School teachers. Ernest Edwards recited this one about his Anglican Sunday School teacher:

> Mrs Harris, tall and thin,
> Is getting whiskers on her chin,
> And everywhere the old girl goes
> The whiskers stick in the children's nose.[31]

While girls' enthusiasm for Sunday School could just be a reflection of their thinking that this was what was expected of them, it could also be that they genuinely did enjoy Sunday School more than boys, since it gave them an opportunity to go out once a week and dress up in their Sunday best. As a Roman Catholic, Bridget Tweed did not go to Sunday School, but she went to Mass every week. Her recollections show something of the freedom which attending church offered to young girls whose lives were more circumscribed than those of their brothers:

> In those days we used to go in a trap, like a buggy affair and we had a lovely horse, called Creamy and I'm the only one that could catch it and the girls and I, France and Ag, we'd go to first Mass, 7 o'clock Mass and some people in Taradale, they had the bread shop, named Jeffares, and they had the shop, they had the bread shop and the daughter Mary, she used to take their lot in the bread cart, not the bread cart but a cart, a gig thing, to church. And they used to try and race us but our, I was driver and Creamy, Creamy wouldn't let them pass. We'd go and strut on and we'd go in when we got there and get to church and on the way back old Creamy would strut out until we'd get to our corner, which we called Jeffares' corner which goes straight down to Murphy Road. As soon as she saw Jeffares' corner she'd stop dead and just trot, trot, trot.[32]

While going to church or Sunday School brought girls and boys together, in many respects this aspect of their week was a gendered experience too. The well-attended Sunday School classes were sex-segregated, as were the Bible Classes for adolescents. If churches could, they made sure girls were taught by women and boys by men. Often, though, a shortage of male teachers meant women took all the junior classes. But the minister or church elders always took the senior boys' classes.

Church, though, was one of the first public places where young women and men could legitimately congregate and socialise. Soon after the Methodist church was built in the area, it began to hold socials where young people could meet amidst the recitations, songs and solos.[33] While Bible Classes were, in the main, sex-specific, the Presbyterian church decided in 1919 to introduce a mixed class, to meet on Sunday afternoons.[34] This group formed a tennis club and discussed topics such as 'The Influence of Man on Woman', said to have been 'introduced very well by the girls of the class'.[35] Girls were becoming more assertive, a trend noted at the national level.[36] The girls continued with their own class as well, organising many socials and gatherings. Louisa Plumb explained some of the attraction of Bible Class for young women:

> So off we would go to Sunday School. Later on we wanted some more excitement really, than just Sunday School there, and we went to the Presbyterian Bible Class, as a group of neighbours and that because they used to have social evenings and we were getting to the stage where we wanted to go to socials.
> *You'd be in your teens?*
> Yes. And this was how you'd gradually go on, and from those socials – they had games and that sort of thing, no dancing in those days, not at the Presbyterian. So after Bible Class then a group of us used to go round to All Saints [laugh] for a dance, once a month. And that's where I met my husband.[37]

Louisa and her group of friends changed their religious affiliations from Methodist to Presbyterian to Anglican as their desire for excitement and different forms of entertainment changed. Ecumenicalism was practised in the name of courting, and practised with a group of friends. Whereas in childhood girls had not gone around in gangs as their brothers had, in adolescence they were far more likely to socialise in a group.

As with Sunday School, it was the women who were interviewed who fondly recalled the church socials and dances they attended as adolescents. The male narrators were far more dismissive of such occasions, often regarding them as too tame and too well chaperoned. Patrick Stevenson's utilitarian attitude to religion is similar to Louisa's, but the tone of his oral account is quite different. Whereas Louisa ended up with the statement about meeting her husband at such a dance, Patrick was far more concerned with conveying the fun he had, as well as indicating his views on the clergy and on female sexuality:

> *You never went to Sunday School?*
> I went twice, no, once. Once to the Methodist. I got a card, that was all. The Boggs talked me into it. Anyhow, that was that. The only other time I got religious was to join the Presbyterian tennis club up here and if you were a Presbyterian Bible Class member you got your half fee so I joined up for the Presbyterian Bible Class . . . Oh I must have gone three or four times because I was going with one of the girls that was going too. I even went to church one night, one Sunday night and went in the choir and it was a sticky night and they'd just painted the church and I was leaning back at the back seat like this and moved and 'Rip'. And the old parson looks down his nose at you like this. Anyhow it got really serious and I think that's when I gave it up was, he decided to let the girls out a quarter of an hour before he let the boys, the silly old coot and here was the girls, just waiting 100 yards up the road for their boyfriends. Well ask yourself, he must have been absolutely illiterate. No, you wonder, it makes you wonder about some of these chaps that have taken up religion as a career. To have a mind like that, knowing, he should have known damn well that the girls would be waiting. They were the worse offenders than the boys.[38]

Patrick may not have had fond memories of the church, but for many the church provided both spiritual comfort and a full social calendar.

For those with no taste for anything religious, there were other activities to indulge in. Although not as frequent as church socials, the Agricultural and Pastoral Show and locally held dog trials were important dates on Taradale's social calendar. Sophie Richardson referred to the Agricultural and Pastoral Show as '*the* annual event'. She recalled that 'from the time the show finished we began to think about the next one which would come along. It really was the highlight of our lives.'[39] Among the women who were interviewed it was often remembered fondly as the time of the year when they got new clothes:

> *What about clothes?*
> Well my mother made all our clothes. I always remember springtime, she'd make us all new clothes, for the Spring Show. We had to have a new hat

and new shoes and your new clothes and it was a great picnic day, to go to the Show in the horse and buggy. We'd take lunch, a packed lunch and I can remember having a marvellous time at the Show.[40]

As with so many aspects of leisure in Taradale, what was fun for some was work for others. Sophie's mother had to make new clothes for all of her children before each Show, and prepare the picnic for the family come Show day. Communal leisure often relied on women's work.

The Show was a great family picnic day, but it was also more than that. It was a place where people could go and just be spectators, and also a place where people could display their skills and expertise in public. Sophie Richardson's father, for example, was a competitor:

My father was a very keen horse man and he took part in horse events, which he continued to do at the present show grounds – mainly the gig with a very smart horse called Molly, who took many prizes. He competed with lots of other people and did very well . . . he started to breed stud sheep, which did very well in the district shows each year.[41]

Such public displays of horsemanship and sheep breeding were masculine pursuits. For although the Show allowed both men and women to enter exhibits, they were not competing against one another. Patrick Stevenson's parents may have won many prizes for poultry at the Show, but as he recalled, his mother won hers for dressed poultry, a suitably feminine competition.[42] It was acceptable for married women to demonstrate their domestic skills on such occasions, just as it was acceptable for men to be competitive when it came to breeding and rearing livestock and showing their control over their horses. The annual Show drew men and women together, but it also separated them.

The same was true at the local dog trials. Again, men were able to display their skills as farmers and show off their control over their dogs. Such shows and competitions were the modern equivalent of harvest celebrations and group activities.[43] Like harvest celebrations, they also performed an important social function. Here women's participation came to the fore. While the men trialled their dogs, their wives faced a different trial. They were expected to produce large quantities of food to feed the hungry sportsmen and onlookers:

Although, in those days, as I mentioned with the dog trials, they used to travel all around the countryside, dog trialling. Not only Hawke's Bay, if they had any luck and won the local trials around Hawke's Bay here and

their dogs qualified and then they would be away up north or way down south.
Was your grandmother interested in that?
Yes, yes, she, in the early stages she used to run the cookhouse round here, supplying meals to them.
Which cookhouse, I haven't heard of this?
Oh yes, there used to be a cookhouse and everything here at the end of O'Dowd Road.
Especially for the dog club?
Yes. They used to hop in there and they'd bake scones and cakes and God knows what.
Who'd make that?
Mostly the competitors' wives or farmers' wives. They'd all pull together . . .[44]

The trials went on for three or four days at a time.

Another constant on Taradale's communal calendar was horse races. These were held locally on what is now Anderson Park.[45] They were attended by large numbers of people, from both the local area and further afield. Men and women, young and old, Pakeha and Maori, workers and employers, all attended the Town and Suburban Race Meetings. Others, most notably practising Presbyterians and Methodists, pointedly stayed away from such leisure activities.

Women were allowed at the local race meetings, indeed they were encouraged to attend. Men had to pay to be admitted, but the course was free to 'ladies'.[46] In 1905, when a patented toilet for ladies was fitted in the grandstand, the appeal of going to the races must have grown for women.[47] Photographs of race meetings show groups of women and men enjoying themselves. It was an opportunity for a day out, and a chance to dress up.[48] But although such photographs often show men and women mingling, we should be careful about concluding that race day offered gender neutral recreation. According to the oral evidence, it did not. While families might travel to and from the races together, they often separated along gendered lines once they reached the course. Race day was another opportunity for families to organise a picnic, and another opportunity for women to be left in charge of the food and young children, while the men went off to look over the horses and place their bets. Men also ran the races. Only men were on the Racing Club's committee; they were the trainers and jockeys, the starters and judges, and they ran the totalisator. Women had to remain on the periphery of this recreational pursuit.

Local men and women attended the Napier Park race meetings at Greenmeadows, but it was not expected that women would go further

A Day at the Races. The grandstand at Napier Park racecourse Greenmeadows, 1902. COLLECTION OF HAWKE'S BAY CULTURAL TRUST–HAWKE'S BAY MUSEUM, NAPIER, NEW ZEALAND, 4301

afield in search of racing entertainment. There were several race courses in the Hawke's Bay area, but it was assumed that only men would want to travel to such meetings, as this notice in the *Daily Telegraph* of 11 February 1892 makes clear:

> Mr Rymer's coach will leave Newton's corner at half-past nine o'clock on Saturday morning to convey those sporting gentlemen from town who intend patronising the Rissington races.

None of the oral narrators' mothers ever went to such meetings, although several of their fathers did.

Race day in the 1880s and in the 1920s was a day for communal leisure. Although some financial outlay was required, it did not need to be an expensive day out. But increasingly leisure came with a price tag, especially the leisure pursuits aimed at the young.

There had long been pursuits designed to meet the needs of young courting couples. In a community where heterosexuality was compulsory, it was important that young women and men got to know one another, as long as this was under the watchful eyes of their elders. Young people did not always play by these rules. In the late 1880s concern was expressed that young men were strolling the streets at night, creating a 'monkey walk', a public parade where they could see and be seen by Taradale's young women.[49] Young women sometimes took the lead and pursued their prey. In 1893 two of the female pupil teachers at Taradale School, Miss Goddard and Miss Gibson, were reprimanded by the headmaster for the bad example they were setting. The school committee reportedly wanted them to be dismissed if their bad conduct continued. Their crime was being familiar with the older boys, many of whom were their age or more. The two young women, aged about 15 years, were told not to walk to or from school with the boys or to fraternise with them in any way. The headmaster noted in his log book that 'these two teachers show so little shame . . . with conduct so unbecoming. Miss Goddard in particular seems totally wanting in womanly modesty.'[50]

When Florence Goddard was reported to have used 'grossly immoral' language to the children during interval, the headmaster decided to take further action. This, after all, was the third complaint about her behaviour: 'she is quite unfit to be placed in charge of children'.[51] He wrote to Florence's adopted father, suggesting that she resign her position rather than suffer an investigation. Her father, a local storekeeper, apparently agreed. So this young woman, who had allegedly overstepped the bounds of decency, left the school. The headmaster could not decide whether 'she [was] entirely destitute of moral sense, or she [was] determined to brazen out the censure she [had] incurred by persisting in her vicious course'.[52] Miss Gibson left at the end of the year.

These young teachers' idea of fun was not shared by others, and they suffered the consequences. While young men were given some leeway to sow their wild oats, the young women of Taradale were not. In the 1890s this meant that the young men Misses Goddard and Gibson were associating with were not disciplined in any way. The oral narrators recalled that by the 1920s, if a young, single woman became pregnant:

> The girl was the lowest thing in the world.
> *What about the boy?*
> Very little blame attached to the boy.[53]

The sexual double standard had not altered, but opportunities had. Increasingly young people could take their leisure away from the censoring eye of the community. There were still church-run socials and dances, but now there were commercially run dances too, held in Napier, Hastings, and the surrounding countryside. With improved roads and better transport, the young were not limited to the local area or to local controls. Little wonder that parents imposed much stricter curfews on their children than their own parents had imposed on them.

The women who recalled attending commercial dances had romantic memories of them. The band played on, they were whisked off their feet by dashing young men, their new store-bought dress caused a sensation. The men recalled the dances in terms of fights they had won and attempts to smuggle alcohol into the hall, rather than the actual dancing. Even at local dances they represented themselves as most interested in getting one over the policeman. When Joseph Barnett was asked about crime in the area and the role of the local policeman, he said:

> I can remember Old Jim [Cartley] kicking me cobber in the backside and shooting him through a hedge.
> *Why was that?*
> Well at the dances we used to have our grog and old Jim didn't like that so he used to chase us and it was Bill Horton and he got his head half way through the hedge and old Jim came along and helped him through the rest. But apart from that, it was only harmless, harmless fun.[54]

The larrikin male, rather than a more romantic figure, lived on in the men's memories. This was how they chose to portray themselves and their mates.

But the more commercially oriented leisure industry of the interwar period did allow young people more privacy. Along with the dances came other consumer-driven leisure activities, many of them reliant on the disposable income of the young. Whereas in the 1880s the only commercial leisure spots were the hotels and local billiard rooms, both masculine preserves, by the 1920s there were places designed for courting couples.

One of these was the Roskilda Tea Gardens, a local establishment serving strawberries and cream and afternoon teas in a pleasant garden setting. James Green and Hannah Field's parents owned Roskilda in the 1920s. They remembered that the tea gardens proved to be a popular spot with young lovers:

> A lot of young couples used to come in because one section of it was down on a lower level and that was all trees and bamboo groves and all that sort of thing and some of the arbours were cut into the bamboo groves, very private and everything and we used to notice the young ones. Dad used to say that they played in the bamboo[laugh].[55]

COMMUNAL LEISURE

Top: Taradale Town Hall, built in 1911, scene of many social and civic occasions.
THE NARRATIVE OF THE PLAINS, 1919, P. 15

Above: Taradale Town Hall interior. The public hall could seat 600 moviegoers or provide a dance floor for many couples. There was also a supper room where 70 could dine. THE NARRATIVE OF THE PLAINS, 1919, P. 16

After an afternoon among the bamboo, another popular haunt for the young was the movies. Taradale, like many small towns at this time, did not have a purpose-built cinema; films were screened in the Taradale Town Hall. Regular screenings began in 1912, after Hayward's Pictures persuaded the Taradale Town Board to lease them the hall for two nights a week. While the decision pleased many young people in the area, within two years the town board's clerk threatened to resign over the inconvenience of the projectionist selling tickets from the board's office. The board supported Mr Nitschke, the operator, and the clerk was forced to resign.[56] The board recognised the importance of film, and the income it would continue to bring them.

Like cinema-goers elsewhere in New Zealand, the people of Taradale enjoyed this relatively cheap form of entertainment, which let them see important current events with only a slight delay, and escape into the glamorous world of Hollywood. While there is no hard data on who went to the movies before 1939, it was estimated in 1916 that 320,000 New Zealanders went to the pictures each week, and many of them were young.[57] Movies were often aimed at young urban women.[58] As Nerida Elliott has said, '[f]ilm-going broke the separation of the sexes for recreation and provided a permanent social freedom for women'.[59] For young women in Taradale, going to a screening at the town hall was a chance to buy some leisure and privacy. Despite the public nature of the town hall, once the lights were dimmed and the film was rolling, Taradale's young could enjoy being out of the communal gaze.

Commercial leisure was not aimed only at the young. Adult men had long spent large amounts of money and time at the local hotels. Grown women and men were not averse to a night at the movies. Nor did the young forsake all communal leisure once tea gardens and the like opened their doors. As in previous generations, Taradale's adolescents continued to have picnics by the river, strolls along Shelly Beach and clandestine meetings in the township. During the Great War one of their regular meeting places was the newly created Taradale Park. When a band rotunda was built in the park in 1918 it acted as a magnet for young couples. It was a sheltered place to meet, not far from home. In the early 1920s tennis courts were laid at the park and mixed doubles became a favourite pastime. Commercial leisure co-existed with communal leisure.

In her study of American courtship, Ellen Rothman points to an irony in family life and leisure in the early twentieth century. With the advent of masculine domesticity and the new family man, men were returning to the home, wanting to be part of their family's emotional life. At the same time, women and children were becoming less home-centred in their work and leisure.[60] Perhaps they passed on the verandah. Or if Margaret Marsh is to be believed, 'the most popular forms of recreation were those families could enjoy together'.[61] Marsh's happy families, based on companionate marriages, went off bicycling together, played tennis and golf, and enjoyed roller skating.

Playing Happy Families I. Mortimer Scott and his motorbike with his sister, Sybil Bennett and her daughter, Thelma, c.1916. It is clear who is in the driving seat.
PRIVATE COLLECTION

There was no roller skating rink in Taradale. Yet as I have argued in this chapter, throughout the period there were communal leisure activities that depended on husbands, wives and their children taking part together. Sometimes these were home based: a sing-song around the piano, or listening to the radio.[62] Sometimes the family went out as a group, paying visits, going to a picnic or to church, spending a day at the races or the Agricultural and Pastoral Show. New opportunities for married couples were emerging too. In the late 1920s the Omaranui Bowling Club was formed in Taradale. Husbands and wives could socialise there together, especially at the weekly '500' tournaments Mrs Ellis and Mrs Kelly organised. On the greens, though, it was a different story. Men bowled and women played croquet. In the pavilion, too, men ran the club and women made the tea.[63] Women could raise funds for the club, but they could not sit on the committee.[64]

This pattern was repeated in many other social situations. Men and women, and often their children too, took part in the same activities, but not as equals. People may have been playing with their families, but they were also playing out gendered roles. The new family man never pretended that he was a democrat. In part, he was there to balance out the influence of his wife, and make sure his son did not grow up effeminate.

Playing Happy Families II. Davis family Christmas party, 1930. Three generations of the Davis family pose in their Christmas hats. The wood in the wheelbarrow was chopped by the men; the women cooked the dinner. PRIVATE COLLECTION

As the youths of Taradale grew up, they continued to enjoy many of the same leisure pursuits their parents and grandparents had enjoyed. Going to the beach, the river, dances at local halls, and Sunday afternoon visits, all remained important on their social calendars. Yet men and women remembered these in different ways. The romantic world women conjured up bore little resemblance to the larrikin antics of men's accounts. This held true both for communal leisure, and for the increasingly commercialised leisure young people were being drawn to. The tension remained between heterosocial and gender-specific leisure. There had to be a courting culture, and young men had to prove themselves by paying for the movie tickets or the cream tea at Roskilda Tea Gardens, but they did not have to talk about it years later. They preferred to focus on the male-only aspects of their leisure, discussed at length in Chapter 8. The women, on the other hand, enjoyed telling stories about their courtships and the carefree years of their youth. They knew that marriage and family were just around the corner, and that once they turned that corner there would be no going back.

CHAPTER 7

Feminine Leisure

When she was young and single, Louisa Gebbie could dress up and go to a ball at 9 p.m. and dance until dawn. She could be swept off her feet, or at least be amused, by Patrick O'Dowd in his stockman's outfit. That was in 1887. Within a decade, as Patrick's wife and already the mother of four children under the age of six, she had little time for such frivolities. Now, like other married women, she snatched moments of leisure at home, in her cash-free social sphere. In between scrubbing the floors and pressing clothes, Louisa might be able to sit down and enjoy a cup of tea. But she did so surrounded by the work that still had to be done.

The boundaries between women's domestic work and their leisure were often blurred. A woman who joined her sister on the freshly scrubbed front verandah, mending clothes, was both at work and at play. While her husband could map his leisure in time and space, hers was very different. Women's work did not finish at 5 or 6 o'clock and there were no half-day holidays. Even if there had been, many women would not have been able to leave their homes easily. Apart from childcare, there were transport problems. Many women were rumoured to be able to ride a horse, but few actually did so. Bicycles were out of bounds for most married women, and the rise of the automobile tended to see men behind the steering wheel. Women had to rely on infrequent public transport, or walk. So their leisure was immediately limited by a lack of cash, time, and transport. By default, the work place of the home became the prime site for married women's leisure.

Women's and men's leisure were based on different value systems. For the most part, the girls and women of Taradale used their leisure to achieve or bolster respectability.[1] The crafts and good works they devoted their time to were a way to confer status on themselves and their families. Not that all women made beaded milk-jug covers or joined the Mothers' Union. Some women refused to play the respectability game, while others changed the rules. By the 1920s, the definition of respectable women's leisure was being challenged, largely because of the behaviour of Taradale's new women.

There were no new women in Taradale in the 1880s, though. Instead, there were hard-working women, such as Louisa O'Dowd, confined for most of their time to the home, who tried to make ends meet while also having some fun. They set up a pattern that generations of women would follow. The women who worked at home, as mothers and daughters, paid and unpaid helpers, knew that if they did not find some way to lighten their daily lives, no one else would. They had to make their work more pleasurable. Hannah Field's mother loved to listen to music, but could rarely afford the time to sit down and do so. So 'she always had the old gramophone playing while she worked'.[2]

But the prime way women managed to grab moments of leisure was to visit their friends and relations during the daytime, when children were at school and husbands were away at work. Visiting, and the gossip that accompanied such visits, was married women's main form of leisure. Many women had an informal arrangement to visit each week, and often centred their visit on food, either lunch or afternoon tea. Florence Rifle could recall her mother's friend, Mrs Burton, being a regular lunch time visitor:

> I can remember Dad saying, 'Gee, they ate a whole pig last winter in bacon'. He killed a pig and cured it and this woman used to come down and Mum used to fry bacon and they'd have bacon and eggs for lunch [laugh]. And they ate the whole pig [laugh]. He was tickled pink.[3]

When women got together and talked about the community and the people in it, they wielded power. Gossip was women's informal power over their neighbourhood. It allowed women to share ideas and information, and so helped to break down the isolation many women felt working most of the day by themselves. The properties in Taradale tended to be some distance apart, so most women could not lean over the back fence or stand in the doorway to chat with neighbours. Often they did not even meet at the local shops, since the butcher, grocer, and baker delivered. Instead they had to rely on visiting to chat, catch up on the news, and even create the news. In a society where physical horizons were limited for most married women, this was often the prime way that they could expand their world.[4]

Girls at home mirrored their mothers' visiting patterns. When Martha Edwards's mother was visited by her sister, Martha and her sisters were joined by their cousin:

> Mum was a very reserved person and so other than the odd relations, her sister who lived at Awatoto used to come over occasionally and her daughter, our cousin. Well she's exactly the same [age] as our sister and she was included because she was the only one in her family. We'd sort of include her in everything, so she used to come and stay with us in the school holidays sometimes. I remember one school holidays we made 21 doll dresses between us [laugh]. Well-dressed dolls.[5]

The nature of girls' play and its values largely reflected what they saw their mothers' lives to be – kin-oriented, domestic and domesticated, concerned with female forms of production such as sewing. The physical boundaries of girls' play reinforced this. Girls had more chores to do and more restrictions on their activities than boys. While their brothers roamed the neighbourhood in groups, Taradale's girls tended to play at home with one or two friends or kin. Like their mothers, they had limited access to the time and resources necessary for a leisurely life. In the nineteenth century the local saddlery did not even bother advertising saddles for girls, and as late as the 1920s the price of bicycles still put them out of reach for many girls.[6] Instead girls' play encouraged and reinforced feminine values of being domestic and decorative. Girls played with dolls, they visited their neighbours or cousins and played house, they learnt the piano or spent time in solitary activities like reading.

This blurring of domestic and leisure roles sometimes occurred at school as well. In 1916, the school inspector commented favourably on Taradale School's habit of providing a hot drink for the children at lunchtime: 'It is interesting to see the elder girls mothering the younger ones, and surely it is an advantage to have this trait of home life imported into our schools'.[7] While Inspector Strachan saw this ritual as promoting the cult of domesticity, Louisa Plumb had more material memories of it:

> I think one of the things, one of the highlights of those years was that there was one school, and all these classes were in one room and they had a stove in the middle, a coal range in the middle of the room which kept the room

warm in the winter and they had a big kerosene tin and had cocoa, you know, at lunchtime, with your lunch. Free. And that's something that's always stood out in my mind was this big kerosene tin of cocoa.[8]

School chores were often gendered for boys too. When Taradale School, in a pioneering mood, introduced toothbrush drill, boys such as Ernest Edwards were entrusted with such masculine, 'scientific' tasks as mixing up the potassium permanganate (Condy's crystals):

At Taradale School they used to mix up Condy's crystals and I offered to do this and we used to go into Mr Williamson's house with a benzine tin and mix up this Condy's crystals and then the school would line up and they'd all have their cups and their toothbrushes and we'd go along and fill them all up with this stuff. And this toothbrush drill used to be quite an episode, but I was distributing it all the time so I didn't have to worry about it [laugh].[9]

Although Louisa Plumb's memories of free cocoa were not quite in line with the inspector's, she was part of the 'mothering' expectation. These were values learnt at home and transferred into the classroom. Some women took this further, and brought their domestic skills and values into the women's organisations they formed and joined.

As the previous chapter demonstrated, not all women went to church on anything like a regular basis. But for those with the time and inclination, church life was one of the very few public avenues of leisure open to adult women. As well as expecting women to clean buildings and provide food, from the early twentieth century Taradale's churches also offered them their own organisations. In 1907 the Presbyterian women formed a ladies' guild, and at around this time the Methodist women also formed themselves into a guild. In 1921 a Mothers' Union was begun at All Saints, and women from all three Protestant denominations belonged to it. Unfortunately the records from these bodies are incomplete, but the surviving material gives some insights into the social activities and church culture of this group of women.

Like the men's church committees, the ladies' guilds met once a month, in the afternoon, whereas the men usually held their meetings at night. But unlike the men on committees, the women paid to belong to these guilds. The payment of a small membership fee marked the guilds off from married women's other social activities. The guilds were the first – and for much of the period the only – public organisation married women in Taradale could belong to. The fee was not only a way to raise funds, but also a means by which women asserted their right to belong to a non-domestic organisation.

Although the guilds and later the Mothers' Union were publicly sited organisations, and despite the fact that women paid membership dues and elected officers, just as their husbands did within friendly societies, the guilds should not be viewed as a rejection of a feminine world, let alone an adoption of masculine ideals. They operated as auxiliaries to the men's church committees. When men decided that the parish needed to raise funds, they informed the women, who then did the fund-raising. Year after year women organised garden parties, cake and apron fairs, sales of work, and bazaars. The effort and organisation involved were magnificent. In August 1919 a group of Catholic women began organising for their church's bazaar. They allocated the stalls and in September began the first of a series of socials in aid of each stall. The bazaar itself was not held until March 1920. It raised over £700.[10] As Alice Parke said when reminiscing about the Catholic bazaars:

> . . . they had all stalls, beautifully done up, all around, like little shops, and they had raffles and I know my uncle won a painting and a beautiful satin cushion and the most beautiful handwork that those women used to do and that would be all sold at these stalls. . . . When the Catholics had their fair it was worthwhile going to because it was really something. You don't see anything like that here now.[11]

Organising socials and providing the refreshments at them was another major function performed by the guilds, and again provided women with a public but still domesticated role. When a minister left or a new one arrived, it fell to guild members to do the right thing and organise a social. They provided the supper while single women and married men provided most of the entertainment.

Not until the Great War did Taradale's women have a secular public organisation to belong to. During the war a group of women in Taradale formed the Ladies Wounded Soldiers' Committee to provide clothes and comfort to wounded soldiers. Like women all over New Zealand, they knitted for victory.[12] Three local women were also included on the Taradale District Soldiers' Committee, which organised the farewell gatherings at the town hall for departing soldiers.

The women on these two committees were the stalwarts of the community. They were from long-established families, tended to be married or older women, and were middle class. Many were related. Ada Martin and Phoebe Dolbel, both on the Taradale District Soldiers'

The Ladies Wounded Soldiers' Committee. *Standing*: Mesdames P. P. Neagle, H. S. Clark, H. C. Ballantyne and Miss Willis. *Sitting*: Mesdames E. Peacock, R. M. Glenny (President), A. B. Davis (Honorary Secretary) and W. W. Brooks. *Absent*: Mrs Dewes, Mrs and Miss Hoadley and Miss Powdrell. Mrs Doctor Swansegar was the first president. Evelina Glenny's husband was a storekeeper, as was Mary Ballantyne's. Phyllis Brooks's husband managed a shop, Annie Davis's husband was a self-employed builder, and Irene Neagle and Laura Clark were married to farmers. The women of this committee were not a cross-section of Taradale's population.
THE NARRATIVE OF THE PLAINS, 1919, P. 51

Committee, were sisters-in-law. Phoebe's husband was one of the area's largest land owners and sheep farmers while Ada's husband was a well-known retailer in Taradale. The other female committee member was a Miss M. Nicol. She was related to Kate Powdrell, a member of the Ladies Wounded Soldiers' Committee. Other members of that committee were married to the doctor, store owners and farmers.

The women who became committee members were very similar to one another, and very different from most women; and there were few of them. Yet they also drew in other women, such as Louisa Plumb's mother, to help with the war effort:

> The only thing that I remember her getting involved in, when we were very young, was the First World War. They used to have cake stalls and all that sort of thing and raise funds for overseas. She used to do a tremendous lot of baking for those bazaars and all those sale days that they had. And that's the only thing I remember her doing. She used to make beautiful butterfly cakes. I remember these trays of butterfly cakes with whipped cream in them. They were gorgeous.[13]

Although the war allowed women a temporary respite from church organisations, their public leisure remained domestically focused. Making butterfly cakes or knitting socks for soldiers hardly redefined women's leisure. The boundaries between work and leisure remained blurred for many women.

But not all were content to play this game. There were always women in Taradale who pushed the boundaries, who scorned the desire for respectability and decided to play by their own rules. For many women challenging the boundaries meant no more than the occasional bet on a horse or having a sherry with their friends. Hannah Field's mother, who dusted while the gramophone played, is a good example:

> Well, Mum liked to have a bet but she used to only have a double that the baker, he was a bookie, Horsefield, he used to deliver the bread and he used to run, of course you weren't allowed to do it but he used to run these little doubles and she'd have a double and then sometimes she'd have a bet on a horse but very seldom, and then sometimes they'd go to the races.[14]

Hannah's brother, who was away at high school all day, did not know that their mother liked to have a flutter. She also took an interest in spiritualism. Several of the female narrators mentioned how superstitious their mothers were and how they flirted with the supernatural. Grace Miner claimed that when her brother ran over a black cat while driving the family car in 1915, her mother took it as an omen. The brother never returned from the war. 'She always said that cat was unlucky. She was very very superstitious.'[15] Hannah Field and James Green's mother took this further:

> She liked spiritualism and that. She used to have these, sometimes all her old cronies and that, they'd have spiritualist meetings over at home. My father didn't believe in that. I sat in once. I only sat in on one. Course James and them, they were all joking about it outside, you know, poking around the window.[16]

Despite her husband's thinking this was a 'huge joke', Mrs Green would hold these gatherings on a regular basis, attended by half a dozen female friends.

Women like Mrs Green occasionally overstepped the expected feminine line, but it was a small step, and they soon retreated. A few women, however, went much further. One of the most fiercely defended rules was that men, not women, drank alcohol and got drunk. As Joseph Barnett said, 'If a woman went into the pub in those days everybody would have dropped dead. It just wasn't done'.[17] But the evidence suggests that some women enjoyed a drink or two.[18] Respectable family women were allowed a wee tipple on special occasions. When one woman bought her Christmas supplies from Cornelius P. Linehan of the Meanee Hotel on Sunday 24 December

1899, the publican ended up in court for selling liquor on a Sunday.[19] Less respectable women, such as Fanny Preston, drank on a more regular basis. Preston, also known as Janet McPherson, was arrested by Constable Rutledge on New Road in Taradale at 5 p.m. on 2 November 1895. At that early hour of the evening she was already drunk. She was fined £1 and costs for being drunk in a public place. Later that month she was arrested again; this time she was sentenced to two months in gaol.[20] Occasionally a prohibition order was taken out against a woman, to prevent her from gaining access to alcohol. An order was granted against Elizabeth Beeham in November 1899.[21] Even Sunday was not sacred to some women. Carol Anderson was arrested for being drunk in Greenmeadows on Sunday at lunch-time in June 1901.[22] But if Anderson was not at home cooking Sunday dinner, hundreds of other women were. It was a very small minority of women whose drinking became a matter of public concern and comment. Most women who drank did so within their own four walls, and in moderation. Sober respectability was the norm.

Although sobriety remained the standard, in other respects Taradale's women were renegotiating ideas of respectability. There is certainly evidence that throughout the period girls were testing what they could get away with at school, rather than at home. On their way to and from school, and in the playground, girls sometimes physically attacked one another. This 'unladylike' behaviour required comment from the headmaster, and teacher patrols in the playgrounds. Brian Sutton-Smith has referred to this as the 'taming of the playground'.[23] In the early 1890s Taradale's school committee and the Hawke's Bay school inspector called on teachers to exercise active supervision of the children's play. As Inspector Henry Hill put it, teachers should be among the pupils at play, 'influencing them in those forms of competition which are the prelude to the higher competition in the business of life'.[24]

Outside of school, too, girls were breaking bounds. In 1903 the library committee of the Taradale Town Board passed the following resolution: 'that owing to the wilful destruction of papers, Illustrated Magazines, books etc. in the Mechanics Institute Reading room, All boys and girls are hereby cautioned NOT to enter or make use of the Reading room from this date unless subscribers'.[25] The behaviour of boys and girls continued to be a worry, and a decade later the by-laws stated that:

> No child under the age of twelve years shall be allowed in the library except in charge of a parent or guardian, and no child under the age of fourteen

years shall be permitted to remain in the library after 8 p.m. without the written permission of its parents or guardians, to be produced when required by the Librarian.[26]

The library had separate rooms for males and females.

Although some girls were breaking the rules, very few of the women interviewed would admit to this. As several other studies have noted, it is rare for adults to recall systematically challenging their parents' authority when they were children.[27] What was interesting about the Taradale material was how the women downplayed all their challenges. If they talked about being naughty at school, they tended to dismiss the incident:

> *What sort of things would the girls do by themselves?*
> Well, nothing very much. We, we had a, in this first school, in the store, we had, there was a little bridge to go over for our playground, it went into Avenue Road and there was a willow tree by the creek and we had a branch there and we used to swing ourselves across that to get into the playground, so we spent a lot of time on that.
> *Did many fall in?*
> Yeah, a few. I had a fall.
> *And then what happened?*
> Oh well, I had to go home and change but fortunately I just lived over the, across the road from it. But we had good times, we played more together than what they do now. And there was very little fighting. In fact I really enjoyed school, especially the first school I went to, the infant school.[28]

Some women recalled other girls being naughty rather than themselves, or focused on the actions of boys rather than girls. When Alice Parke was asked who her teachers were, she told the story of Mr Engelbretsen:

> We used to have some boys that went to school there and they hated their teacher, Mr Engelbretsen, and they used to play tricks on him . . . and on one occasion they buried his bicycle up to the handlebars and they'd hide his tools and all that sort of thing because they disliked him so much.[29]

Arthur Bishop's memory of the same event is somewhat different. He recalled that 'even the girls helped' to bury the bike.[30] When the women told such stories they did not place themselves at the centre of the narrative, as Martha Edwards's story about Taradale School's headmaster shows:

> And the headmaster, Mr Williamson, who lived over next along, had a cow at the back of his place and the boys used to pitch the onions, the rotten onions over to the cow and of course Mr Williamson complained because it rather gave the milk a funny taste.[31]

Girls such as Martha were meant to watch boys break the rules, and then go home and make countless dresses for their dolls. If they either wanted to or did lob a couple of onions over the fence, this was not something to be proud of, and certainly not something to recall years later.

Yet within a few short years the Marthas of Taradale did start to challenge and ultimately to change ideas about women's leisure. This renegotiation did not happen overnight, and it did not affect all women in the same way or at the same time. But the changing nature of girls' education, and their increasing participation in paid work outside the domestic sphere (discussed in Chapter 4), had a profound impact on what young women regarded as leisure, and what was accepted as respectable feminine behaviour. Girls who left home to go out to work or attend secondary school had already expanded their geographical boundaries. But the ideas and experiences of higher education and a changing work culture meant that these young women's opportunities expanded in other ways too.

Sport was centrally important. It was mainly at secondary schools and technical colleges that young women came into contact with teachers who believed in physical freedom for them. At primary school these girls had had only limited instruction in callisthenics. Now playing the game took on a whole new importance. By 1900 the girls at NGHS were playing croquet and hockey, rounders and tennis. Within two years there were tennis competitions with Woodford House, a private girls' school. In the winter of 1902 they began to play basketball, described in the school magazine as a 'capital winter game'. By the 1920s a school cricket club was formed, and annual athletic sports were being held at McLean Park.[32] While some no doubt saw all these games as preparing young women to be physically fit mothers, they also gave young women new freedoms. Clothing had to be reformed so that the players could run and jump, and the gym frock was adopted. Courts and fields had to be provided for girls to play on. NGHS, like many girls' schools, did not have the space for anything more than a few tennis courts doubling as basketball courts. So each Friday afternoon the girls walked down Clyde Road, boarded waiting trams, and went to Nelson Park, where they had room to play.[33] The importance of sport can be seen by the fact that from 1899 NGHS had a school games captain. Team sport built team spirit and loyalties, useful qualities for young women to take with them when they left school and entered paid work. These sporting girls were 'creating a new discourse of femininity'.[34]

In Taradale, some girls carried on with their games after leaving school. By 1909 Taradale boasted two women's sports teams, the St Joseph's Ladies' Cricket Club and the Airini Ladies' Hockey Club. Miss Murnane was the captain of the cricket club, and Miss Nicholl captained the hockey players.[35] Miss Rundle, a pupil teacher at Taradale School, was in the representative hockey team, but found it difficult to obtain leave to play games. Just before the headmaster, Mr Williamson, denied her leave to attend a tournament, he gave the whole school a half-day holiday to go and watch Hawke's Bay play Britain at football.[36] The situation did not improve for Miss Rundle. In 1911 the headmaster was still refusing to give her time off for hockey, stating that 'the whole matter of obtaining so much leave for these Games is most objectionable'.[37] Miss Rundle left the school at the end of the year.

The girls at Taradale School did not have their first experience of team sports until some years later. The women teachers at the school,

Taradale ladies' hockey team, probably the Airini Ladies' Hockey Team, in the early years of the century. COLLECTION OF HAWKE'S BAY CULTURAL TRUST–HAWKE'S BAY MUSEUM, NAPIER, NEW ZEALAND, 5625

no doubt influenced by the experiences of girls' secondary schools, tried to persuade the headmaster to introduce games for girls. At the turn of the century, against the headmaster's wishes, callisthenics for girls was begun, although the school inspector felt that the girls' physical training was 'wanting' in the area of deportment: 'Gracefulness in walking in the case of a woman is worth striving for'.[38] It was not until 1920 that the 'lady teachers' were able to convince the headmaster that more physical and team activity for girls was desirable.[39] Basketball courts were prepared and girls' team sport began. It was not a coincidence that in their smaller playground girls played a game requiring little space.[40]

Recently there has been much debate about the historical importance and role of sport for girls and young women. It has been claimed that an emphasis on change through sport, in terms of dress and behaviour, overlooks the limitations which continued to be placed on women. There was also an argument at the time that sport could be sanctioned, since it prepared women physically for motherhood.[41] Yet we should not assume that the women who took to the hockey field listened to or agreed with this rationale. The Taradale School headmaster's annoyance about female sport needs to be understood in this context. While callisthenics for girls or the slow introduction of the gym frock may not be great leaps forward, they were, nonetheless, important steps taken by women, for women.

While organised team sports were an important new development, they were not the only physical activities that this new breed of women were engaging in. Young women were also able to join in non-organised sporting activities, such as bicycle riding and swimming, to a degree that had not been possible when they were children. Girls did not own their own bikes, but young women frequently did. From 1901 NGHS pupils were wobbling around the school tennis court, learning to ride a bike. Their task was not made any easier by the fact that others were often playing tennis at the same time.[42] Girls did not have time after school to go down to the local river or beach to swim, but young women frequently did. By 1905 sea bathing was popular among the pupils at NGHS. With the opening of the Municipal Baths in 1909, even more young women took to swimming. A swimming club was formed and within a few years the school held annual swimming sports.[43] As a young girl Harriet South had not been allowed out to play. She had chores to do after school, so she never got to go to Shelly Beach. But once she went to tech and then began paid work, the situation changed. Harriet would get the Napier to Greenmeadows bus at 6 o'clock, and by 6.45 p.m. be down at the beach with a group of friends. They would swim and have supper on the beach. Harriet's group of friends included her sister and neighbours. Sometimes boys were included, but Harriet's network was dominated by female friends. Like many other young women, she was no longer as bound by house or chores as she had been in childhood.

These young women were able to indulge in leisure in these ways partly because of the changing economy. The money they earned bought them leisure time – since they paid board at home, they were partly relieved from domestic chores. The consumer economy they were part of offered them many ways to spend their wages. For the period before the Great War it is impossible to determine how Taradale's young women spent their earnings. But in the post-war period the oral evidence indicates that young women used their limited financial means to distinguish themselves both from young girls and from their mothers.[44]

One way they did this was through their physical appearance. It was the young single women of Taradale who bobbed their hair, put on make-up, and wore fashionable clothes. As a young working woman, Ellen Store wore make-up: 'Just a little. I used to put very light colouring on, you could hardly see it. And the lipstick . . . Just enough to make a difference.'[45]

Even though Ellen only wore 'a little' make-up, it was 'enough to make a difference', to mark her off both from the girl she had been and from her mother. Whereas Ellen worked for the Town Board, Sophie Richardson had to stay at home and help her mother. But she defiantly bobbed her hair. Doing this physically differentiated her from her mother, even if the work they did was the same. Adolescent women also asserted their independence through the clothes they wore on social occasions. As Ellen Store pointed out, ball dresses were best if bought from Blythe's or McGruer's in Napier, rather than being home-made by mother, even though 'you might do without something to pay for it'. Louisa Plumb once paid over a week's wages for a hat. She still fondly recalled splashing out this way:

> I know I went very extravagant one day, on a Wednesday afternoon I went into town to do some shopping, to get a new hat and I paid the large sum of 30 shillings. Now that was really extravagant. It really was. I've never forgotten that.[46]

Like other young women in New Zealand at the time, Louisa was 'putting on style'.[47] The clothes revolution of elite and middle-class women in New Zealand has received more attention than the changing fashions of young working-class women.[48] Yet these young women, too, were moving away from cumbersome, maternal clothes to a more boyish, slender look. The change is instructive, for it represents more than a simple rejection of uncomfortable, closely fitted boned necklines. The young women of Taradale were using their consumer power to buy a different look, a look that challenged conventions about feminine beauty and respectability. It was often a look modeled on the silver screen. Young women who flocked to the cinema were imitating the stars they adored. When Ellen Store and her girl friend went to the pictures every Saturday night, they were buying glamour.[49] No wonder that Ellen then rejected homemade party clothes. Some young women went so far as to smoke, although even in the 1920s that was rare and considered something of a scandal: 'I can remember two well-known girls in Taradale here, well, they were adults, but they were seen smoking and oh my God that was a terrible thing.'[50] It was the young single women who did the 'terrible things', rather than the girls or married women.

I am not suggesting that once the girls of Taradale turned 14 they all suddenly became rebellious. Many did not, of course. Nor am I suggesting that these new freedoms were without costs. Although the available evidence from Taradale is slim, girls who went out in the evenings or socialised away from the communal gaze could find themselves in danger, as Harriet Ogden did in 1897. This young woman had gone into Napier for the evening. At 10 p.m. a Greenmeadows jockey, John Sweeney, indecently assaulted her.

Yet despite the risks, even the leisure pursuits associated with 'good' girls took a new direction, as church-related activities show. At adolescence, sex-segregated Sunday School was replaced with sex-specific Bible Class. In 1907, for example, St Columba Presbyterian church began a class for young women's Bible study.[51] Each week, up to a dozen young women would gather and discuss a set topic and were then meant to write on a particular subject, such as 'The Spirit of Anzac'.[52] The classes provided an opportunity for the young women to organise socials, midnight picnics and camps. Sunday School had offered girls a yearly picnic only; Bible Class provided young women with regular leisure opportunities. Although young women's leisure time was still often gender-specific, they used these opportunities to plan for leisure shared with young men. They did this in two ways: by organising 'mixed' events such as socials, and by preparing themselves for these events by discussing masculine topics.[53]

A few young women took this further and entered the previously masculine domain of friendly societies. In 1909 Miss Daisy Button, an

18-year-old engaged in domestic duties, became the first female member of the Ancient Order of Foresters, Court Redclyffe. She left in 1913, the same year that the second young woman, Miss Lucy Harris, joined. Two years later Annie Ellison, a 36-year-old lady's help, joined the lodge, and in 1926 Miss E. Harris, a 16 year old domestic, was initiated into Court Redclyffe.[54] The Manchester Unity Independent Order of Odd Fellows, Meanee Lodge, remained a male preserve until 1925, when six women between the ages of 17 and 21 joined. Over the next five years they were joined by another half dozen women.[55] The women who joined the lodges were all in paid employment, all were single, and most were minors. As Mary Ann Clawson has pointed out, as women's public role increased, so did their participation in lodges.[56] Young women's earning power and their increasing role in Taradale's public life led to their membership of previously male preserves.

The gradual movement of a group of young women into the lodges, onto the playing fields and down to the beach, marks an obvious break between them and the women of their mothers' generation. What is interesting about such developments is that these young women often asserted their public roles through masculine institutions and activities. As girls, they had acted like boys on the rare occasions that they negotiated the gendered boundaries; as young women, they took this further and joined in masculine leisure activities as well as using public space for their leisure. Simply by purchasing their own bicycle and taking to the roads, they were redefining Taradale's gender boundaries.

They were not alone in this redefinition. While their mothers and grandmothers were not offered the same opportunities, by the 1920s they were following the young women's lead. The married women of Taradale did not suddenly take up hockey or demand the right to drink at the Greenmeadows Hotel. Young women may have been able to yell and run around, wear make-up and still be considered 'proper'; but adult women knew that that sort of behaviour was still unacceptable for wives and mothers. However, in other ways their leisure time was changing.

Within church organisations, women were increasingly asserting their independence from men and moving away from a purely domestic focus. By the 1920s men were no longer members of the ladies' guilds. Although fund-raising and the organising of socials continued to be important, women began to use the guilds to perform other functions too. In 1929 the Methodist guild set out its 'syllabus' for the next six months. At each meeting a speaker would offer some intellectual stimulation to guild members.[57] Women were also organising meetings with other guilds.[58] They were becoming more inter-denominational, as the 1920s records of the Protestant Mothers' Union show.

Although their fund-raising role remained, women were now being consulted about how the money they raised would be spent. In 1915 the Methodist church trustees asked the ladies' guild for the money the women had recently raised. The trustees had had the church painted and there was a bill to be paid. Though the women had not been consulted about this, they handed over the money. But by 1924, when it came to discussing the installation of electric light in the church, members of the ladies' guild were invited to the trustees' meeting to talk about this proposition. Once it was decided to go ahead with the plan, the women were consulted over the question of fund-raising. The guild responded by holding a concert and coffee supper.[59] The changing nature of the guilds indicates wider changes in the role married women played within the churches. In the 1880s women did not even attend their parishes' annual general meetings. By the late 1920s, at those same meetings, women were proposing and seconding motions and voting for vestrymen. In 1928 two Methodist women became communion stewards, and in 1929 two were appointed church visitors. In the 1920s, rather than the 1880s, it would be more accurate to say that married women had a social and public role within the churches.

But it was a new organisation in the 1920s, the Women's Institute, or WI, which epitomises the changes for married women's leisure. The Institute was the first permanent, non-religious, public leisure organisation for women in Taradale. When the Taradale branch of the WI began in 1925, it was the fifth branch formed in New Zealand. In July of that year seven local women met with Elizabeth Jerome Spencer, the instigator of the WI, with the hope of founding a Taradale branch. These women invited another seven women to join them, and began to hold monthly WI meetings in the Taradale Town Hall. Within a decade the Taradale branch had over 100 members, and a separate Greenmeadows branch was formed.

Unfortunately most of the local WI's early records were destroyed in the 1931 earthquake. However, some material has survived. Used in conjunction with the oral histories, it gives insights into the first five years of Taradale's WI. The WI's constitution and rules demonstrate Miss Spencer's aims when she began it. Like masculine leisure organisations, the Institute aimed to be inclusive within rural communities. All women and girls were welcome to join. A rule preventing the discussion of sectarian and party political matters at Institute meetings was intended to ensure that no group felt alienated. Although each

FEMININE LEISURE

member had to pay a subscription fee, it was only 2 shillings a year. The WI did not aim to be exclusive on any basis apart from gender: no men were allowed to join. The rapid growth of the Taradale branch is testimony of the inclusive nature of the Institute, and also of married women's strong desire for organised public leisure.

But although the WI rules were designed to enable a wide range of women to join, with no stipulations about age or marital status, it was still the older married women of Taradale who tended to become members. The surviving records identify fifteen of the WI's earliest members. All were married women, and most had children. But unlike the committee women of the Great War, these women tended not to be long-term residents, and typically were not married to middle-class business men. As well as the wives of a local clergyman and of a schoolteacher, the wives of dredge hands and storemen were also inaugural members and office holders.

The main purpose of the WI was to improve and develop the conditions of rural life. It aimed to stimulate interests in agricultural pursuits, give instruction and training in domestic science, hygiene, social welfare and home handicraft, and encourage women to engage in co-operative enterprises. In other words, it focused on the lives and needs of married women and continued the long history of blurring women's work and leisure. Single women with some discretionary spending power and few domestic responsibilities preferred to go shopping or see a movie in their leisure time. Yet the WI's attraction for married women was wider than the practical instruction it offered. Its main drawcard was the social life it gave women. That is why it is classed here as leisure, rather than as work.

Louisa Plumb's mother enjoyed a brief foray into the public world during the war, but it was not until the WI began that she really had a social life beyond her home and family:

> . . . but until we were all married she was very housebound, until somebody got her to join the Country Women's Institute and that was the turning point in her life, where she was going out and meeting people. So she belonged to the Taradale Institute and then they formed the one in Greenmeadows and she was president for a number of years there, but that was really something that she was able to do, for the first time, that she wanted to do.[60]

Much of what Louisa's mother and other members did as WI members could be defined as traditional feminine activities. At meetings they learnt how to refoot a silk stocking, make paper lampshades, sew gloves and create bead-trimmed jug covers. On Anzac Day they played a supporting role, laying a wreath at the war memorial. Like the guilds before them, they also held socials to raise funds.

However, again like the guilds, the WI was also part of the slowly changing focus of adult women's organised leisure. Women's domestic skills were gaining public recognition. They began to hold annual flower shows and send pieces of their handiwork into the Agricultural and Pastoral show. At the Autumn Show in 1929, Mrs Ellis won the glove competition and Mrs Simpkin came second. Both were on the Taradale WI committee.[61] Women's domestic skills were taking on much more of an organised, competitive edge.

The Institute also offered married women new opportunities. It had an educative role, giving women the opportunity to manage and run their own organisation from the outset. Each branch had to elect officers and run itself in line with the Institute's overall rules and constitution. An annual Dominion conference was held, attended by at least one delegate per branch. Like men who belonged to lodges, married women could now belong to an organisation which was not only national, but also had international ties.

Nevertheless, many women were also happy to participate in less structured leisure activities. Married women's leisure remained far more communally focused than single women's. But like their daughters and nieces, adult women also indulged in some commercially organised activities. Although young courting couples made the back row of the Taradale Town Hall their own on movie nights, going to the pictures was not exclusively for the young. Married couples also walked or drove to the hall to catch the latest film, and many married women went with their female friends and relations. While William Cliff's father stayed at home working, his mother went to the movies with her friend, Mrs Campbell. Hannah Field's mother would go to the pictures with her neighbour Mrs Goeffic on the nights when her husband had work meetings. Patrick Stevenson and Grace Miner's mother was also a regular moviegoer, although for her it was the Gaiety Theatre in Napier rather than the Taradale town hall. When her husband began a regular 'service car' run into Napier on Saturday nights, she went along for the ride. Like the young people Mr Stevenson ferried into Napier, Mrs Stevenson enjoyed her night out. For a couple of hours she could escape from the housework and live a fantasy life.

By the time movies arrived in Taradale, Louisa O'Dowd was dead. She missed out on the excitement of the cinema and the development of women's organisations. As the mother of six, she did not even have regular Plunket visits to break up her week. All of these came after her time. Some of Louisa's contemporaries, though, were beginning to enjoy new leisure activities as their daughters grew up and became wives and mothers. It was when young women married that their leisure lives matched those of their mothers. Kathleen Thomson's mother was born a little later than Louisa O'Dowd. When asked about her mother's leisure, Kathleen replied:

> No, Mum never went out much, never went out at all. Only in later years when the daughters got married. Well I took her out more than anything. We used to go to cards and we joined the Institute together, that's the only time.
> *This was after you were married?*
> After I was married. That was the only time she was, she'd go out, just with us girls.[62]

Before Kathleen married she socialised with people her own age. Ladies' guilds and the WI held little attraction. Nor was it physically possible for most single women to attend them, since they held their meetings in the afternoons, when young women were away at work. Young women took their leisure at night and in the weekends, and increasingly were paying a price for it. It was after marriage that daughters began to mirror their mothers' lives, in work and leisure. As these younger women joined the Mothers' Union, their different experiences and expectations had some impact on the organisation. Women who had shouted along the sidelines at hockey matches and wore enough make-up to 'make a difference' were less deferential and domesticated than their mothers and grandmothers. From one generation to the next, the gendered boundaries were slowly being renegotiated. Respectable feminine behaviour was experiencing a minor redefinition. Although these changes were small, they were significant, especially when they are compared with the inclusive nature of masculine leisure. As the next chapter shows, age and marital status rarely divided men, and a shared set of values often prevailed.

CHAPTER 8

Masculine Leisure

Louisa Gebbie's life changed markedly on Wednesday 18 June 1890, the day she married Patrick O'Dowd. Within weeks she was pregnant with their first daughter. Rather than fancy dress balls and picnics, her life now revolved around keeping house and sewing her baby's layette. Patrick's life was also fundamentally altered. Within ten months of getting married he was a father. A couple of years later there was another daughter, then the first of four sons was born.

Patrick was an only child. He did not have Louisa's experience of living in a household full of children. But at least he could escape the noise and work his land. With over 20 acres to farm, and various sheds and stables to potter about in, Patrick could fulfil his responsibilities as a good provider while also gaining some peace and quiet. Unlike Louisa, he also found some time for leisure away from the family. Before he and Louisa started to see one another, Patrick had joined a local friendly society, the Foresters. He remained a member after their marriage, although within a couple of years he was struck off, because his membership fees were in arrears. A decade later he joined the Odd Fellows, but his membership lapsed after three years when he again fell into arrears.

It is unclear whether Patrick O'Dowd could not afford his friendly society fees, or simply chose to spend his discretionary income in other ways. He had inherited money from his mother in 1903, and his land holdings were increasing in value all the time. Either way, Patrick's leisure life was less constrained than Louisa's. As a general rule, the men of Taradale had more time for leisure than the women, were able to leave the home and family environment more easily, and had access to more money for leisure. As a result they were better catered for. Besides the hotels and the billiard saloon, there were lodges, sporting organisations, and public buildings which men made their own. Particularly in the period before the Great War, the provisions for men's organised leisure were far superior to anything provided for women. Then there was the informal, unorganised recreation that men indulged in. Hunting and shooting, fishing, chatting to friends in the main street or at the dairy factory – all were part of men's leisure and part of their identity.[1] A man who could afford to play, in terms of both money and time, was making a statement about his capacity to provide for his family and also about his power over his family.

Many aspects of men's leisure remained consistent over the period. In the 1880s and the 1920s men could enjoy recreation away from the home and the influence of women. Commercially oriented leisure and organised group activities were always important, and a wide variety of men could be found within any organisation or event. Masculine leisure was inclusive. The temperance crusader and the social drinker may have chosen to spend an evening in different ways, but in another situation they may well have joined together. Moreover, a range of men could be found mixing together at the lodge, in the hotel, or on the sports field. This inclusiveness was another way that men's leisure signalled men's power.

But men's leisure, like women's, also experienced some changes over the years. Although commercial leisure was always an option, new forms, such as motor bike races, arose to compete for men's spare time and money. New challenges also developed. As previous chapters mention, from the late nineteenth century concerns were being expressed about the undue influence of women on young boys. Men decided that they had better take more interest in the lives of their sons. The feminising impact of mothers and female teachers had to be countered by masculine pursuits and values. School cadets, team sports and new organisations such as Boy Scouts all developed in the early twentieth century, and were all led by local men. Fathers may long have taught their sons to fish or shoot, but there was an additional imperative now. The inclusiveness of masculine leisure expanded even further as boys and young men were brought into the fold.

The masculine leisure culture they were drawn into was not defined by domesticity and respectability. Young women may have struggled to redefine feminine leisure and bring it into a more public and competitive world, but these were not battles young men had to face. Masculine leisure simultaneously challenged ideas of respectability and was an avenue for men to show what good providers they were. It was also a way to control the community, in the name of being a good citizen.

Like men in other western societies at that time, the men of Taradale placed great importance on the physical aspects of life and on the capabilities of their own bodies.[2] As Jock Phillips has discussed, as their work became more organised and the Saturday half-holiday was introduced, so more organised recreation became possible.[3] For some this may have meant more family picnics, but for many it was a chance to either play or watch team sports. In this way sport perpetuated the sexual division of labour. It encouraged men to trust their team mates and enjoy their company, rather than the company of women. Since the best male sportsmen became local heroes, women were further marginalised from this masculine world.[4] Team sports came to embody a certain type of masculinity. The bowling club might not require the physical strength and power of the rugby field, but it did need cunning, tactics, team work and loyalty. These were the values and skills that had to be instilled in the boys and young men of the area.

One way to do this was through team sports at school. For most of the day the boys were taught by women teachers, but the senior master or headmaster always took them for games. The Taradale School headmaster's diary does not clearly show when boys' sports teams began. They were definitely playing competitive football in 1907, since in that year football teams from Standards 5 and 6 went to Napier to play High School, who had challenged them.[5] Cricket developed later. In 1917 the headmaster noted: 'I took the senior boys for a game of cricket near the Rifle Range. Great interest is evinced in this recreation'.[6] From that time on he regularly took the senior boys over to the park to 'indulge' in a game of cricket.[7] He never noted down what the senior girls were doing while he was off playing with the boys.

Boys were also encouraged to be sporting spectators. In 1908 the headmaster authorised a half-day holiday 'in honour of Football match Britain v. H.B.'.[8] After that occasion, whenever the senior boys wanted to watch a special match of football or cricket he tended just to let them leave school early.[9] In the early 1920s the Hawke's Bay Ranfurly Shield team often trained in Taradale, so the boys would rush off to watch them. Team games such as cricket and football were meant to encourage masculine virtues and values in Taradale's schoolboys. They were the toast of the school when they won. In 1919 they were runners-up to the Ross Shield and in 1920 they were 'victorious', winning two cups.[10] When they lost they were encouraged to 'persevere'.

Taradale-Meanee Districts Schools Football Team, 1919. Posing with their headmaster, Mr Williamson (middle row, third from left), the boys were runners-up in the school competition. COLLECTION OF HAWKE'S BAY CULTURAL TRUST–HAWKE'S BAY MUSEUM, NAPIER, NEW ZEALAND, 7348

The headmaster recorded that: 'A gallant stand [was] made against Clive boys who were much heavier than they were'.[11] No doubt this defeat was particularly galling since the girls had recently taken up basketball and won the B grade championship in their first year.[12]

Outside school, boys were being encouraged in other manly sports. When James Green was asked 'Who taught you how to shoot?' he replied that his father had:

> He took a fair interest in us. He taught us how to shoot, he also was pretty good on self defence, that's one thing he was good on. He wasn't frightened of anyone and he taught us. He insisted that we learnt and we even had a boxing ring at the back, built at the back [of the house], a home-made one and on a weekend he'd put the gloves on us and take us out and teach us boxing. And then he'd teach us other forms of self defence too. So that in later years, I kept the boxing up for a long while and in later years we found we, that we could defend ourselves and personally I wasn't scared of anyone – when I was in my twenties and that I found I wasn't scared of anyone and I think it all came from that skill he taught us. Perhaps I should have been frightened, I don't know, but I wasn't. But he insisted on that, that we learnt this.[13]

James's father seems like the archetypal man about the house Margaret Marsh writes of.[14] He taught his sons to shoot and box, and he even tended to his children's injuries if they hurt themselves. His wife had an arthritic hand, so when the children cut themselves they turned to their father to bathe their wounds. But when it came to other types of illnesses Mr Green exercised a form of masculine domesticity. As his daughter Hannah recalled, 'But I used to get sick a lot, get bilious attacks and Mum would always look after me then, but he looked after the boys, sort of. Mum sort of looked after me more and he'd look after the two boys.'[15]

Not all sons were happy with the level of attention their fathers paid to their physical development. William Cliff's father took a great interest in his son's physical fitness, much to William's chagrin. His father had been a European athletic champion over middle distances, and imposed a harsh regime on his son. William had to have a cold bath every morning before primary school, and when he went on to Napier Boys' High School his father insisted that he rode his bike there every day, rain or shine. Even on the coldest days Mr Cliff forbade his son to wear a scarf or gloves.

These recollections are from after the Great War. But before that men were also taking an interest in the physical prowess of young men. In 1893 a local gymnasium was begun for the young males of Taradale. The initial meeting to discuss forming the gym was held in the Taradale Hotel. Twenty young men enrolled, and another 20 agreed to join.[16] Adult men organised the gym and led classes there. A few years later a gymnasium class began in the All Saints Sunday School room, led by a former physical fitness instructor in the British Grenadier Guards, who was happy to share his expertise with the young men of Taradale. No girls attended these classes.

Once the boys of Taradale left school they could continue to play games such as rugby and cricket, and take up new sports such as polo and bowling. Taradale had its own cricket club from at least 1896, and by 1907 it sported two men's hockey clubs.[17] Boys could also keep up their shooting skills by joining the Taradale Defence Rifle Club. In these organisations males of all ages mixed. Fathers and sons were often members, as Sidney Anderson and his son Francis were at the rifle club. Married and single men joined together in these clubs, and men from a wide range of occupations found themselves playing in the same team.[18]

Perhaps the most inclusive game of all at this time was rugby. Like males all over New Zealand, the boys and men of Taradale were quick to embrace what was fast to become New Zealand's national game.

MASCULINE LEISURE

From the late 1880s Taradale had a club, affiliated to the Hawke's Bay Rugby Football Union.[19] As Jock Phillips has so convincingly argued, rugby soon came to epitomise a certain type of masculinity in New Zealand: the rugged colonial man, tamed to a degree by the rules of the game, but still looking out for his mates. Rugby was the perfect vehicle for men to retain their frontier notions of team work and mateship, egalitarianism and the importance of strength.[20] It was also a way for males to emphasise their power, not just over their opponents, but also in a more general sense. The fragments of available information on rugby in Taradale before 1930 make it clear that rugby united wide groups of males, and was an almost exclusively male sport.[21] Those who played and took part in the rugby culture ranged in age from school boys to grandfathers. They were single and married, white collar workers and labourers, old timers and newcomers to the area, and not invariably Pakeha. They were united by gender and the game.

Given its highly physical nature, rugby was played mainly by the relatively young and fit. Schoolboys, adolescents and young adults took to the field, while men over the age of 30 tended to stay on the sidelines. Brothers often played in the same rugby team. Between 1901 and 1905, for example, there were seven cases of brothers playing in the Taradale team. Three of the McCutcheon boys took to the field together, as did three Hepburn brothers. Men's involvement in rugby did not necessarily diminish because they could no longer play on a regular basis, however. Before Matthew Silk and Emily Jones's father married, he used to play in the Taradale team. After his marriage, he became the coach and a regular spectator. Emily recalled how 'very keen' their father was on football:

> Yes, he'd go to most of the football games that were held in the Park and he coached a team at one time for two or three years and there was great days when they won.
> *Was he in a good mood then?*
> Yes, oh very [laugh]. Oh he loved to see his team winning, just the same as it is today, rugby.
> *Would the whole family go down and watch?*
> Well, I don't remember going to see them but I know that we were all greatly excited because Dad was excited [laugh].
> *Would your mother go and watch?*
> Oh I don't think so. I don't remember her going, not really. She was very busy in the house, you know. She didn't have time to go, waste time with sport or anything like that. No, they had a hard life, you know, really did.[22]

While the women were busy at home, boys and men were joined together, watching the local team and also following the national team. In the 1920s the local postmaster was a rugby fan. During the 1924 Invincibles tour of Great Britain, the men and boys from the area could keep in touch with the play:

> On Sunday morning there, outside, he'd put a notice outside the post office with results of the game the All Blacks were playing in the UK, the Invincibles, in 1924. Through his contacts with the post office he'd get the score and he'd put it out in the front window. We'd all toddle down and have a look and see what the score was.[23]

Few of Taradale's rugby players were married men, although some, such as sailmaker Albert LeRoy, did continue their active involvement in the game after marriage. Instead married men such as Matthew and Emily's father took on different roles, as coaches, administrators and spectators. Occasionally charity games were held where married men played single men. There were also annual matches between Greenmeadows and Taradale for the Dolbel-Currie Cup. The men who played in these teams ranged from auctioneers to labourers. Few of them had lived long in the area or owned land. If you could play the game, then it almost did not matter who you were.[24]

To an extent this inclusiveness extended to ethnicity. A quarter of the men known to have played rugby in Taradale were Maori. They were important members of the team, and were sorely missed when they could not make a match. When Taradale lost 8–0 to Te Aute in 1890, the reporter noted 'Taradale lacked the assistance of the much talked about Hoani and Ngahoro'.[25] A few years later Chinese market gardener W. Ah Keong was the Honorary Secretary and Treasurer of the Taradale Football Club. To point to Maori and Chinese men participating in predominantly Pakeha sporting organisations is not to suggest that there was no discrimination or racism in the Taradale area. But it does indicate that there were times and occasions when Pakeha men were prepared to accept the sporting and administrative prowess of non-white men. To this extent, masculine sporting cultures admitted non-Pakeha men.

Like other team sports, rugby strengthened the bonds between men, and against women. Yet women did have certain roles in Taradale's rugby culture. At a very practical level they washed the kits. William Cliff's mother kept his football gear 'immaculate', a way of showing the rugby world her particular skills. There were also attempts by rugby bodies to include women in their sport. 'Ladies' were encouraged to be spectators, in order to provide an admiring audience. It was common for 'ladies' to be admitted free to games, while everyone else, including the players, had to pay. This happened when Taradale played the Pirates rugby team in 1890.[26] The Taradale team was either distracted by the presence of so many ladies, or disappointed that more did not take up the offer: they lost, 9–0.

Women were meant to be sidelined in men's sports. They could watch, and they could do the washing, but they could never belong. In a similar way they were excluded from another aspect of masculine leisure, larrikinism. This was not limited to leisure, just as strength and team spirit were not confined to the sports ground. But when the boys and men of Taradale went out to play, their larrikin inclinations often came to the fore. If sisters, wives and mothers were meant to use their leisure to reinforce their respectability, brothers, husbands and fathers often used it as a time to flout the rules. Keeping rules was associated with femininity; breaking rules was a masculine pursuit. From childhood, Taradale's males used their leisure time as an opportunity to challenge authority figures. This was a way to demonstrate that they were outside the control of feminine, domestic, law-abiding influences. On the whole these challenges had at most a nuisance value, but they also served to reinforce certain masculine traits.

At school, boys were more likely than girls to be hauled in front of the headmaster on charges of fighting and bad behaviour. While most of the male narrators had been physically punished at school, the consensus was that they deserved it and it had not done them any harm. But if they were going to be punished, then they preferred a man to administer the cuts, as Thomas Raven did:

> . . . old Ma Shugar. She must have been a good teacher. She told me to bend over and she was going to strap me and there was nothing doing and she, 'I'll ask you again and I'll send you to the headmaster.' So, sooner than drop my tweeds and let her belt my backside I went to schoolmaster. I didn't mind him belting me but I wasn't going to have her . . . Gilchrist [the headmaster] was a man. He used to beat hell out of you but I liked him. He was a real man. He never, ever, like some of them got nit picking, he'd belt you but he never ever held a grudge. He was a good sports master and I think everybody that ever went, the men that I know, boys that I went to school with, all adored him. He was a terrific teacher and a good fella. Gilchrist, he was terrific.[27]

Thomas Raven's obvious admiration for this 'real man' of a teacher was echoed in other men's oral accounts. All the men interviewed could and did recount incidents when they overstepped the adult imposed boundaries of proper behaviour. But their memories were full of masculine bravado rather than the understated reminiscences of the women.

The only children recorded as officially committing crimes were boys, and most of these cases were associated with boyhood bravado and 'fun' rather than more serious matters. When Walter Clegg was charged with breaking a telegraph insulator by throwing stones at it, the Resident Magistrate said that 'he wished to caution all the boys in the district that they were liable to a penalty of £10.'[28] Often local boys who were caught stealing, or for some other misdemeanour were dealt with informally by the local constable. If they went to court, they were admonished or convicted and discharged. Almost every man interviewed had a story about how the local policeman, Constable Gartley, used to kick young offenders with his size 13 boots, rather than officially charge them. The long arm of the law became the big boot of the law in Taradale. When William Cliff was out riding his bike at night without a light, he tried to avoid running into Slim Jim Gartley: 'If I had no light on my pushbike I tried to make sure that he wasn't on the road because otherwise you wouldn't be able to sit on the seat of your pushbike on the way home [laugh].'[29] When James Green was asked about Gartley, he said:

> I used to pinch a few things myself. We'd have all that fruit and stuff here but I'd love to go down pinching someone else's because they always tasted different, I suppose. The old story, something to do. A bit of devilment but if he caught you, yes you'd get the old boot and 'If you ever do that again, look out next time' and as I say, in the boys, and most of them, amongst my age group, Gartley was known as a good joker. He was a good joker, although he was a cop.
> *What about the girls, did they get into that sort of trouble?*
> Oh crumbs, no. No. They never got into any kind of trouble much, although perhaps some of them did now and again but in those days the girls were very sheltered. I've never know them to take up stealing, I can't recall anything like that.[30]

The women interviewed could not or would not recall anything like that either.

The Taradale Police Station's Charge Book indicates that few young men were officially charged with crimes. If they were local lads, they were more likely to be convicted and ordered to come up if called upon than to suffer any other form of punishment. Only two youths were sent to borstal, and neither of them had local ties.[31] But the policeman's diary of duty shows that young males were in trouble more often than the charge book reflects. In 1896 Constable Riordan had to take young Alf Lewis in hand after Lewis stole two packets of cigarettes, a box of matches and a jar of jam from George Scotcher's house.[32] The previous year Scotcher himself had been in trouble for using indecent language. Sometimes these petty thefts were group activities. Riordan was forced to stake out a Greenmeadows property in 1899 to try to 'catch some young men suspected of stealing grapes'. Despite his vigilance from 7.30 until 11 p.m., he failed.[33] Youths sometimes committed these offences with older men. In 1900 Riordan made inquiries about Robert and James Leslie and youths said to be exposing themselves in an undue manner at Taradale Bridge.[34] A few years later he was again making inquiries about 'larrikinism' in the area.[35] While in some cases a lack of evidence may have prevented prosecution, it seems that in many instances this was not deemed appropriate. It was enough that the young men were dealt with informally by the constable.

As the boys grew into young men and adults, their flirtations with larrikinism continued. For Thomas Raven this involved fighting:

> I can remember one part, I went to ten dances and had ten fights and the girl that I was knocking around with at the time, her father said that if I got into any more trouble that was the finish. Not that I minded fighting at all.[36]

For other men it involved participating in legal activities that were nonetheless frowned upon by certain sectors of the community. The local billiard room offered men a form of unorganised sport and a place away from the influence of their mothers, girlfriends or wives. Local by-laws stated that persons under the age of 18 were not allowed on the premises, but young men in Taradale flouted such rules:

> Well, at Taradale, where the Post Office is on the corner, a man named Tad Jeffares had a billiard saloon. Well, you had to be, I think 18 or 19 or something before you were allowed in there. Well, there was about five or six of us that got together, one or two from Meanee and the rest from Taradale. And Mr Gartley used to come round so often, you know, from the police station, walk around. And he heard about us kids being in there, playing billiards, because Jeffares didn't mind because it was sixpence a game or something that we paid so he didn't mind. But Gartley knew that

we were there, but what we used to do. I don't know whether he woke up to it, because he wasn't a fool. One of us had to stay on the corner of the Post Office and watch and when we seen Gartley coming we had to tear into the billiard room and tell the rest to get out, see. Anyway, we'd all go out and be out in the street somewhere, and he'd give us a silly look and I think he knew what we was up to. Anyway, one day instead of coming down the main street of Taradale he come around the back road and he caught us in there. Oh, he give us a kick in the pants, hunted us out, chased us out. But oh, he was good, that's all he done. He was good. We never got up to any mischief or anything. We liked a game of billiards and we were out of the road . . .[37]

It was not just the underage Henry Nolan and his mates who enjoyed the saloon. Around the billiard table they were joined by many older men. Sometimes these games spilled over into the hours when the saloon was meant to be closed. When this happened in February 1908, Constable O'Halloran took Edward Roberts to court. Roberts had allowed men to keep playing after 11 o'clock on a Sunday night. For transgressing the Sabbath, he was convicted and discharged. After Roberts, local man Tad Jeffares took over the parlour. Jeffares was Taradale born and bred, and by the time of his marriage in 1908 he was already listing his occupation as billiard marker. By the late 1920s his status had improved to billiard saloon proprietor. Jeffares was never charged with keeping a disorderly house or breaching the by-laws, although oral testimony and comments in the policeman's diary of duty indicate that there were occasions when he too broke the law.

Some men did not have to leave their homes in order to play a game of billiards. Emma Needle and Edward McLean's father had a table at home. Emma had very mixed feelings about this. When asked if her father went to the local hotel, she replied:

Well, I think he must have gone a bit but I really think as much as anything they had it, you see, when we had the place in Avondale [Road] it was quite a nice house . . . we did have a bathroom and we did have a toilet and as I say we did have the carbide lights but there was a room at one side of the house and he had a billiard table, you see, he had the billiard table there and he had lots of different ones, they came, that's why I feel, I feel that Mum had a fairly hard life because I was only a kid and before the different ones went to the war they'd always be there because once they sort of started going away, but they used to come and any amount of time they'd play all night. I would sleep but I know a lot of the time Mum didn't get her sleep which she should have got.[38]

Billiard players often lubricated their game with alcohol, as Emma's father and his mates did. If anything epitomised the larrikin male, it was his fondness for alcohol. The centrality of the hotel and drinking to some men's leisure is clear. Hotels such as the Duke of Edinburgh and the Waverley in Greenmeadows were major sites of masculine leisure. Hotels were strongly masculine institutions. The only women allowed were publicans, such as widow Hannah Dineen, who took over the running of the Meanee hotel after her husband John died. But female publicans were the exception. For the most part women did not darken the doors of Taradale's hotels. Indeed, this was a period when the government passed a series of laws restricting women's access to hotels.[39] Instead pubs served as a male refuge from work, home and women. Here men could enjoy a quiet drink with mates or a rowdy booze-up and fight.

Not all of the men who frequented the hotels ended up in a fist fight, of course. The pub drew in a wide range of men, some wanting to drown their sorrows, others merely after a bit of male companionship before they headed home. In both cases, going to the hotel demonstrated men's ability to indulge in leisure as they chose. While some men handed over their entire wage packet or earnings to their wives each week, others retained their own form of 'pin money' to ensure that they could have a few pints, and some spent regardless of their family's financial predicament. These men were consumers. While much of the recent literature about consumption has focused on women's changing status from household producer to consumer, the men of Taradale had a long and continuous history of buying themselves goods and services.[40]

When people were asked about the role of the hotel in their father's lives, it was the women who replied in terms of the financial costs. Interestingly, those who did so chose words that expressed how reasonable they saw this to be, or made it clear that despite his drinking, their father was still a good provider. Sisters Jane McNight and Florence Rifle explained how their mother was in charge of the family's finances. She received the milk cheque from the dairy factory. But when their father went out cutting hay for people, he would keep the cash he earnt as 'pin money':

> If he was out working, you know, doing a pin job, doing a little job, like cutting hay for somebody, there was always an odd place, where he'd say 'That was my pin money today, Mum' . . . Or he wouldn't draw the money from the hotel if he was cutting their hay. He'd leave it there and he'd pop in on the way home and have a drink.[41]

Men and their dogs outside the Plumpton Park Hotel in Meanee, c. 1897. Men gathered at the hotel to drink, and also used it as a meeting site before leaving for other activities, like hunting and dog races. COLLECTION OF HAWKE'S BAY CULTURAL TRUST–HAWKE'S BAY MUSEUM, NAPIER, NEW ZEALAND, 7593

Jane and Florence's sister, Theresa Pond, had been interviewed a year before, and made the same point about the cheque from the Heretaunga Dairy Company.

Kathleen Thomson was at pains to indicate that although her father had a drink and went to the hotel, 'he was always good to us':

Did your father have a lot of friends?
Yes, Dad had a lot of friends. Dad was well liked.
Would they come over, the men?
Oh yes. Dad used to have, the men friends used to come and see him. But he liked his drink but he never took it out on us and we never went short of anything.
Did he go to the Greenmeadows Hotel?
Um. But he was always good to us. We never starved, we were always dressed well.[42]

Again, respectability won out in the women's accounts. This was not true of the men's reminiscences about alcohol and hotels.

Henry Nolan left school on the day he turned 14. Within two years he was frequenting a local hotel: 'When I was about 16 I'd be in there,

MASCULINE LEISURE

O'Rourke's Taradale Hotel with staff, family and assorted hangers-on, c. 1890s. Women and girls stand over to the right, while men and boys congregate near the main entrance. COLLECTION OF HAWKE'S BAY CULTURAL TRUST–HAWKE'S BAY MUSEUM, NAPIER, NEW ZEALAND, 7164

you know. Even the cops came in one day and I was in the pub there and they didn't bother.'[43] Henry was one of the few who risked being caught by the big boot of the law for underage drinking in a hotel. Yet this did not mean that minors had nothing to do with alcohol. Those who would not risk getting caught drinking at the pub were happy to smuggle alcohol into the local dances. Nor did it mean that the boys and young men of Taradale were ignorant of the area's pub culture. They may not have taken an active part in it, but they did actively observe it:

> The local drunks, mainly they were harmless. We had two here, that had been to the war, one bloke was decorated but they would get, they were trying to forget what they'd been through . . . . And these two blokes, they'd go through hell. I think it was the military medal he got for bravery and they would get that drunk that you would find them in the creek, not a creek, a ditch, with no water in it. And you'd see that quite often around here. For instance, we had a chap who came round here to Murphy Road to one of the Jeffares' places, he went to back his horse and gig and he was so drunk that he backed into the drain, fell out of the gig and the gig held him down and he drowned. We did have, well, I suppose about half a

145

Hill's Taradale Hotel, built in 1904, showing the 'Private Entrance' doorway. This was built on the site of O'Rourke's hotel, after O'Rourke's burnt down. Hill's Hotel was destroyed in the 1931 earthquake. THE NARRATIVE OF THE PLAINS, 1919, P.18

dozen to eight around here. They would get so drunk that they couldn't walk, they'd fall into a ditch or something or rushes or something like that and that was it. But you see a drunk person doesn't cause much trouble, he's too drunk to know what he's doing.[44]

While Patrick Stevenson saw such men and remembered the stories surrounding them, his sister, Grace Miner, was unaware of the existence of local drunks and claimed that people drank more today. The women who were interviewed had never set foot inside a hotel until well into their adulthood, and had little sense of the area's pub culture. Unlike their brothers, they were not allowed to play out on the streets, nor were they taken to the hotel as children by their fathers. Despite the fact that in 1893 it was made illegal for hotels to sell alcohol to children, some of the male narrators went to the hotel as young boys to buy alcohol for their neighbours. Others occasionally risked buying alcohol for themselves when they were adolescents. In 1920 Constable Gartley heard of youths being served liquor at the Meanee hotel, although his inquiries did not lead to any charges being laid.[45] So it is not surprising that it was the men who recalled tales of drinking and drunks.

These men could also recount lengthy alcohol-related stories. Philip Manners had this to say when asked about the role of alcohol locally:

My father, he smoked. He had a drink, he wasn't a wowser. Now and again he'd go to the pub for some reason, with friends or something like that.

They'd call into the hotel and have a drink. Sometimes he had a drink at the hotel. I don't remember my mother touching it. In those days there were terrible drunkards around, you know. That was all they lived for. Some of them were hard drinkers, the hotel was everything to them. Their social life was made from the hotel. The drink, I forget the percentage alcohol but they've cut it down about four times, since then. Old Speights beer, I remember the ads. It was a beer then in those days. It came from Dunedin, although there were breweries round here. Speights beer was looked upon as the best beer. And some of them used to get rolling drunk. They'd be all over the blooming road, some of them, on bikes. They'd try to ride home, and those with horses, the old horses used to take them home. They were well known jokers. There was old Percy Jones who had teams, he lived down Meanee Road. And there was O'Shannassey used to get into his cart and he wouldn't have any reins and he'd just let the horse take him home and he'd be singing at the top of his voice, rolling round in the cart. He used to sing old Irish songs and if he saw someone he didn't like he'd abuse him. Then there was Pat O'Shannassey, another joker that was always tight. And one or two of the Maoris. Some of them were barred from going to the pub because they got so nasty with their drink. There was quite a lot of old identities. Even some of the leading lights in the town were quite heavy drinkers, like Rymer. I remember Rymer because he lost an eye in a fight. He was quoting in the hotel, to one of the Irish jokers. Anyway, he picked up a glass and said, 'Here's to King William and to hell with the Pope' and the other bloke just threw a glass and hit him in the eye and knocked his eye out. So old Rymer had one eye. They were a little bit touchy about their ancestors, the Irish and the Protestants.

Not only did Philip recall names and events in a way that no woman who was interviewed could or would; he also told the tale of Rymer losing his eye as though he himself had been present at the event. Yet George Rymer lost his eye over 30 years before Philip was born. In June 1873, Rymer was wounded in the eye by a glass tumbler broken by James Lawton. Both men were drinking at Mr T. Peddie's Taradale Hotel when a discussion about Orangemen and Fenians turned nasty. Rymer allegedly tried to end the conversation by saying 'Well here's to King William, the Pope and rest of them'. At that point, Lawton struck him. Lawton claimed, in court, that Rymer said 'To hell with the Pope'. James Lawton was sent to the Supreme Court and sentenced to six months for actual bodily harm.[46] Ironically, Rymer was elected to the Meanee Licensing Committee in 1886 and the Taradale Licensing Committee in 1888.[47]

As Philip's story makes clear, one of the repercussions of taking part in this form of leisure could be a run-in with the law. It is the area's police records that give much of the information about drinking in Taradale's hotels. This, of course, distorts the picture of drinking somewhat, since many of the men who went to the pub were never charged with being drunk and disorderly, or needed a prohibition order taken out against them. However, the official police records, along with the unofficial policeman's diary of duty, oral accounts and newspaper reports, allow us to step inside Taradale's hotels.

In any of the area's hotels, men could be found at the bar drinking with their kin. Fathers and sons, cousins and brothers often had a pint together – and sometimes more. In 1897, when blacksmith James Hollis was reunited with his brother Arthur after a long absence, they celebrated with what the newspaper reported as 'too much liquor'. James, Arthur and friend Frank Moran imbibed to excess, and James and Frank ended up being charged with breaching the peace when they hit fellow blacksmith George Bradley.[48] If men thought that their kin were drinking too much, they were not averse to taking out prohibition orders so as to stop their son or brother from being allowed to enter licensed premises. In March 1899, June 1900, and March 1902 James Davis requested orders against his son Ernest. Not that a prohibition order necessarily prevented men from drinking. William Cunningham had a prohibition order against him, but he went into the Waverley Hotel in Greenmeadows with his mate Arthur Edwards in October 1913. Arthur ended up being charged with being drunk and disorderly too.

Kin, neighbours and work mates all gathered together at the local hotels. There does not seem to have been any particular hotel for manual workers, Catholics, or any other group. It was not unknown for Maori and Pakeha to stand together at the bar. Since Maori men could only be sold alcohol to be consumed on the premises, if they wanted to drink they were forced into this masculine leisure world. The area's pubs were differentiated by geography rather than by class, ethnicity or religion.

It is clear from oral and written accounts that drinking at Taradale's hotels was not always a peaceful occupation. Fights and brawls broke out from time to time, although the male narrators' accounts of such incidents always stressed the 'civility' of such encounters: no knives, no kicking while a man was down, shaking hands once the dispute was settled, and having a drink together as a peace offering. The local policeman seems to have investigated such fracas without laying any charges. When drunken brawls and disturbances were reported at the

Waverley Hotel in 1918, Constable McIvor investigated, but took no further action.[49]

The men who tested the patience of Taradale's policeman were those who, after drinking to excess, were repeatedly disorderly in public rather than in the sanctity of the hotel, uttered profanities as they stumbled down Main Road, fought on the streets with fellow drinkers, and drove dangerously. While those with horses could often rely on their animal to lead them home, with the advent of the motor car drink-driving became a more serious menace. When this happened the constable used his discretion. A local could be escorted home, or given an informal talking to; but if he persisted with this sort of behaviour, he ended up in court. Most of the men officially charged with alcohol-related offences were not long-term residents.[50] The fact that so many of the men charged with offences were just passing through is consistent with J. A. Sharpe's theory that locals were taken to court only when other informal means of control had failed.[51] If the offender was new to the area, or only visiting, then local leniency did not apply. These crime statistics should not be interpreted as indicating that local men did not drink. The oral evidence shows that they did, and that some drank to excess. However, the locals who were charged tended to be repeat offenders, those who had worn out the constable's tolerance. When these men appeared in court they tended to fare less well than non-locals. Of the men who were not on the local electoral roll and who were charged with being drunk, half were convicted and discharged, and many of the others were fined no more than £1. Of the men who *were* on the electoral roll, few were simply convicted and discharged. Most were fined and some were imprisoned.[52]

Although very few women were part of the inner workings of Taradale's hotels, many felt the effect of alcohol in their lives. Some created their own private drinking world, and others suffered the ill effects of men's drinking. While few of the women interviewed had any detailed knowledge about local hotels and drunks on the streets, it was only the women who told of alcohol-related domestic violence:

> I remember mother saying that the hotels were open in the evenings and some men drank too much and went home and beat up their wives. One man in particular, he was very, he would go home drunk and he would give his wife a beating. My grandmother was sitting in that house I told you about, just past the hotel and you don't lock your doors and windows in those days and this dear lady, I won't mention her name, he was going to beat her up and she rushed out of her house, which was next door and she rushed in my grandmother's back door and right through the house and

out the front door. And what's more her pet sheep followed her. It was tremendous. My grandmother was terrified.[53]

Little wonder that wives were the most common group of people requesting that prohibition orders be taken out, in their case against their husbands. Some even went back to court later and took out a second order.[54] Women like Mrs Joseph Jeffares and Mrs William Lord became involved in Taradale's alcohol culture when they tried to curtail their husbands' drinking and spending.

Both men and women consumed alcohol in Taradale, but only the men could do so in public places. Men drank in the hotels and were drunk on the streets. They did so when they were young and old, single and married, regardless of whether they were driving home, and often in spite of having a prohibition order taken out against them. By treating their mates to a round of drinks they showed that they held the family's purse strings, or at least had enough 'pin money' to be a real man. This notion of being a good provider was not important only to men's sense of identity at work. In leisure too, the provider ethic competed with the larrikin tendencies. Men who could spend hard-earned money at the hotel or at the races were making a statement about their role as head of the household. Other men, who kept a tight control on their personal spending, were also making a statement.[55] Central to their identities was providing for their families. In their leisure as well as their work, this ethos sometimes won out.

A good provider might spend his leisure time at home, digging his vegetable garden. He might take the family for a picnic, and combine that with a spot of fishing or hunting. Or he might take his sons off to learn how to spear a flounder or shoot a swan. Fishing and hunting occurred at family picnics, but for the most part these were separate, masculine activities, which took place away from the home and away from women. Even when men only went duck shooting for the day, or floundering at night, the times they went stressed that this was a masculine pursuit, an activity in which women, with their domestic chores and child-care responsibilities, could not join.[56] James Green went duck shooting and fishing with his father, while his mother stayed at home and looked after the household:

> I bought a shot-gun, that's right, I bought a shot-gun and I used to go duck shooting on the lagoon, that was before the quake and I built a maimai out in the lagoon and I used to go duck shooting, swan and duck used to be thick. And he [father] did go with me then. And also if we were going spearing flounders, the flounders were quite thick, there in the inner

MASCULINE LEISURE

harbour and he would always go floundering, the two of us and cave it in case of accidents, in case anything happened. And we used to get anything, three dozen to five dozen flounders of a night.[57]

It was expected that men would go out hunting with only the bare necessities for survival. Their aim was definitely not to create a home away from home when they built their maimai or bush camp. They were proving that they could survive, living rough, even if they did so only in short bursts, as George Davies's father and uncle did:

> I can remember times when he [father] and my uncle Ron Taylor, they used to go out rabbit shooting and all this sort of thing. They would go out and take a tent out and be out perhaps two or three days, just for the fun of it [laugh].[58]

It was common for males to go hunting and fishing with their male kin, and for fathers and uncles to teach their sons and nephews. A man's family was crucial in defining his leisure networks.[59]

The camps of a man's childhood did not change drastically in his adult life, and neither did his attitude to killing large numbers of animals and fish. These mass killings performed important functions in the definition of masculinity in Taradale. In an increasingly modernizing world, men could prove that they were still real men by engaging in large-scale destruction. The five dozen flounder James Green and his father killed were a measure of their skill and control over nature, crucial elements in their notion of what it was to be manly. At the same time, these boys and men were proving that they were the family's providers. Richard Jackson recalled that his mother was a great cook of game 'because we was always out getting rabbits or hares or ducks. Dad would bring ducks and swans home'.[60] On one occasion three of them got over 100 swans.

Killing game was an obvious way that boys and men could use their leisure time to provide for their families. But it was not the only way. The men who joined the area's friendly societies were also blurring the boundary between work and leisure, making sure that they were good providers in sickness and in health. In April 1882, bootmaker Samuel Golding was initiated into the Meanee Lodge of the Manchester Unity Independent Order of Odd Fellows. Samuel was a married man and a father. In 1871, the same year that the Odd Fellows began in Taradale, he had married Ann. The following year he and Ann had their first son, William, followed three years later by Charles. After another son their daughter Elizabeth, known as Fanny, was born, and just before

Samuel joined the Odd Fellows he and Ann became the proud parents of Arthur. A couple of years later they completed their family when son James was born. For Samuel, a self-employed bootmaker, joining the lodge could be seen as the sensible thing to do. After all, lodges provided married men with a form of security lacking in the pre-welfare era. Should Samuel have an accident at work he could rely on his lodge to provide him with sick pay. When Samuel took ill in 1899 and again in 1904 he received over £5 from the lodge both times. When Ann died in 1905 he could also turn to the Odd Fellows for a funeral benefit. Such economic benefits are often seen as the main or indeed the only reasons for joining fraternal organisations.[61] Undoubtedly such considerations must have influenced some men. As Chapter 3 showed, men often had to turn to their lodges in times of need. Lodges also allowed men to make important commercial contacts. Men such as Samuel, who owned and operated businesses, could use their lodge ties to create and strengthen business contacts, while men who relied on casual work could also foster important links with local employers.

But to see fraternal organisations solely as economic bodies is to miss the point. Friendly societies were also about leisure. Once a fortnight the men of Taradale who belonged to one of the area's lodges would gather at the lodge hall for an evening of ritual and fraternalism. On Monday night it was Odd Fellows, and on Tuesday night it was Court Redclyffe, Ancient Order of Foresters, No. 7083. A Roman Catholic lodge met from 1910 to 1916, and in 1917 the Masons arrived when Lodge Omaranui No. 216 began to meet in Bill Jarvis's home. They soon built a temple for their brethren to gather in.

The language of the Masons – temple, brethren – gives some indication of the rituals these men engaged in. For those who did not attend church, and even for those who did, here were their own masculine ceremonies. New members had to be initiated into the fold, learn the customs, wear the correct regalia, and progress through the lodge, taking new degrees or levels of membership.[62] At the Odd Fellows or Foresters a man could forget that he was plain old William Brown, gardener, or Alfred Harrison, contractor. Now he was part of the brethren, and one day might obtain the title 'Master'. Unlike the church, lodges were at that time solely masculine institutions run by men, for men.

Joining a lodge gave men a refuge from the home, but not necessarily from their male kin. It was common for brothers and cousins to join the same lodge, as it was for fathers and sons. Samuel Golding was a member of the Odd Fellows until his accidental death at sea in 1914. Ten years after he joined the lodge his eldest son, William, also became a member. William was 20 years old at the time. The following year 18-year-old Charles Golding joined the Odd Fellows. When Samuel's youngest son, James, reached the age of 18 he also became an Odd Fellow, and the following year, in 1903, Samuel's last surviving son, Arthur, joined too. The Golding boys illustrate several important features about lodge culture in Taradale. None of them were over the age of 21 when they joined the lodge and none of them were married when they were initiated. In both respects they were fairly typical of lodge members. A third of the men who joined Taradale's lodges were minors, that is, they were under the age of 21 at the time of their initiation.[63] From the age of 16 young men were joining lodges and taking part in the fraternal culture. It is hard to believe that young men, still living at home, joined lodges solely for economic benefit. Two thirds of the men were single when they joined.[64]

Many, of course, did not remain bachelors. Five years after joining the Odd Fellows William Golding married and became a father. Arthur Golding married much later than his brother. By the time he tied the knot with Annie Brown, in 1920, he was no longer an Odd Fellow. But during the years of his membership he had been an Odd Fellow with Annie's father, William, and her brothers Howard, Henry and Philip. Howard and Henry were the witnesses at Annie and Arthur's wedding. Arthur Golding was a fictive relation of William, Howard, Henry and Philip Brown long before he married into their family. Not only did lodges provide men with business networks, they also served a very important role in introducing men into a social network based on the idea of brotherhood. With male kin and fictive kin, a new family was born, a family that, for the most part, excluded women. Lodge members knew that family was the key to Taradale's social organisation and power, so they recreated male familial situations in their leisure time.

Taradale's lodge members included men as young as 16-year-old Robert Thompson, an orchardist who joined the Odd Fellows in 1929, and as old as Sidney Anderson, a foundation member of the Foresters in 1886, who was a member continuously right up to 1930. Sidney was born in 1849. But men often did not last as long in a lodge as Sidney did. Some, such as Patrick O'Dowd or Arthur Golding, were struck off for being in arrears with their lodge payments. Others, such as Arthur's father Samuel, died. Some members resigned and some were given clearance. If a member was leaving the area, he could gain clearance from his lodge and rejoin the same order in his new town. This is what Anglican vicar Charles Tuke did when he left Taradale in

1893. Tuke had been a foundation member of the Foresters. Other men joined the lodge by clearance rather than initiation. When baker David Hastie arrived in town in 1888 he was able to join Court Redclyffe because he had been a Forester elsewhere. In a society used to geographical mobility, institutions such as lodges made it easy for men to establish networks quickly.

Friendly societies offer another example of the inclusive nature of masculine leisure. Age, marital status, length of residence or class were not barriers to joining a local lodge. As Erik Olssen found in Caversham, each lodge drew together men who were petty proprietors, skilled, semi-skilled and unskilled workers.[65] They reinforced ideas of egalitarianism. Rather than men being divided by class, they were united by gender – providing they were Pakeha. No Maori or Chinese men were lodge members before 1930.[66]

To an extent this brotherhood was rocked when women began to join the lodges in their own right. When Daisy Button joined Court Redclyffe in 1909, fraternalism was challenged. The Odd Fellows held out until 1925, but finally women members were initiated into the organisation. On the one hand, this should be seen as a negotiation of Taradale's gendered boundaries by these young, working women. But on the other, the fact that they joined male lodges rather than setting up female auxiliaries meant that they were not able to use their separateness to negotiate the maleness of the lodges. The women who joined the Odd Fellows and Foresters in Taradale had to take on a masculine guise.[67] Although there was a female presence in some of the lodges by 1930, they remained masculine institutions.

The friendly society member might seem very different to the man who drank his family's money away at the hotel, but sometimes he was one and the same. Joseph Jeffares and William Lord were both paid up members of the Odd Fellows when their wives took out prohibition orders against them. Both also held positions of responsibility in the community. Joseph was a lodge official, and William was a member of the Town and Suburban Racing Club's committee. When they were sober they were upstanding citizens.

Citizenship was an important concept in masculine leisure. The power men wielded in the community had to be used to good effect. Boys and men had to learn about their rights and obligations as citizens. This training began at an early age. At Taradale School there was a growing concern with instilling the right values into the future citizens and soldiers of New Zealand. Military training was introduced in 1899. Rifle drill began in 1901, although rifles were not obtained until 1902. In that year the Taradale Corps boasted a captain, lieutenant, sub-lieutenant, three sergeants and 34 privates. The ironically named Major Chicken, veteran of the New Zealand Wars, distributed the prizes at the annual firing competition that year, and advised the boys: 'to take their duties as cadets seriously in particular to yield a ready, active, alert and implicit obedience to their boy officers. Discipline was the essence of a good soldier and obedience was the essence of discipline.'[68]

In 1910 a local land owner, Philip Dolbel, gave the school permission to erect a rifle range on his property. Now the 900 rounds of ammunition the school had received could be used.[69] Boys such as Richard Jackson were taught to shoot by their fathers. Richard and his brother '[a]lways went out with me Dad. Wherever he went with a gun, we were there.'[70] Richard won the medal for best shot in the cadets. Even at the annual school concert, boys were encouraged to be martial. As the newspaper reported: 'the elder girls sang a solo and chorus, "Welcome Lovely May", a really excellent item. Then came a boys' marching song.'[71]

Outside school the training continued. Scouts arrived in Taradale in 1916 when the Presbyterian minister, the Reverend Fish, inaugurated the Greendale Troop. Meetings were held in the Presbyterian church hall. Led by men such as Mr Hookings of Auckland Road, and clerk Alf Burr, young boys in Taradale learnt all about Baden Powell's masculine ideals.[72] Here again adult men were making sure that boys and youths were learning to be proper men: disciplined, martial, in control and self-reliant.

Once the Scouts came of age they could move into more public positions of responsibility. Men were the official leaders of the community. They took on the obligation of running the district, and by doing so they increased their power and control over the area.[73] Taradale was not run by a small group of men who acted as a united body. In his study of Johnsonville, David Pearson found that until the 1930s, 'the link between wealth, occupation and leadership was a common one'.[74] In Taradale there were men who fitted this profile. John Drummond was one: between 1886 and 1905 he served the area as a JP, a member of the Licensing Committee, and a Road Board member, sat on the Library Committee, helped administer Taradale's cemetery, was a Town and Suburban Racing Club official, belonged to Taradale School's committee, led his lodge, ran the rifle club, and was a Taradale Town Board commissioner. But Drummond was atypical. Two thirds of the men who took office held a position on only one committee. A further fifth of the men who held office served on only two committees.[75]

Like other aspects of men's leisure, inclusiveness is one of the hallmarks of public office holding. Apart from their gender, the only other factor that most of them had in common was that they were married at the time they were first elected to office. Only a fifth of the office holders are known to have been single at the time of their accession to power.[76] Given that most of these men were married, few of the office holders were minors, but men in their twenties through to old age pensioners could and did sit side by side on committees.[77] Similarly, religious affiliation was not a barrier, nor did it seem to matter whether a man held land in the area, how long he had lived there, or what his occupation was.[78] At times ethnicity was not an issue either. Te Roera Tareha, from the Waiohiki pa, served on the Taradale School's committee and was a member of the Taradale War Memorial committee, while the Chinese market gardener William Ah Keong was a rugby official. But generally the all-embracing nature of office holding reached only as far as Pakeha men. Often those men were related to one another.

Patrick O'Dowd seems never to have held any public office in Taradale, unless being a hotel keeper is considered a public office. For a few years at the beginning of the century Patrick was a publican, the occupation that allowed men to blend their work and leisure most easily. On either side of his stint behind the bar, Patrick was a lodge member. Like many of the men of Taradale, he was involved in organised and commercial leisure activities in a way that his wife never was. He could afford to be a leisure consumer. It is no coincidence that this chapter on masculine leisure is longer than the previous one on feminine leisure.

Men's leisure differed from women's in several ways. There was more of it, it was better organised and it often required cash resources. The rugby players had to buy their own kit, shooting required a good gun, lodges demanded regular subscription fees. These differences reflect men's power in the area. They were able to establish leisure times and opportunities for themselves in a way that their wives, for the most part, were not.

But men's leisure is not an uncomplicated story. There was an ongoing tension in many men's recreation, between their desire to have a good time and their need to retain their status as respectable citizens. The twin goals of being both a larrikin and an upstanding citizen came through in men's oral accounts. What also came through was a heavy emphasis on the gender-specific nature of their leisure. All the men I interviewed had married; indeed, some of them were courting or got married in the 1920s. Yet their recollections of this period were more about their pranks and sporting successes than about romance. The homosocial world of leisure took precedence in what they were prepared to say. Again, this was in contrast to women's accounts where heterosocial leisure reigned supreme.

There was no unitary masculine leisure world or culture in Taradale. The men who propped up Patrick O'Dowd's bar tended to be different from those who attended local temperance meetings. I say tended, because a couple of Taradale's temperance advocates ended up in court, charged with breaching their prohibition orders. The point is not that all males did the same things in their spare time, but that almost any male could join in any activity. Masculine leisure was far more inclusive than its feminine counterpart. If you were not yet old enough to actually drink in the pub, you could still be part of the culture. If you were too old to play rugby, you could still be involved as coach or spectator. If you were a clergyman or a labourer, you could belong to a temperance group, a lodge, or the cricket club. Age, marital status and occupation were far less important in men's leisure than they were in women's.

What mattered in men's leisure was the way it reinforced ideas about manly men. How a 'real' man was defined varied. Masculinity could be performed through being temperate and showing self-control. Or you could perform it by drinking large amounts of alcohol in short amounts of time, shouting rounds of drinks and showing what a good mate and provider you were. These competing notions often played out in individuals' lives, hence the tension in the oral accounts. Men's leisure was a demonstration of their power, and power is never unproblematic.

Conclusion

In many ways, the Taradale into which Noel Robert Tong was born in 1930 was very different from the community which had greeted James Rundle on his birth in 1886. Over the years the population had doubled, new buildings had been erected, electricity had been switched on, new industries had developed, and there were more leisure opportunities and organisations. Yet in other ways, Noel and James shared a common history. Both were born into close-knit, local, extended families. They also both grew up in an area that was never so large as to prevent face-to-face community. In the 1920s the recently formed Taradale Scout troop used to draw a map of the area:

> We used to be able to draw a map, this was when I was in the Scouts . . . we used to be able to draw a map of every house in Taradale and put the name of the people who lived in them all. Now that's what it was like. Everybody knew everybody and you knew where everybody lived.[1]

Had there been a Scout troop in the 1880s, I am sure they could have done the same.

The community of Taradale has been the focus of this book, but I have not attempted to write a general history of the area, or even of the people of the area. Rather, I have used Taradale as my site to explore the performance of gender. My aim when I embarked on the project was to examine the historical importance of gender in the everyday lives of ordinary New Zealanders. I decided to focus on one geographical area, since that provided me with certain boundaries. More important than the physical geography, though, was the human geography of the area. I soon realised that gender was central to the way these people lived their lives. There were far more social boundaries constraining and dictating what people should do, and how they should behave, than the hills and rivers marking out the physical area. I also realised that it was often easier to change the physical landmarks than it was to rewrite the gendered script these people performed. The Tutaekuri River was rerouted in the 1920s to prevent flooding; the 1931 earthquake changed the lie of the land as the inner harbour disappeared. But girls and boys at Taradale School continued to enter their classroom through gender-specific doors; the iron fence, erected in 1890 to divide their playgrounds, remained.

The other thing that soon became apparent was the centrality of kin to the people of Taradale. The strength of the kin-based core of this community's life might surprise those enamoured of Miles Fairburn's atomisation thesis. The people of Taradale were not lonely, kinless, bondless atoms, wandering around colonial New Zealand in search of an ideal society. In both the nineteenth and the early twentieth century, they were members of dense kin networks.[2] Yet these kin networks, discussed at length in Chapter 2, were not gender neutral. As Elizabeth Bott has argued, albeit for a different society and period, when women and men both enter a relationship with a well-developed network of their own, they often turn to their relatives, friends and neighbours for support, rather than to their spouse. In such situations, there is a strong degree of gender segregation in the tasks and activities they perform. Men continue to work and socialise with their male kin, friends and workmates; women turn to their female kin and neighbours.[3] This was often the pattern in Taradale too.

I am not suggesting that there was no interaction between women and men in the area. That would be foolish indeed. Gender is a relational concept. How the men and women, boys and girls, of Taradale interacted on a daily basis is an important part of the story. Most adults in this community married. Therefore I began with a chapter on family, using the quintessential family rituals of birth, marriage and death, to show how men and women turned to one another and to their kin at these times. I also began the sections on work and leisure with chapters exploring women's and men's shared world. In the mixed economy of Taradale, all members of the family contributed to the family's economic well-being. Rather than viewing this as a male breadwinner economy, I argued that it was a household economy, built on a mutuality in men's and women's work. The husband may have milked the cow, and his wife churned the butter, but they were working for a common goal. The symbiosis in men's and women's contributions to the household's economy also existed in their leisure lives. Family picnics and days at the races or at the Show saw men, women and children playing together. But as in the way they ran the household's economy, when they did so their gender was often made to matter. Fathers and sons left the picnic site to fish or swim while mothers and daughters prepared the food. The presence of invisible iron fences continued to make itself felt.

Since there were iron fences in Taradale, both real and imagined, I decided to explore the meaning of gender in people's lives through their gender-specific worlds, both at work and in leisure. Although gender is a relational concept, that does not mean we should focus solely on the relations between women and men, or between femininities and masculinities. How different groups of women understood their femininity, or different groups of men acted out their masculinity, is also an important part of the story.

In Chapter 3 I turned my attention to female work, looking at the ways young girls were expected to follow in their mother's footsteps, as wives and mothers, earning respectability and status through keeping the floors scrubbed, the tins full and the clothes pressed. That understanding of femininity was increasingly challenged as young women attended high school and tech, eschewed domestic service and entered the public wage-earning economy. Such tensions were less apparent in the separate world of men's work. Fathers and sons continued to work together and share the same values. No new man arrived to rival the new woman of Taradale. A similar pattern emerged as I explored the separate worlds of female and male leisure. The new women of Taradale wanted to take to the hockey fields or go to the movies. They did not expect to be housebound as their mothers were, or have their leisure limited to doing good works and attending church groups. Even their mothers were less content with their lot by the 1920s. They too started to expect to use public spaces for their leisure and have their voices heard in community matters. The masculine world of leisure was not particularly threatened by these developments. Men had long had a grip on the public leisure institutions of Taradale, and they were not about to let go. Power may be problematic, but it was something Taradale's males were prepared to go on puzzling over.

When I decided to divide the sections on work and leisure into three chapters, it seemed obvious to me that the first chapter in each section should be on shared experience. Family ties were of crucial importance to the life of this community, and family ties are shared. It also seemed right to me that the second chapter in each section should be on women's gender-specific experiences. As a feminist historian, I wanted to give women's lives their due. This decision had a consequence I had not anticipated. Women appear in the chapters on men's work and leisure, but few men are present in the women's chapters. In part this is because, having already discussed women's work or leisure, it makes sense to refer back to women's lives when a

CONCLUSION

similar or sometimes very different situation is discussed for men. But it is also due to my use of oral history, and to my argument, running through this book, that oral accounts are gendered both in content and in form. For the most part I have relied on the interviews with women for stories and insights into the worlds of women's work and leisure, and on the interviews with men for their worlds. Since these people spent so much of their time living within the iron fences, it follows that each knows their gender-specific worlds best. However, the form of the oral accounts is also gendered. What people remember, what they choose to recount, who they choose to tell, and how they position themselves within the narrative is often determined by their gender. The women I interviewed were far more likely to remember details about their fathers' work and life than the men were about their mothers. These women understood, from an early age, the significance and consequences of their fathers' actions.

The differences, tensions, and sometimes contradictions between women's and men's oral accounts have been invaluable in exploring the ways femininities and masculinities were understood and acted out in Taradale. I interviewed brothers and sisters whose stories were so at odds it was as if they had grown up in different families. More generally, women and men not only had gender-specific experiences, but understood those experiences in gendered ways. The girl who, in a fit of desperation, heaved her younger brother out of his pram, knew that she was acting in an unfeminine, unladylike, and unacceptable way. Decades later, she still had not told her brother. The boy who stole from local orchards had no such compunction. Instead he celebrated his daring acts. This may strike some readers as a very reductionist reading of these gendered tales. There were, of course, women in the area who scorned 'proper', ladylike behaviour; there were men in Taradale who thought a 'real' man was an upstanding citizen, who lived by the rules and never questioned authority. My point is that most of the people, most of the time, understood and tried to live by a certain set of gendered rules – that is, by what I referred to in the first chapter as a hegemonic understanding of femininity and masculinity. The proper women of Taradale were meant to be domesticated and hard-working, to be good wives and mothers who looked after their nuclear and extended families, raised money for charity and never got into trouble. The real men of Taradale were meant to be hard-working too, contributing to the household economy and looking after their wives and children. They performed what I have referred to as masculine domesticity: they were a real presence in the home, balancing rather than overshadowing the feminine influence of their wives. But the real man was also meant to play hard. The larrikin spirit was not extinguished when he came of age.

It was within this context that the new women of Taradale emerged. These young women had access to secondary education, worked in the non-domestic sector, played team sports and bought ready-to-wear clothing. They offered the most sustained attack on the iron fences of Taradale. Their understanding of femininity was often at odds with their mothers' and grandmothers' understanding. They did not see that their respectability was in question if they wore a little make-up; they could not see how they were un-sexing themselves if they joined a male friendly society. Although these new women were an important force in Taradale, they were hardly able to rewrite the gendered script. At best they managed to add a few new stage directions. I could not argue that these were egalitarian times, as Rollo Arnold has claimed in his recent study of a frontier community.[4] There were too many tensions between the different groups of women in Taradale; their competing ideas about femininity lessened the force of any attack. And then there was the impressive defence mounted by the males of the area.

If femininities in Taradale are best characterised over these years by generational conflict, then inclusiveness is the key to understanding masculinities. The masculine domesticity of the manly family man saw fathers, uncles and grandfathers keep a watchful eye over their sons, nephews and grandsons. In work and leisure alike, they made sure that the boys and young men of the area were exposed to, and became part of, a certain set of masculine values and behaviours. This inclusiveness crossed generational lines; it also encompassed men of different classes and religions. The new settler and the old timer were both part of the same masculine world. At times even ethnicity was ignored. Males were already the most powerful group in the area in terms of their economic resources and physical strength. They built on this as they gathered together at work and at play.

My focus in much of this book has been on actual events and measurable results. Masculine domesticity can be seen as more men involve themselves in family rituals. New women's attempts to challenge ideas of femininity are visible when they start up their own sports teams and play in public. This is what we expect in a social history. Yet it is important to remember that the discursive plays out alongside material changes and continuities. For many of the women I interviewed, modernisation was a state of mind. Their lives and their mothers' lives were more similar than dissimilar. In their oral accounts these women were happy to discuss the household chores they did as children, or the work their mothers did in the home. But when their

CONCLUSION

own full-time job was as an unpaid domestic at home, or even as a domestic servant in someone else's home, they had little to say. Their identity at this time was not defined by their work. They saw themselves as new women even if all the material evidence pointed in a different direction. When we think about changes in the gendered script, it is important to bear this in mind.

That the males of Taradale retained their power and hold over this community is not in doubt. There was no watershed in Taradale's gender relations between 1886 and 1930. But then there rarely are watersheds in gender relations. Rather, there are ebbs and flows. Slowly, over the years, people, attitudes and ideologies are repositioned. The story is less dramatic than some might hope for, but it takes many years for an iron fence to rust away. By 1930, in Taradale, the corrosion had at least set in.

APPENDIX A

Oral Informants

For the purposes of this study I interviewed 35 men and women who lived in the Taradale area before the 1931 Hawke's Bay earthquake. Nineteen of my informants were women, all but two of whom had married at least once. All of my 16 male informants had married. The people I spoke with were born between 1892 and 1925, and of these 26 were born between 1905 and 1914. Most of the people I interviewed were either born in the Taradale area or born in Napier of Taradale parents. However, only a minority have always lived in the Taradale area. Most have spent a considerable period of their lives away from the district and some of them continue to live in Napier or Hastings. Many have moved back to Taradale in their retirement. Some are working class, some middle class. I have spoken with Anglicans, Catholics, Methodists, Presbyterians and agnostics. Some of the people I interviewed belong to Taradale families of long standing; others had only a temporary stake in the area. Since some of the oral informants requested anonymity, I decided to give everyone a pseudonym. Brief biographies follow.

Women

MARTHA EDWARDS
Interviewed in Taradale, 30 January 1987.
Born in Greenmeadows in 1912. Father a carpenter, born in Rissington (H.B.); mother born in Greenmeadows. Oldest daughter in family of six children. Educated at Taradale School and Napier Technical College (two years). Worked in a factory and in domestic service during the 1920s. Later employed as a shop assistant. Never married. Anglican. Spent early child-

hood in Palmerston North area, returned to Taradale when aged about nine years, spent most of time since living in the Taradale area.

HANNAH FIELD
Interviewed in Taradale, 20 May 1987.
Born in Napier in 1909. Father a tearoom owner, born in the South Island; mother born in England. Oldest in family of three children, with an older half-sister from her mother's first marriage. Sister of James Green. Educated at Napier West School, Hastings Street School and Taradale School. Worked at home, later owned and operated a cake shop. Married in 1931 in Napier, two children. Anglican. Lived in Taradale since c.1920.

EMILY JONES
Interviewed in Taradale, 29 August 1988.
Born in Taradale in 1908. Father a painter-decorator, born in the South Island; mother born in Napier. Oldest in family of nine children. Sister of Matthew Silk. Educated at Taradale School and Napier Technical College (18 months). Worked as a shop assistant until marriage. Married in Napier in 1927, four children. Presbyterian. Lived away from the area for much of her married life, but retired to Taradale.

JANE McNIGHT
Interviewed in Napier, 5 February 1988, with sister, Florence Rifle.
Born in Napier in 1916. Father a fellmonger born in Taradale; mother born in Napier. One of ten children. Younger sister of Theresa Pond and Florence Rifle. Educated at Greenmeadows School and Meanee Convent. Worked at home and as fruit picker. Married in 1938 in Napier, four children. Since marriage has not lived in Taradale.

GRACE MINER
Interviewed in Taradale, 13 February 1988.
Born in Greenmeadows in 1905. Father a storeman, later a taxi driver, born in England; mother born in Greenmeadows. Oldest daughter in family of eight children. Sister of Patrick Stevenson. Educated at Greenmeadows School and Taradale School. Helped at home after leaving school, and worked for a short time at the Greenmeadows Post Office. Married in Napier in 1927, three children. Methodist. Retired to Taradale after living much of her adult life in Napier.

EMMA NEEDLE
Interviewed in Napier, 9 February 1987.
Born in Taradale in 1909. Father a carrier-farmer born in Scotland; mother born in Napier. Oldest daughter in family of ten children. Sister of Edward McLean. Educated at Greenmeadows School and Taradale School. Worked

at home, helping mother and as housekeeper for brother, Edward, until her marriage. Married in 1931 in Meanee, six children. Roman Catholic. Spent most of her life in the Taradale area.

ALICE PARKE
Interviewed in Greenmeadows, 1 September 1988.
Born in Taradale in 1914. Father a builder, born in Dunedin; mother born in Napier. Only child. Educated at Taradale School, Hastings Street School and Wellington High School (two years). Worked as a housemaid in Greenmeadows and as a shop assistant. Married in Wellington, 1939, one child. Brought up as a Baptist, but later became a Presbyterian. Retired to Greenmeadows after living in a variety of New Zealand towns.

ANN PEARCE
Interviewed in Taradale, 11 February 1987.
Born in Napier in 1917. Father a baker. Only daughter in family of two children. Educated at Puketapu School (H.B.) and Wellington Technical College. Worked as shop assistant, factory worker and domestic servant. Married in 1939 in Puketapu, five children. Anglican. Spent early childhood in Taradale area, moved to Wellington but returned to area when a young adult and has lived locally ever since.

ELIZA PETERSON
Interviewed in Awatoto (H.B.), 22 January 1987.
Born in Greenmeadows in 1907. Father a farmer. Both parents born in Ireland. Oldest child in family of five children. Educated at Meanee Convent. Worked as a dressmaker all of working life – first as employee, then established own one-person business. Never married. Roman Catholic. Lived all her life in the Meanee-Awatoto area.

LOUISA PLUMB
Interviewed in Taradale, 20 January 1987.
Born in Greenmeadows in 1909. Father a labourer-farmer; mother born in Greenmeadows. Oldest in family of six children. Educated at Greenmeadows School and Taradale School. Worked at home then as a shop assistant in Greenmeadows. Married in 1930 in Napier, three children. Anglican. Resident of Taradale and surrounding area all her life.

THERESA POND
Interviewed in Greenmeadows, 3 February 1987.
Born in Napier in 1911. Father a fellmonger, born in Taradale; mother born in Napier. Oldest in family of ten children. Sister of Florence Rifle and Jane McNight. Educated at Greenmeadows School, Meanee Convent and Taradale School. Worked at home, in a Napier factory and as a domestic

servant. Married in 1941 in Meanee, four children. Roman Catholic. Lived all her life in the Taradale area.

SOPHIE RICHARDSON
Interviewed in Hastings, 7 February 1987.
Born in Napier in 1913. Father a farmer, born in Pakowhai (H.B.); mother born in Greenmeadows. Oldest child and only daughter in family of five children. Educated at Taradale School and Napier Girls' High School (three years). Helped at home after leaving school until her marriage. Married in Taradale in 1939, two children. Anglican. Since marriage has not lived in Taradale.

FLORENCE RIFLE
Interviewed in Napier, 5 February 1988, with sister Jane McNight.
Born in Taradale in 1912. Father a fellmonger, born in Taradale; mother born in Napier. Second in family of ten children. Younger sister of Theresa Pond and older sister of Jane McNight. Educated at Greenmeadows School, Meanee Convent and Taradale School. Helped at home on leaving school and also worked in a Napier factory. Married in Meanee in 1933, five children. Roman Catholic. Since marriage has not lived in Taradale.

CHARLOTTE ROSE
Interviewed in Taradale, 16 January 1987.
Born in Greenmeadows in 1896. Father a gardener-drover. Both parents born in Ireland. One of 15 children. Educated at Taradale School. Worked helping at home until marriage. Married in Taradale in 1920, four children. Anglican. Lived all her life in Taradale and the immediate surrounding area.

HARRIET SOUTH
Interviewed in Taradale, 19 January 1987.
Born in Napier in 1903. Father a carter-labourer from Auckland; mother from Dannevirke. Oldest of two daughters, with nine older half-brothers and -sisters (both of her parents had been married before). Educated at Greenmeadows School, Taradale School and Napier Technical College (two years). Worked at Greenmeadows Post Office until marriage. Married in 1954, no children. Presbyterian. Lived in Taradale area since 1906.

SARAH STEVENSON
Interviewed in Taradale, 15 and 16 February, 1988.
Born in Ashburton in 1910. Father a carrier-farmer. Both parents born in England. Oldest child in family of three children. Educated at Taradale School and Napier Girls' High School (three years). Worked helping at home, part-time shop assistant and then office worker in Taradale garage,

until marriage. Married Patrick Stevenson in Taradale in 1932, two children. Anglican. Lived in Taradale since 1914.

ELLEN STORE
Interviewed in Greenmeadows, 12 January 1987.
Born in Greenmeadows in 1902. Father was Manager of Greenmeadows Fruit Farm and then Town Clerk. Only child. Educated at Greenmeadows School, Taradale School and Solway College, Masterton (three years). Worked as an office worker-librarian until her marriage. Married in 1944 in Taradale, no children. Anglican. Lived in area all of her life.

KATHLEEN THOMSON
Interviewed in Napier, 8 February 1988.
Born in Greenmeadows in 1903. Father a carrier, born in Auckland; mother born in Patangata (H.B.). Oldest in family of eight children. Educated at Greenmeadows School, Taradale School and Napier Technical College (one year). Worked as a shop assistant until marriage. Married in Taradale in 1924, two children. Anglican. Lived in Taradale after marriage and then moved away c.1930. Has not lived in Taradale since then.

BRIDGET TWEED
Interviewed in Napier, 12 February 1987.
Born in Taradale in 1896. Father a farmer-road overseer, born in Tasmania; mother born in Ireland. One of 11 children. Educated at Meanee Convent. Worked helping at home and during WWI was a shop assistant in Taradale. Married in Meanee in 1923, three children. Roman Catholic. Since marriage has not lived in Taradale.

Men

JOSEPH BARNETT
Interviewed in Taradale, 26 August 1988.
Born in Greenmeadows in 1911. Father a taxi-driver from Ireland; mother born in Clive (H.B.). Youngest son in family of seven children. Educated at Taradale School and Napier Technical College (one year). Worked for Electricity Department and in viticulture. Married in Napier in 1951, three children. Methodist. Lived in Taradale area most of his life.

ARTHUR BISHOP
Interviewed in Taradale, 30 August 1988.
Born in Meanee in 1909. Father a wool classer. Both parents born in Scandinavia. Youngest child in family of 12 children. Educated at Meanee School, Napier West School, Taradale School and Napier Technical College (two years). Worked as a printer. Married in Napier in 1936, six children.

Anglican. Left the area for much of his adult working life, but retired to Taradale.

WILLIAM CLIFF
Interviewed in Taradale, 8 February 1988.
Born in Napier in 1913. Father a plumber. Both parents born in Ireland. Oldest child in family of four sons. Educated at Greenmeadows School, Taradale School, and Napier Boys' High School (two years). Worked in farming, plumbing and as a welder. Married in Napier in 1950, one child. Presbyterian. Moved to Taradale area as a young child, moved away when a young adult but retired to Taradale.

GEORGE DAVIES
Interviewed in Taradale, 9 February 1988.
Born in Meanee in 1914. Father a labourer, born in the Waikato; mother born in Greenmeadows. Oldest son in a family of seven children. Educated at Greenmeadows School, Taradale School and Napier Technical College (two years). Worked as a labourer and carpenter. Married in Napier in 1940, three children. Methodist. Lived in Taradale area most of his life.

ERNEST EDWARDS
Interviewed in Napier, 5 February 1988.
Born in Greenmeadows in 1908. Father a builder from North Auckland; mother born in Napier. Oldest in family of three children, including an adopted sister. Educated at Greenmeadows School, Taradale School and Napier Boys' High School (three years). Worked as a builder. Married in Napier in 1931, three children. Anglican and then Methodist. Lived most of his adult life in Napier.

JAMES GREEN
Interviewed in Taradale, 13 May 1987.
Born in Napier in 1911. Father a tea room owner, born in the South Island; mother born in England. Oldest son in family of three children, with an older half-sister from mother's first marriage. Brother of Hannah Field. Educated at Napier West School, Hastings Street School, Taradale School and Napier Boys' High School (four years). Worked in banking and the public service in accounts and administration. Married in Napier in 1931, one child. Anglican. Lived in Taradale in the 1920s, then moved to Napier. Retired to Taradale.

CHARLES HORSE
Interviewed in Taradale, 1 and 3 February 1988.
Born in Otago in 1892. Father a stock inspector. Both parents born in England. Oldest child in family of two sons. Educated at South Island

APPENDIX A

primary schools and Mosgiel District High School (three years). Worked as an electrician-engineer. Married in Dunedin in 1916, two children. Presbyterian. Moved to Taradale in the 1920s and lived in area ever since.

FRED JACKSON
Interviewed in Taradale, 16 February 1988.
Born in Taradale in 1912. Father a gardener-ranger, born in Napier; mother born in Meanee. Only son in family of five children. Cousin of Richard Jackson. Educated at Greenmeadows School, Taradale School and Napier Technical College (one year). Worked in agriculture, as labourer and in wild life service. Married in Hastings in 1931, three children. Anglican. Lived in Taradale area most of his life.

RICHARD JACKSON
Interviewed in Taradale, 4 February 1987.
Born in Taradale in 1910. Father a gardener. Both parents born in Napier. One of seven children. Cousin of Fred Jackson. Educated at Greenmeadows School and Taradale School. Worked as a gardener and in agriculture. Married in Meanee in 1937, three children. Anglican, converted to Roman Catholicism on marriage. Lived in Taradale area most of his life.

EDWARD MCLEAN
Interviewed in Greenmeadows, 21 January 1987.
Born in Taradale in 1907. Father a carrier-farmer, born in Scotland; mother born in Napier. One of ten children. Brother of Emma Needle. Educated at Taradale School. Worked in viticulture, first as employee, then self-employed since 1927. Married in Dannevirke in 1931, two children. Presbyterian. Lived in Taradale area all his life.

PHILIP MANNERS
Interviewed in Taradale, 10 February 1987.
Born in 1909 in Hastings. Father a builder-carpenter, born in Dunedin; mother born in Taradale. One of eight children. Educated at Taradale School and Napier Technical College (two years). Worked for Railways most of his life. Married in Meanee in 1936, one child. Presbyterian. Lived in Hawke's Bay most of his life, retired to Taradale.

HENRY NOLAN
Interviewed in Meanee, 14 February 1987.
Born in Meanee in 1905. Father a butcher and farmer, born in England; mother born in Greymouth. One of six children. Educated at Meanee Convent and Meanee School. Worked as labourer and farmer. Married in Napier in early 1920s, five children. Anglican. Lived all his life in the Taradale area.

ORAL INFORMANTS

THOMAS RAVEN
Interviewed at Poraite (H.B.), 8 February 1987.
Born in 1911 in Waipukurau. Father a blacksmith-farrier, born in Dunedin; mother born in Opunake. Second in a family of six sons. Educated at Meanee Convent and Taradale School. Worked for father and later took over the Taradale business. Married in Meanee in 1943, four children. Roman Catholic. Lived in Taradale and its surrounding area since c.1914.

MICHAEL ROPER
Interviewed in Taradale, 10 February 1987.
Born in Taradale in 1925. Father a farmer, born in Taradale; mother born in Greenmeadows. Oldest in family of four children. Educated at Taradale School and Napier Boys' High School (two years). Worked as a farmer. Married in Napier in 1947, three children. Lived in Hawke's Bay all his life, largely in the Taradale area.

MATTHEW SILK
Interviewed in Taradale, 2 September 1988.
Born in Taradale in 1912. Father a painter-decorator, born in the South Island; mother born in Napier. One of nine children. Brother of Emily Jones. Educated at Taradale School and Napier Technical College (two years). Worked as painter-decorator. Married in Napier in 1931, 11 children. Presbyterian. Lived in Taradale until 1933, then moved away. Retired to Taradale.

PATRICK STEVENSON
Interviewed in Taradale, 12 February 1988.
Born in Greenmeadows in 1909. Father a storeman and then taxi driver, born in England; mother born in Greenmeadows. Youngest child in family of eight children. Brother of Grace Miner. Educated at Greenmeadows School and Taradale School. Worked in agriculture, as a stonemason and then for the post office. Married Sarah Stevenson in Taradale in 1932, two children. Lived in Taradale area all his life.

APPENDIX B

Occupational Categories for Men

The six major categories men's occupations have been grouped under are as follows:

1. High White Collar: Professionals, Major Proprietors, Managers, and Officials
2. Low White Collar: Clerks and Salesmen, Semiprofessionals
3. Petty Proprietors, Managers and Officials
4. Skilled
5. Semiskilled and Service Workers
6. Unskilled Labourers and Menial Service Workers

Some men had no occupation listed for them or else were listed as being 'retired'. These men were grouped under occupational category '0'.

The following lists the occupations contained within each of the six major categories.

1. *High White Collar: Professionals, Major Proprietors, Managers, Officials*

Architect	Banker
Brewer	Broker
Clergy	Doctor
Editor	Lawyer
Manufacturer	Merchant
Minister	Priest
Professor	Runholder
Sheepfarmer	Solicitor

OCCUPATIONAL CATEGORIES FOR MEN

2 *Low White Collar: Clerks and Salesmen, Semiprofessionals*

    Accountant   Agent
    Auctioneer   Book keeper
    Civil Servant   Clerk
    Commercial   Traveller
    Customs Officer   Insurance Agent
    Journalist   Law Clerk
    Musician   Photographer
    Secretary   Student
    Surveyor   Teacher

3 *Petty Proprietors, Managers and Officials*

    Boarding-house Keeper   Cab Proprietor
    Chemist   Clothier
    Coach Proprietor   Dairyman
    Dealer   Draper
    Farmer   Foreman
    Fruit Grower   Fruiterer
    Gaoler   Gentleman
    Grocer   Harbour Master
    Inspector   Ironmonger
    Master Mariner   Minor Govt. Official
    Nurseryman   Orchardist
    Overseer   Postmaster
    Publican   Sawmiller
    Settler   Ship Master
    Small Manager   Station Manager
    Storekeeper   Taxi Proprietor
    Well Sinker

4 *Skilled*

    Baker   Basketmaker
    Blacksmith   Boilermaker
    Bookbinder   Bootmaker
    Builder   Butcher
    Cabinet-maker   Carpenter
    Coachsmith   Compositor
    Confectioner   Contractor
    Cordial Maker   Currier
    Electrical Engineer   Electrician

APPENDIX B

Engineer	Fitter
Iron turner	Jeweller
Joiner	Linotype Operator
Lithographer	Machinist
Mason	Mechanic
Motor Engineer	Moulder
Painter	Patternmaker
Plasterer	Plumber
Printer	Ropemaker
Saddler	Sailmaker
Shipwright	Shoemaker
Slaughterman	Tailor
Tanner	Tinsmith
Turner	Upholsterer
Watchmaker	Wheelwright

5 *Semiskilled and Service Workers*

Barman	Billiard Marker
Bricklayer	Brickmaker
Cabman	Caretaker
Carrier	Carter
Cellarman	Chauffeur
Chimney Sweep	Coachman
Cook	Cooper
Cowboy	Driver
Drover	Expressman
Fellmonger	Fireman
Fisherman	Gardener
Guard	Hairdresser
Hawker	Horse Breaker
Horse Trainer	Jockey
Linesman	Milkman
Ploughman	Police Constable
Railway Guard	Ranger
Sawyer	Sexton
Shearer	Shepherd
Shop Assistant	Stableman
Storeman	Stevedore
Teamster	Telegraphist
Trainer	Warder
Wardsman	Wool Classer
Wool Sorter	

OCCUPATIONAL CATEGORIES FOR MEN

6 *Unskilled Labourers and Menial Service Workers*

Bushman	Farm Hand
Farm Servant	Fencer
Gas Stoker	Groom
Labourer	Mariner
Miner	Porter
Quarryman	Seaman
Stablehand	Watersider
Yardsman	

Per centage breakdown of men's occupational categories for the electoral rolls 1887–1928.

Year	0	1	2	3	4	5	6	No.
1887	3	2	1	26	15	17	36	375
1890	0	2	2	27	18	15	34	507
1893	0	4	5	28	19	19	26	362
1896	0	4	6	24	19	22	25	367
1899	0	2	5	24	20	23	24	356
1902	0	3	7	28	16	23	22	438
1905	0	2	6	27	18	23	24	563
1908	0	2	8	24	18	23	24	671
1911	0	3	9	26	24	20	19	596
1914	0	2	10	23	21	24	20	578
1919	0	2	9	25	19	24	22	716
1922	0	2	6	25	19	25	22	656
1925	1	3	6	27	19	23	21	581
1928	1	2	7	25	19	23	23	701
TOTAL	0	2	7	26	19	22	24	7479

Notes

CHAPTER 1 *Gender and the Taradale Community*

1. Taradale School Committee Minutes, 13 December 1890.
2. Taradale School Committee Minutes, 11 April 1891.
3. Taradale School Committee Minutes, 11 March 1893.
4. Taradale School Committee Minutes, 6 January 1894.
5. William Cliff, interviewed Taradale 8 February 1988. Pseudonyms have been given to all of the oral narrators. All interviews were conducted by the author. A brief biographical sketch of each interviewee is contained in Appendix A.
6. The literature on separate spheres is extensive, but is summarised well in Linda K. Kerber, 'Separate Spheres, Female Worlds, Woman's Place: The Rhetoric of Women's History', *Journal of American History*, 75, June 1988, pp.9–39.
7. On gender and oral history see Caroline Daley, '"He would know but I just have a feeling": gender and oral history', *Women's History Review*, 7, 3 1998, pp.343–59.
8. Claire Toynbee, *Her Work and His: Family, Kin and Community in New Zealand 1900-1930*, Wellington, 1995.
9. Joan W. Scott, 'Gender: A Useful Category of Historical Analysis', *American Historical Review*, 91, 5, 1986, pp.1053–75. This essay is reprinted in Joan Wallach Scott, *Gender and the Politics of History*, New York, 1988, pp.28–50.
10. See, for example, Joan Hoff, 'Gender as a Postmodern Category of Paralysis', *Women's History Review*, 3, 2, 1994, pp.149–68, and the ensuing debate in *Women's History Review*, 5, 1, 1996, pp.5–30.
11. Gisela Bock, 'Women's History and Gender History: Aspects of an International Debate', *Gender & History*, 1, 1, Spring 1989, p.21. Emphasis in original.
12. Bock, 'Women's History and Gender History', pp.10–15.
13. Judith Butler, *Gender Trouble: Feminism and the Subversion of Identity*, London and New York, 1990, and *Bodies That Matter: On the Discursive Limits of 'Sex'*, London and New York, 1993.
14. On the concept of 'hegemonic masculinity' see Tim Carrigan, Bob Connell, and John Lee, 'Towards a New Sociology of Masculinity', in Harry Brod, ed., *The Making of Masculinities: The New Men's Studies*, New York and London, 1992, p.86. Jill Matthews discusses 'true' or hegemonic femininity in her study of post-war femininity in Australia: Jill Julius Matthews, *Good and Mad Women: The Historical Construction of Femininity in Twentieth-Century Australia*, Sydney, 1984.
15. On the crisis in gender relations see Michael S. Kimmel, 'The Contemporary "Crisis" of Masculinity in Historical Perspective', in Harry Brod, ed., *The Making of Masculinities: The New Men's Studies*, New York and London, 1992,

pp.121–53; Barbara Ehrenreich, *The Hearts of Men: American Dreams and the Flight from Commitment*, London, 1983.

16 Jock Phillips has written about the family man in New Zealand, arguing that from the 1880s there was a transition from a 'father-dominated, functional family to a mother-dominated, sentimental' one. It is hard to see this transition in Taradale. Jock Phillips, *A Man's Country? The Image of the Pakeha Male – A History*, revised edition, Auckland, 1996, p.222.

17 Margaret Marsh, 'Suburban Men and Masculine Domesticity, 1870–1915', in Mark C. Carnes and Clyde Griffen, eds, *Meanings for Manhood: Constructions of Masculinity in Victorian America*, Chicago and London, 1990, pp.111–27. See also Ralph LaRossa, *The Modernization of Fatherhood: A Social and Political History*, Chicago and London, 1997.

18 Peter Gibbons, 'Non-fiction', in Terry Sturm, ed., *The Oxford History of New Zealand Literature in English*, Auckland, 1991, p.73.

19 Rollo Arnold, *Settler Kaponga 1881–1914: A Frontier Fragment of the Western World*, Wellington, 1997; Erik Olssen, *Building the New World: work, politics and society in Caversham 1880s–1920s*, Auckland, 1995; Maureen Molloy, *Those Who Speak to the Heart: The Nova Scotian Scots at Waipu 1854–1920*, Palmerston North, 1991; David Pearson, *Johnsonville: Continuity and Change in a New Zealand Township*, Sydney, 1980.

20 Miles Fairburn, *The Ideal Society and its Enemies: The Foundations of Modern New Zealand Society 1850–1900*, Auckland, 1989, Ch. VI. For critical responses to Fairburn see *New Zealand Journal of History*, 25, 2, 1991.

21 References to Taradale can be found in most regional histories of Hawke's Bay, or studies of Napier. No histories of Taradale per se exist. Indeed, the area is better represented in literature than in history. See Kitty O'Sullivan, *The Curse of the Greenstone Tiki*, Auckland, n.d. (c. 1945) and Lauris Edmond, *Hot October: An Autobiographical Story*, Wellington, 1989, especially Part One.

22 It has been claimed that Taradale was named after Tara in County Mead, Ireland, where Henry Alley was born. Matthew Wright, *Hawke's Bay: The History of a Province*, Palmerston North, 1994, p.196, fn. 11. It has also been claimed that Taradale was named after Ngai Tara, who occupied the nearby Otatara pa before Ngati Kahungunu. See Kay Mooney, *History of the County of Hawke's Bay: Part II*, Napier, n.d., (c. 1974), p.103.

23 Greenmeadows gained its name because of the native *Danthonia* grasses covering it when Henry Stokes Tiffen purchased the land from the Crown. Wright, *Hawke's Bay*, p.44.

24 Meanee is named after the Meeanee area in the Scinde Province of India, scene of a battle in which Sir Charles Napier was the victor. Mooney, *History of the County of Hawke's Bay: Part II*, p.91. Today, the common spelling for the area is Meeanee, but in the period covered by this study it was spelt Meanee. I have adopted the contemporary spelling here.

25 D. W. Meinig, quoted in John Mack Faragher, *Sugar Creek: Life on the Illinois Prairie*, New Haven, 1986, p.xiv.

26 For the history of the pa see *Otatara Pa Historical Reserve*, Napier, 1983 and Wright, *Hawke's Bay*, pp.11–23.

27 Wright, *Hawke's Bay*, p.55.

28 Wright, *Hawke's Bay*, p.70 and J. G. Wilson, *History of Hawke's Bay*, Dunedin and Wellington, 1939, p.419.

29 Wright, *Hawke's Bay*, pp.115–16; Wilson, *History of Hawke's Bay*, p.419.

30 *Hawke's Bay Herald*, 22 December 1876.

31 *A Return of the Freeholders of New Zealand, October 1882*, Wellington, 1884.

32 *Daily Telegraph*, 3 October 1884.

33 *Hawke's Bay Herald*, 13 October 1885.

34 *New Zealand Gazette*, 1886, Volume II, pp.1536–7, 1541.
35 *Census*, 1936, Volume III, Maori Census, Table 4, p.5.
36 For a discussion on the geographical mobility of the people of the area see Caroline Daley, 'Taradale Meets The Ideal Society and Its Enemies', *New Zealand Journal of History*, 25, 2, 1991, pp.129–46, especially pp.136–42.
37 On the essential woman see Denise Riley, *'Am I That Name': Feminism and the Category of 'Woman' in History*, Minneapolis, 1988.
38 Giovanni Levi, 'On Microhistory', in Peter Burke, ed., *New Perspectives on Historical Writing*, Cambridge, 1991, pp.93–113; Barry Reay, *Microhistories: Demography, society and culture in rural England, 1800–1930*, Cambridge, 1996, especially pp.xxii, 259–62.

CHAPTER 2 *Family and Community*

1 Matthew Wright, *Hawke's Bay: The History of a Province*, Palmerston North, 1994, p.55.
2 Information on individuals discussed here and in the following pages is taken from the Taradale Database, unless otherwise noted.
3 Miles Fairburn, *The Ideal Society and its Enemies: The Foundations of Modern New Zealand Society 1850–1900*, Auckland, 1989, p.162.
4 Raewyn Dalziel, 'Emigration and Kinship: Migrants to New Plymouth 1840–1843', *New Zealand Journal of History*, 25, 2, 1991, pp.112–28; Maureen Molloy, *Those Who Speak to the Heart: The Nova Scotian Scots at Waipu 1854–1920*, Palmerston North, 1991.
5 Births, Marriages and Deaths records, held by the Napier Justice Department. I would like to thank the Registrar of Births, Deaths and Marriages for granting me free access to these records.
6 The aim of this sampling procedure is to allow me to touch on the family lives of a cross-section of people in the area, some of whom had lived in the area for many years, some of whom were newly arrived, and some of whom were just passing through. If the study covered a longer period I would have been inclined to follow through on all of the marriages, to trace the subsequent creation of a family and interactions with the bride's and groom's families. However, the families of many of the couples who married in the area were not completed by 1930.
7 Of the 501 births that have been studied in depth, some immediate extended family could be established in 253 cases.
8 The figures are:

Year	No. Births	No. With Extended Family	% With Extended Family
1886	39	19	49
1890	57	20	35
1895	52	27	52
1900	60	29	48
1905	47	32	48
1910	43	26	60
1915	52	30	58
1920	57	27	47
1925	49	26	53
1930	45	17	38
TOTAL	501	253	50

9   In total, paternal extended family was traced in 167 cases, and maternal in 181 cases. Since in 95 cases extended family was traced on both sides, this explains why the two figures add up to 348, rather than the 253 quoted above. Over 1886–1905, 255 births were studied, of which 127 had some extended family. Of those 127, 79 (62%) had paternal and 88 (69%) had maternal kin. In 1910–30, 246 births were studied, of which 126 had some extended family. Of the 126, 88 (70%) had paternal and 93 (74%) had maternal kin.
10 Of the 2200 births, 67 (3%) were illegitimate; of the 501 births whose family ties were explored, the same percentage were illegitimate.
11 Nationwide in 1920, two-thirds of births still took place at home or in unlicensed maternity homes. Philippa Mein Smith, *Maternity in Dispute, New Zealand 1920–1939*, Wellington, 1986, p.1.
12 Matthew Silk, interviewed Taradale 2 September 1988.
13 Emily Jones, interviewed Taradale 29 August 1988.
14 Theresa Pond, interviewed Greenmeadows 3 February 1987.
15 Martha Edwards, interviewed Taradale 30 January 1987.
16 Of the 501 births studied in detail, fathers registered the birth in 205 cases, mothers in 104, male kin in five and female kin in 27. The other births were registered by a non-family member acting on behalf of the parents. This means that in just over two-thirds of all births, kin registered the birth.
17 Molloy, *Those Who Speak to the Heart*, pp.99–100.
18 Some of these children were named after non-resident branches of the family – an indication that out of sight was not out of mind when it came to kin – but as many were named after locally living members of the extended family.
19 cf. Nancy Grey Osterud, *Bonds of Community: The Lives of Farm Women in Nineteenth-Century New York*, Ithaca and London, 1991, pp.111–12.
20 In total, 42 of the 186 first births, 1913–1930, were pre-nuptial conceptions. Andree Levesque's work on New Zealand as a whole indicates that the Taradale findings were not uncommon: Andree Levesque, 'Prescribers and Rebels: Attitudes to European Women's Sexuality in New Zealand, 1860–1916', in Barbara Brookes, Charlotte Macdonald and Margaret Tennant, eds, *Women in History: Essays on European Women in New Zealand*, Wellington, 1986, pp.6–7.
21 I have been unable to secure any information regarding local abortion practices, although it is assumed that some unmarried and married women would have resorted to illegal terminations during this period.
22 Kathleen Thomson, interviewed Napier 8 February 1988.
23 Since there were 67 illegitimate births, this means that overall 12% of these children were adopted out. In the 1920s there were 18 illegitimate births locally, so for that decade 28% were officially adopted.
24 Theresa Pond, interviewed Greenmeadows 3 February 1987.
25 Henry Nolan, interviewed Meanee 14 February 1987.
26 A similar trend has been noticed in other societies. See Osterud, *Bonds of Community*, p.107, and Derek Thompson, 'Courtship and Marriage in Preston Between the Wars', *Oral History*, 3, 2, 1975, p.43.
27 Bridget Tweed, interviewed Napier 12 February 1987.
28 Hannah Field, interviewed Taradale 20 May 1987.
29 Hannah Field, interviewed Taradale 20 May 1987.
30 I have employed a different definition of extended family here, since on marriage the couple created their own family and family relations changed. Many of those with immediate extended family in the area (parents, siblings, siblings' partners and children) also had grandparents, aunts, uncles and

NOTES TO PAGES 22-24

cousins in the area. Couples who married in the area were not necessarily resident in the area. The figures are:

Years	No. of Marriages	No. with Extended Family	% with Extended Family
1886	11	5	45
1890	10	7	70
1895	15	11	73
1900	9	7	78
1905	12	12	100
1910	17	13	76
1915	21	18	86
1920	25	21	84
1925	13	13	100
1930	17	11	65
TOTAL	150	118	79

31   Of the 118 weddings where extended family could be traced, in 33 cases it was found for both bride and groom, in 63 only the bride's family was located, and in 23 only the groom's family was traced. So, overall, in 96 cases bridal kin was found, and in 56 groom's kin.
32   Of the 587 weddings in the area, in 163 cases (28%) no kin could be positively identified among the witnesses. This was a consistent pattern throughout the period 1891–1930. Of the 51 marriages, 1886–1890, kin ties could not be established in just under half the weddings.
33   At 424 weddings kin could be positively identified among the witnesses. In 273 cases only kin on the bridal side was identified, in 63 only kin on the groom's side, and in 88 kin on both sides. So, in total, bridal kin was identified in 361 (85%) of the weddings and groom's in 151 (36%).
34   In total, the brides had 434 known kin as witnesses. Of these half were female and half male. At the beginning of the period more female kin acted as witnesses. Of the 33 witnesses at the marriages 1886–1890, two-thirds were female kin. But from 1910 onwards it was slightly more likely that the bride's male kin acted as her witnesses. Of the 218 bridal kin witnesses at weddings, 1911–1930, 118 were male kin. Among the grooms, three-quarters of their known kin who acted as wedding witnesses were male. Of the 166 people involved, 121 were men. For the period 1921–1930, there were 19 weddings where only the groom's kin could be identified among the witnesses. At those 19 weddings, in 14 only male kin was noted.
35   On sibling exchange in Waipu see Molloy, *Those Who Speak to the Heart*, pp.79–80, 84–5, 89.
36   Of the 1263 witnesses at the 587 marriages, 215 did not live in either the Taradale area or Napier. Of that 215, 151 were men and 64 were women. A kin connection could be found for 105 of these witnesses – 56 on the bride's side, 49 on the groom's. Of the bride's kin 24 were female and 32 were male, while eight of the groom's kin were female and 41 were male. For the period up to 1910, 48 non-local kin are known to have acted as witnesses. In 29 instances they were the bride's kin, in 19 cases the groom's. After 1910, 57 non-local kin were identified, 27 on the bride's side and 30 on the groom's.
37   Using the five-yearly sample, 59 of the 133 couples who married 1886–1925 had family in the area, but did not themselves register to vote locally once married (those who married in 1930 were not included since electoral rolls

NOTES TO PAGES 24-26

after 1928 were not considered). In 41 (69%) of those cases the bride had family living locally, in 13 (22%) the groom had local kin.
38 Of all births, 122 (6%) died within the first 12 months. Broken down by decades, the figures are:

Years	No. of Deaths	No. of Births	% of Deaths Within First Year
1880s	25	275	11
1890s	44	498	9
1900s	14	453	3
1910s	22	530	4
1920s	17	444	4
TOTAL	122	2200	6

For a comparative overview of infant mortality in this period see Philippa Mein Smith, 'Truby King in Australia: A Revisionist View of Reduced Infant Mortality', *New Zealand Journal of History*, 22, 1, 1988, pp.23-43, especially pp.23-5.
39 Every Wednesday afternoon the Plunket nurse used the Supper Room of the Taradale Town Hall. Taradale Town Board Minutes, 10 July 1919.
40 Charlotte Rose, interviewed Taradale 16 January 1987.
41 Mein Smith, 'Truby King in Australia', especially pp.23-5, 34.
42 Only 3% of births in the area were illegitimate (67 of 2200), but seven (10%) of these children died before their first birthday. Andrée Lévesque notes that the death-rate of illegitimate infants was more than twice the death-rate of legitimate babies: Levesque, 'Prescribers and Rebels', p.4.
43 In the 1880s, 14 of the 25 infant deaths (56%) were due to diarrhoea and dysentery related complaints. By the 1890s, these illnesses led to ten of the 44 deaths (23%), in the 1900s three of the 14 deaths (21%), in the 1910s four of the 22 deaths (18%), and in the 1920s none of the 17 deaths were diarrhoea or dysentery related. This information is based on the causes of death given on death certificates.
44 See the *Daily Telegraph* reports, 8, 13, 15, 23, 24 November 1920.
45 *Daily Telegraph*, 24 November 1920.
46 That is, of those adults who died in 1886, 1890, and then at five-yearly intervals until 1930.
47 The figures are:

Years	No. of Deaths	No. with only Nuclear Family	No. with Extended Family	No. with some Kin
1886	5	2	1	3
1890	6	2	1	3
1895	9	1	6	7
1900	5	1	4	5
1905	17	6	6	12
1910	6	1	2	3
1915	11	6	4	10
1920	23	7	15	22
1925	21	8	9	17
1930	22	6	6	12
TOTAL	125	40	54	94=75%

48 For the period 1886-1905, 42 death records were studied – 28 male and 14

181

female. Thirty of these people left behind some kin (71%); 12 (86%) of the women and 18 (64%) of the men. In 12 (29%) cases only nuclear family was traced – the proportion was the same for men and women. Eighteen of the deceased left behind nuclear and extended family (43%). Only ten (36%) of the men did, whereas eight (57%) of the women did.

49 For the period 1910–30, 83 death records were examined – 48 male and 35 female. Overall 64 (77%) left some kin – 35 (73%) of the men and 41 (83%) of the women. Twenty-eight (34%) left just nuclear family – 16 (33%) of the men and 12 (34%) of the women. Thirty-six (43%) left nuclear and extended family – 19 (40%) of the men and 17 (49%) of the women.

50 Of the 125 death records examined, 76 were for men and 49 for women. Some family was found in 94 (75%) of the cases – 53 (70%) of the men's and 41 (84%) of the women's cases. When that is broken down by marital status, 51 of the dead men were married and kin was found locally for 45 of them – 20 just had nuclear family living locally, 25 had nuclear and/or extended family in the area. Twenty-five men were single and kin was traced for eight of them. Of the women, 47 were married and some kin was found in 40 instances – in 15 cases only nuclear family, in 25 cases nuclear and/or extended family. One of the two adult single women who died in Taradale left behind nuclear family.

51 In 104 of the 146 wills studied, all the beneficiaries lived in Taradale, and in six cases they lived in Taradale and Hawke's Bay. Of the 146 wills studied, 114 left everything to the nuclear family, and six to the nuclear and/or extended family. Only four of the wills left everything to non-family members, and three of those were written by members of a religious order.

52 The wills of 103 men were studied. In 84 cases they left everything to their nuclear family and in five cases to nuclear and extended family. The wills of 43 women were studied. In 31 cases they left everything to their nuclear family, and in one case to nuclear and extended family. In all six cases of women's wills, 1886–1900, everything was left just to their nuclear family.

53 The wills of 74 men who were married at the time of their deaths have been studied. In 27 cases they left their estates to their spouses, absolutely; in 12 instances to their wife while she remained widowed; in 17 wills the widow benefited only while alive; and in 14 cases the estate was left to the deceased's spouse and children. In four of the wills other arrangements were made. If the period is divided into two, 1886–1907 and 1908–30, we can see changes occurring. For the first period, 23 wills are extant, seven leaving everything to the spouse, five only while she remained a widow, six while she was alive and five to widow and children. For the period 1908–30, 51 wills were studied. In 20 cases the widow was left the entire estate, unconditionally. Seven of the wills left her property only while she remained a widow (only two of those were from the 27 wills of the 1920s), five left her the estate while she was alive, and nine wills left wife and children property. In four cases other arrangements were made.

54 Justice Files, National Archives, Napier Probates, 726/1894.
55 Justice Files, National Archives, Napier Probates, 416/1925.
56 Justice Files, National Archives, Napier Probates, 929/1897.
57 Justice Files, National Archives, Napier Probates, 851/1928.
58 Justice Files, National Archives, Napier Probates, 505/1890.
59 Fairburn, *The Ideal Society and its Enemies*, pp.162–8.
60 Joan Wallach Scott, *Gender and the Politics of History*, New York, 1988, p.44.
61 Claire Toynbee, *Her Work and His: Family, Kin and Community in New Zealand*

1900–1930, Wellington, 1995, p.133.
62 Ralph LaRossa's study of interwar fatherhood in America offers many other avenues for exploring new types of fatherhood: Ralph LaRossa, *The Modernization of Fatherhood: A Social and Political History*, Chicago and London, 1997.

CHAPTER 3   *The Household and Local Economy*

1. Information taken from the land valuation records for 1905, 1908 and 1918. In 1905 Thomas owned the land but it was unimproved. By 1908 it contained a dwelling and shed. By the time of the 1918 roll, the additional acre of land had been purchased.
2. Patrick Stevenson, interviewed Taradale 12 February 1988.
3. ibid.
4. Grace Miner, interviewed Taradale 13 February 1988.
5. Patrick Stevenson, interviewed Taradale 12 February 1988.
6. Claire Toynbee, *Her Work and His: Family, Kin and Community in New Zealand 1900–1930*, Wellington, 1995; Erik Olssen, *Building the New World: work, politics and society in Caversham 1880s–1920s*, Auckland, 1995; Rollo Arnold, *Settler Kaponga 1881–1914: A Frontier Fragment of the Western World*, Wellington, 1997.
7. Wally Seccombe, 'Patriarchy stabilized: the construction of the male breadwinner wage norm in nineteenth-century Britain', *Social History*, 11, 1, 1986, pp.53–76, especially p.54.
8. Raewyn Dalziel, 'The Colonial Helpmeet: Women's Role and the Vote in Nineteenth-Century New Zealand', *New Zealand Journal of History*, 11, 2, 1977, pp.112–23.
9. *The Cyclopaedia of New Zealand, Volume Six*, Christchurch, 1908, pp.436–9.
10. ibid., p.436.
11. Records exist for 511 men and 158 women who owned land. Of the 730 plots that men owned from 1905 onwards, 361 (49%) were under one acre in size. Of women's plots, 86 (46%) were less than an acre. A further 306 (42%) of men's plots were between one and nine acres in size, as were 82 (44%) of women's plots. Only 63 (9%) of men's plots were between 10 and 99 acres in size, while 18 (10%) of women's were. Of the male landholders, 138 (27%) were multiple landowners, whereas this was true for only 23 (15%) of the women landowners.
12. Of all women's land plots, 52% contained a dwelling and 61% contained fencing. Of women's first land plot only, 49% contained a dwelling and 52% were fenced. Of all men's land plots, 43% contained a dwelling and 53% contained fencing. Of men's first land plots only, 47% contained a dwelling and 55% were fenced.
13. Of the 158 women who owned land, 12 (8%) were single, 108 (68%) were married, 29 (18%) were widows and the marital status of 9 (6%) is unknown. It is possible that some of the women counted as married were in fact widows by the time they owned land. Of the 511 male landowners, 282 are known to have been married (55%), and 229 (45%) appear to have been single.
14. Men were listed under a variety of occupations related to the rural sector. The following table, based on electoral roll data, shows the numbers and percentages who said they had a rural occupation (defined as labourers, gardeners, farmers, dairymen, orchardists or fruit growers, farm hands and servants, nurserymen, fencers, drovers, ploughmen, shearers and shepherds).

Although labourers also engaged in non-rural work, as Thomas Johnson (discussed below) did, they were often involved in the rural sector as well.

Year	Rural Occupation	Rural Occupation as % of All Males on Electoral Roll
1887	240	64
1890	326	64
1893	205	57
1896	189	51
1899	189	53
1902	237	54
1905	316	56
1908	346	52
1911	274	46
1914	258	45
1919	329	46
1922	306	47
1925	253	44
1928	309	44
TOTAL	3777	51

15 *The Cyclopaedia of New Zealand*, p.437.
16 Roman Catholic Archives, Regnier I (Box) 208/20.
17 *Hawke's Bay Almanack and Directory for 1908*, Napier, 1907, p.189.
18 *Industries of New Zealand (Illustrated)*, Auckland, 1898, pp.62–3.
19 J. M. Thorp, *The History of Tiffen Lodge, Avenue Road, Greenmeadows, Hawke's Bay*, Napier, 1971, p.27.
20 Kay Mooney, *History of the County of Hawke's Bay: Part II*, Napier, c.1974, p.31.
21 Roman Catholic Archives, Regnier I (Box) 208/20.
22 Advertisement in the *Hawke's Bay Almanack and Business Directory for 1908*.
23 Figures for the Taradale area taken from the annual sheep returns for the Napier District of Hawke's Bay County, *Appendices to the Journal of the House of Representatives*, 1886–1930, H-23.
24 *Daily Telegraph*, 15 February 1886 and 22 August 1898.
25 *Hawke's Bay Herald*, 26 February 1889 and *Daily Telegraph*, 19 February 1892.
26 Taradale Town Board Minutes, 7 June 1888.
27 Taradale Town Board Minutes, 3 April 1891.
28 Taradale Town Board Minutes, 20 June 1896.
29 Taradale Town Board Minutes, 9 February 1909 and 14 February 1918.
30 Taradale Town Board Minutes, 23 October 1920 and 25 May 1922.
31 Taradale Town Board Minutes, 29 June 1922.
32 Harriet Bradley, *Men's Work, Women's Work: A Sociological History of the Sexual Division of Labour in Employment*, Cambridge, 1989, p.43.
33 John Mack Faragher, 'History From The Inside-Out: Writing the History of Women in Rural America', *American Quarterly*, 33, 5, 1981, p.544.
34 Sophie Richardson, interviewed Hastings 7 February 1987.
35 Information from wills, probate records and testamentary records was located for 159 men and 67 women. The worth of 156 of the male estates and 63 of the female estates is known. In 81 (53%) of the male cases the estate was valued at over £1000, while this was true in 23 (37%) of the female cases. Thirteen men (8%) left estates valued at over £10,000, and a further 10 (6%) left estates valued between £5000 and £10,000. Only one woman, Amelia Randall, left an estate of over £10,000.

36 Justice Files, National Archives, Napier Probates, 1005/1898.
37 The wills of 74 parents with children were examined. In nine cases daughters inherited on reaching the age of 21 or on marrying. In a third of the cases (26) the wills left property to sons and daughters in an unequal manner, although it was almost as common for daughters to be favoured as sons. In 39 of the wills the estate was equally divided between sons and daughters. There was almost no difference in how fathers and mothers divided up their property.
38 Justice Files, National Archives, Napier Probates, 173/1919.
39 *Daily Telegraph*, 7 May 1886.
40 *Daily Telegraph*, 23 November 1897, 16 May 1898 and 23 May 1898.
41 *Daily Telegraph*, 23 November 1897.
42 *Daily Telegraph*, 22 February 1899.
43 See Margaret Tennant, *Paupers and Providers: Charitable Aid in New Zealand*, Wellington, 1989.
44 United Districts Charitable Aid Board Minutes 1893–1900, 9 October 1893.
45 ibid. 14 November 1893, 13 February 1894, 13 March 1894, and 16 May 1894.
46 Register of Patients, Napier Hospital, 24 August 1909. The family's surname was variously written as Bryon and Bryan.
47 United Districts Charitable Aid Board Minutes 1907–1910, 11 October 1909.
48 Hawke's Bay Hospital and Charitable Aid Board Finance Board Minutes, 1910–1917, 11 August 1911.
49 Register of Patients, Napier Hospital, 24 July 1914.
50 *Daily Telegraph*, 18 August 1890.
51 *Daily Telegraph*, 2, 5 and 10 August 1898.
52 cf. Nancy Grey Osterud, *Bonds of Community: The Lives of Farm Women in Nineteenth-Century New York*, Ithaca and London, 1991, p.123.
53 From 1886 to 1930 148 men joined AOF, 186 joined MUIOOF and 25 belonged to HACBS. Eight of these 359 men belonged to two lodges, so in total 351 men in Taradale were lodge members. All figures are taken from the membership rolls of the lodges.
54 P. H. J. H. Gosden, *Self Help: Voluntary Associations in the Nineteenth Century*, London, 1973, pp.26–7; Nancy Swinburne Renfree, 'Migrants and Cultural Transference: English Friendly Societies in a Victorian Goldfield Town', PhD thesis, La Trobe University, 1983, passim.
55 David Thomson, *A World Without Welfare: New Zealand's Colonial Experiment*, Auckland, 1998, p.45.
56 Of the 351 men who belonged to the area's three lodges, 158 received at least one sick pay. Two of the 17 women who belonged to the lodges also received sick pay.
57 Justice Files, National Archives, Napier Probates, 838/1893.
58 Taradale Town Board Minutes, 8 October 1914.
59 ibid. 1 July 1927.

CHAPTER 4 *Women's Work*

1 Sophie Richardson, interviewed Hastings 7 February 1987.
2 For a similar argument regarding American women see John Mack Faragher, 'History From The Inside-Out: Writing the History of Women in Rural America', *American Quarterly*, 33, 5, 1981, p.544, and Carol Groneman and Mary Beth Norton, 'Introduction', in Carol Groneman and Mary Beth Norton, eds, *'To Toil the Livelong Day': America's Women at Work, 1780–1980*, Ithaca and London, 1987, p.16. For Britain see Diana G. Gittins, 'Marital

Status, Work and Kinship, 1850–1930', in Jane Lewis, ed., *Labour and Love: Women's Experience of Home and Family 1850–1940*, Oxford, 1986, p.249.
3   Glenna Matthews, *'Just a Housewife': The Rise and Fall of Domesticity in America*, New York and Oxford, 1987; Christina Hardyment, *From Mangle to Microwave: The Mechanization of Household Work*, Cambridge, 1988; Ruth Schwartz Cowan, *More Work for Mother: The Ironies of Household Technology from the Open Hearth to the Microwave*, London, 1989.
4   Jane McNight, interviewed Napier 5 February 1988.
5   Thomas Raven, interviewed Poraite 8 February 1987.
6   *Appendices to the Journal of the House of Representatives* (AJHR), E-1B, 1895, p.18.
7   Taradale School Headmaster's Log Book, 5 February 1924.
8   Martha Edwards, interviewed Taradale 30 January 1987.
9   Henry Nolan, interviewed Meanee 14 February 1987.
10 Hannah Field, interviewed Taradale 20 May 1987.
11 Susan Strasser, *Never Done: A History of American Housework*, New York, 1982, p.41.
12 Martha Edwards, interviewed Taradale 30 January 1987.
13 Hardyment, *From Mangle to Microwave*, p.10.
14 For example, in 1926 only 4600 homes in New Zealand had an electric stove. Sandra Coney, ed., *Standing in the Sunshine: A History of New Zealand Women Since they Won the Vote*, Auckland, 1993, p.214.
15 Kathleen Thomson, interviewed Napier 8 February 1988.
16 Ellen Store, interviewed Greenmeadows 12 January 1987.
17 On 'scientific' housework see Margaret Tennant, 'Natural Directions: The New Zealand Movement for Sexual Differentiation in Education During the Early Twentieth Century', in Barbara Brookes, Charlotte Macdonald and Margaret Tennant, eds, *Women in History: Essays on European Women in New Zealand*, Wellington, 1986, pp.87–100, especially p.93; Coney, *Standing in the Sunshine*, pp.202–4.
18 Bev James and Kay Saville-Smith, *Gender, Culture and Power: Challenging New Zealand's Gendered Culture*, revised edition, Auckland, 1994, p.27.
19 Ellen Store, interviewed Greenmeadows 12 January 1987.
20 Harriet South, interviewed Taradale 19 January 1987.
21 Martha Edwards, interviewed Taradale 30 January 1987.
22 Louisa Plumb, interviewed Taradale 20 January 1987.
23 Charlotte Rose, interviewed Taradale 16 January 1987.
24 Jane McNight, interviewed Napier 5 February 1988.
25 Sophie Richardson, interviewed Hastings 7 February 1987.
26 See for example the report in *Hawke's Bay Herald*, 2 February 1889.
27 Marilyn Lake, 'Helpmeet, Slave, Housewife: Women in Rural Families 1870–1930', in Patricia Grimshaw, Chris McConville and Ellen McEwen, eds, *Families in Colonial Australia*, Sydney, 1985, p.179.
28 Theresa Pond, interviewed Greenmeadows 3 February 1987.
29 Ann Pearce, interviewed Taradale 11 February 1987.
30 There were 261 private dwellings in the Taradale Town District in 1926. One hundred and ninety of these households (73%) kept some form of poultry. *Census* 1926, Volume XVI, Poultry, p.8.
31 The account book is held by one of Sarah Ridley's descendants, who kindly showed it to me.
32 Joan M. Jensen, 'Cloth, Butter and Boarders: Women's Household Production for the Market', *Review of Radical Political Economics*, 12, 2, 1980, pp.14–24.
33 ibid. p.15.
34 John Modell and Tamara K. Hareven, 'Urbanization and the Malleable Household: An Examination of Boarding and Lodging in American Families',

Journal of Marriage and the Family, 35, 3, August 1973, pp.467–79.
35 Erik Olssen, 'Towards a New Society', in Geoffrey W. Rice, ed., *The Oxford History of New Zealand*, second edition, Auckland, 1992, p.263. Given the limited data, it is impossible to calculate average completed families specific to the Taradale area over this period.
36 Bridget Tweed, interviewed Napier 12 February 1987.
37 Emma Needle, interviewed Napier 9 February 1987.
38 On women's involvement in childbirth see Adrian Wilson, 'The Ceremony of Childbirth and Its Interpretation', in Valerie Fields, ed., *Women as Mothers in Pre-Industrial England: Essays in Memory of Dorothy McLaren*, London and New York, 1990, pp. 68–107; Mary Chamberlain and Ruth Richardson, 'Life and Death', *Oral History*, 11, 1, 1983, pp.31–43.
39 Harriet South, interviewed Taradale 19 January 1987.
40 Trying to determine how many adult women were married at any one time is not an easy task, especially since it was not until the 1926 census that official figures on conjugal condition by age were given for the Taradale Town District. In that year, 75% of the women in the area aged 16 or over were married. By the time Taradale's women reached the age of 25, 89% had married. *Census*, 1926, Volume IV, Conjugal Condition of the People, p.54.
41 The differences in boys' and girls' attendance at Taradale School are discussed in detail in Ch.5.
42 In 1890 the school had 47 pupils and in 1900 it had 59 pupils. *Statistics of New Zealand*, 1890 p.338; 1900 p.408. In a more general sense, in 1900 only 10% of primary school pupils went on to secondary school. Of that 10%, 45% were girls. Ruth Fry, *It's Different For Daughters: A History of the Curriculum for Girls in New Zealand Schools, 1900–1975*, Wellington, 1985, p.29.
43 By 1910 there were 113 pupils at Napier Girls' High School; in 1920 there were 136, 110 of whom were on scholarships and free places. *Statistics of New Zealand*, 1910, p.585 and 1920, Volume IV, pp.5, 7.
44 J. Garnham and G. Cowlrick, eds, *Ad Lucem: Napier Girls' High School 1884–1984*, Napier, 1984, pp.14, 135–6, 138.
45 By 1916 there were 34 convent girls. *Census*, 1916, Section VII, Education, p.72.
46 In 1915 there were 11,958 pupils at secondary education; by 1924 the figure had increased to 23,276. *New Zealand Official Year Book*, 1926, p.229.
47 John Nicol, *The Technical Schools of New Zealand: an historical survey*, Wellington, 1940, pp.62, 114.
48 By 1911 Napier's technical school had 231 pupils. *Statistics of New Zealand*, 1911, Part VII, Education, p.727. By 1920 it had 335 students. *Statistics of New Zealand*, 1920, Volume IV, Education, p.12. In 1916, 104 males and 103 females attended Napier Technical School. *Census*, 1916, Section VII, Education, p.72.
49 Nicol, *The Technical Schools of New Zealand*, p.115. See also Fry, *It's Different For Daughters*, p.63.
50 Martha Edwards, interviewed Taradale 30 January 1987.
51 It is very difficult to quantify these women. There are no census figures on women's breadwinner or dependent status for the Taradale Town District. Electoral roll material is of little help here. First, it does not cover women under the age of 21. Second, from 1908 a woman's occupation was listed by her marital status. The only census figures available are for dependent women in the Hawke's Bay province and from 1916 for the Napier urban area. In 1896 and 1901, 84% of these females were dependants, while in 1906 and 1911, 83% were dependants. In 1916 79% of the females from Napier were dependants, in 1921 76% were dependants, and in 1926 79% were dependants. All figures are derived from the *Census*, Occupations of the

People, and cover females of all ages. By 1926, 54% of all 16–20 year old females in New Zealand were classified as breadwinners. *Census, 1926,* Volume IX, Industrial and Occupational Distribution, p.7.
52 Theresa Pond, interviewed Greenmeadows 3 February 1987.
53 On the moral economy of domestic work and women's desire to escape from it see, John Springhall, *Coming of Age: Adolescence in Britain 1860–1960,* Dublin, 1986, pp.90–2, and Anne M. Boylan, 'Growing Up Female in Young America, 1800–1860', in Joseph M. Hawes and N. Ray Hiner, eds, *American Childhood: A Research Guide and Historical Handbook,* Connecticut, 1985, pp.168–9.
54 Louisa Plumb, interviewed Taradale 20 January 1987.
55 Harriet South, interviewed Taradale 19 January 1987.
56 Theresa Pond, interviewed Greenmeadows 3 February 1987.
57 Kathleen Thomson, interviewed Napier 8 February 1988.
58 AJHR, 1893, E1, Table 8, p.29.
59 AJHR, 1924, E2, Appendix E, p.l.
60 Elizabeth Roberts, *A Woman's Place: An Oral History of Working Class Women 1890–1940,* Oxford, 1984, p.68, noted a similar pattern in Lancashire.
61 This is a common phenomenon, noted in other societies. See, for example, Roberts, *A Woman's Place,* pp.40–5.
62 Available sources make it very difficult to quantify these women. From 1908 onwards women were listed on the electoral roll by marital status, and about a fifth of them were spinsters. The census of 1926 indicates that 13% of Taradale's women aged 16 and above were widows, while 16% of women aged 25 or over were widows. A further 11% of women aged 25 and over were unmarried. In that year there were only two legally separated women in the area, although how many were living separately from their husbands we cannot tell. *Census,* 1926, Volume IV, Conjugal Condition of the People, p.54.
63 Information taken from the marriage certificates of widows and divorcees who remarried. None of these women worked in the growing white collar sector.
64 Taradale School Committee Minutes 10 August 1889, 4 March 1899 and 23 April 1906.
65 Taradale School Committee Minutes 19 July 1909, 10 August 1910, 30 June 1915 and 27 February 1918. St. Columba Presbyterian Church, Manager's Minute Book 29 November 1920 and 11 April 1924.
66 Taradale Town Board Minutes 13 August 1914, 10 June 1915, 12 August 1915, and Taradale Town Board General Committee Book 8 November 1916.
67 Beryl Hughes, 'Women and the Professions in New Zealand', in Phillida Bunkle and Beryl Hughes, eds, *Women in New Zealand Society,* Auckland, 1980, p.133.
68 For example, Toynbee's evidence for women and girls doing farm work relies almost exclusively on one woman's oral recollections. Claire Toynbee, *Her Work and His: Family, Kin and Community in New Zealand 1900–1930,* Wellington, 1995, pp.52–5. In *Bonds of Community: The Lives of Farm Women in Nineteenth-Century New York,* Ithaca and London, 1991, Chapters 6–7, Nancy Grey Osterud argues for a flexible sexual division of labour. However, on p.160 she admits that women's diaries show more knowledge about men's work than men's do about women's work.
69 On the idea of true womanhood in New Zealand see Erik Olssen and Andree Levesque, 'Towards a History of the European Family in New Zealand', in Peggy G. Koopman-Boyden, ed., *Families in New Zealand Society,* Wellington, 1978, pp.1–25, especially pp.6–12.
70 The idea of interwar New Zealand as a modern society is discussed in Danielle Sprecher, 'The Right Appearance: Representations of Fashion, Gender, and Modernity in Inter-war New Zealand', MA thesis, University of Auckland, 1997, especially the introduction.

CHAPTER 5 Men's Work

1. Caroline Ramazanoglu, 'What Can You Do With a Man? Feminism and the Critical Appraisal of Masculinity', *Women's Studies International Forum*, 15, 3, 1992, pp.339-50, especially p.339.
2. The categories are based on the definitions used in Michael B. Katz, *The People of Hamilton, Canada West: Family and Class in a Mid-Nineteenth-Century City*, Cambridge, 1975.
3. See Appendix B for more information on this point.
4. Thomas Raven, interviewed Poraite 8 February 1987.
5. William Cliff, interviewed Taradale 8 February 1988.
6. David G. Pearson, *Johnsonville: Continuity and Change in a New Zealand Township*, Sydney, 1980, p.111.
7. Overall, of the 587 marriages, there were 157 cases where the groom and his father had exactly the same occupation (27%). Decade by decade the figures are: 1880s = 13 of 51 (25%), 1890s = 35 of 115 (31%), 1900s = 36 of 131 (27%), 1910s = 39 of 147 (27%), and 1920s = 34 of 144 (24%). The slight decrease in the 1920s could be due to the increasing specialisation of jobs.
8. Of the 157 cases, ten of the grooms and fathers belonged to occupational category one, three to category two, 65 to category three (most of whom were farmers), 27 to category four, 17 to category five and 35 to category six (most of whom were labourers).
9. Information supplied by Eliza Peterson, interviewed Awatoto 22 January 1987.
10. New Zealand Biographies, Alexander Turnbull Library, 1953, vol. 1 p.100.
11. New Zealand Biographies, Alexander Turnbull Library, 1959, vol. 1 p.152.
12. *Daily Telegraph*, 7 August 1886.
13. *Daily Telegraph*, 9 May 1892.
14. Elizabeth Roberts, *A Woman's Place: An Oral History of Working Class Women 1890-1940*, Oxford, 1984, p.23, notes a similar pattern among the boys of late nineteenth and early twentieth century Lancashire.
15. Patrick Stevenson, interviewed Taradale 12 February 1988.
16. Henry Nolan, interviewed Meanee 14 February 1987.
17. *Daily Telegraph*, 7 May 1900.
18. *Daily Telegraph*, 27 and 28 February 1894.
19. Richard Jackson, interviewed Taradale 4 February 1987.
20. AJHR, 1895, E-1b, p.16; 1904, p.19.
21. Colin McGeorge, 'School Attendance and Child Labour 1890-1914', *Historical News*, 46, May 1983, also highlights the paid, part-time work boys did, p.18, although he does not specify whether boys or girls or both were engaged in seasonal harvesting, p.19. In another paper he shows that overall girls had a slightly lower attendance rate at primary school 1880-95 than boys, but is aware that the overall figure does not allow for differences by district; Colin McGeorge, 'How Katy Did at School', *New Zealand Journal of Educational Studies*, 22, 1, 1987, p.103. Kerry Wimshurst's study of school attendance and child labour in late nineteenth and early twentieth century South Australia indicates that boys were more likely to be poor attendees. Wimshurst argues that this was due to the sexual division of labour. Kerry Wimshurst, 'Child Labour and School Attendance in South Australia 1890-1915', *Historical Studies*, 19, 1981, p.392.
22. Taradale School Headmaster's Log Book 28 May 1905.
23. ibid. 31 May 1905.
24. ibid. 26 July 1915.
25. ibid. 4 May 1888.

26 ibid. 24 June 1908.
27 ibid. 10 September 1908.
28 ibid. 11 March 1898.
29 The 1877 Education Act did not make attendance for seven- to 13-year-olds compulsory, unless the local committee declared it to be so. Not until 1910 were children expected to be at school whenever the school was open. See McGeorge, 'School Attendance and Child Labour 1890–1914', p.17.
30 AJHR, 1891, E-1b, p.16.
31 Forty summonses were served on parents; in 25 cases the offending child was a boy, in 15 cases a girl.
32 For a fuller discussion and explanation for the change in attitude towards school attendance over this period, see C. T. Paxton, 'Childhood in New Zealand, 1862–1921: Child Labour and the Gradual Popular Acceptance of Primary School Attendance', MA thesis, University of Auckland, 1987. Colin McGeorge, 'Schools and Socialisation in New Zealand 1890–1914', PhD thesis, University of Canterbury, 1985, also notes that 'By 1911 irregular attendance was hardly the problem it had been in the nineteenth century', p.87. Taradale School's examination results, listing annual attendance, are not available before 1915, but for the period 1915–28 the average attendance for Standard 6 pupils has been studied, and it was found that boys and girls both attended, on average, 351 half days a year.
33 Harriet South, interviewed Taradale 19 January 1987.
34 George Davies, interviewed Taradale 9 February 1988.
35 *Daily Telegraph*, 6 May 1893, 6 February 1894, 14 May 1888 and 7 May 1891.
36 Matthew Silk, interviewed Taradale 2 September 1988.
37 Louisa Plumb, interviewed Taradale 20 January 1987, and George Davies, interviewed Taradale 9 February 1988.
38 See the list of wages and prices in Hawke's Bay in 1891 in AJHR, 1892, H-14, pp.15-18.
39 Sarah Stevenson, interviewed Taradale 16 February 1988.
40 Florence Rifle, interviewed Napier 5 February 1988.
41 Thomas Raven, interviewed Poraite 8 February 1987.
42 ibid.
43 Henry Nolan, interviewed Meanee 14 February 1987.
44 Edward McLean, interviewed Greenmeadows 21 January 1987.
45 ibid.
46 Michael Roper, interviewed Taradale 10 February 1987.
47 *Hawke's Bay Herald*, 27 August 1887.
48 *Hawke's Bay Herald*, 1 September 1887.
49 David H. J. Morgan, *Discovering Men*, London and New York, 1992, p.77.
50 ibid. p.91.

CHAPTER 6 *Communal Leisure*

1 *Hawke's Bay Herald*, 19 November 1887.
2 Charlotte Rose, interviewed Taradale 16 January 1987.
3 Miles Fairburn, *The Ideal Society and Its Enemies: The Foundations of Modern New Zealand Society 1850–1900*, Auckland, 1989, pp.161-2.
4 Sarah Stevenson, interviewed Taradale 16 February 1988.
5 Ted Ownby, *Subduing Satan: Religion, Recreation, and Manhood in the Rural South, 1865–1920*, Chapel Hill, 1990, pp.110-11.
6 Joseph Barnett, interviewed Taradale 26 August 1988.
7 William Cliff, interviewed Taradale 8 February 1988.

8   See Margaret Marsh, 'Suburban Men and Masculine Domesticity, 1870-1915', in Mark C. Carnes and Clyde Griffen, eds, *Meanings for Manhood: Constructions of Masculinity in Victorian America*, Chicago and London, 1990, pp.111-27; E. Anthony Rotundo, *American Manhood: Transformations in Masculinity from the Revolution to the Modern Era*, New York, 1993; Ralph LaRossa, *The Modernization of Fatherhood: A Social and Political History*, Chicago and London, 1997.
9   *Daily Telegraph*, 25 November 1889.
10 James Green, interviewed Taradale 13 May 1987.
11 George Davies, interviewed Taradale 9 February 1988.
12 See, for example, Joan R. Gundersen, 'The Local Parish as a Female Institution: The Experience of All Saints Episcopal Church in Frontier Minnesota', *Church History*, 55, 3, 1986, p.320; Jama Lazerow, 'Religion and the New England Mill Girl: A New Perspective on an Old Theme', *New England Quarterly*, 60, 3, September 1987, p.430; Ownby, *Subduing Satan*, p.129.
13 Sophie Richardson, interviewed Hastings 7 February 1987.
14 The figures are taken from the All Saints list of communicants, 1885-90; the Roman Catholic Register of the Association in Honour of the Sacred Heart of Jesus, 1894; and the Methodist Members Roll 1910-15. The figures on church attendance by gender are:

	Anglican	RC	Methodist	Total No.	Total%
Women	160	94	41	295	64
Men	78	65	26	169	36
TOTAL	238	159	67	464	100

15 The figures on church attendance by marital status are:

	Anglican	RC	Methodist	Total No.	Total%
Single Women	88	31	19	138	34
Single Men	22	4	10	36	9
Married Women	72	28	22	122	30
Married Men	56	35	16	107	27
TOTAL	238	98	67	403	100

It was not possible to ascertain the marital status of all of those attending the 1894 Roman Catholic Mission, hence the figure of 98, rather than 159.
16 From the three congregations, 61 married couples were noted. There were 122 married women among the attendees, so 50% attended with their husbands. Of the 107 married men, 57% attended with their wives.
17 See, for example, the All Saints Anglican Church Vestry Minutes, 1 June 1889, and St Columba Presbyterian Church Session Minutes, 8 September 1896.
18 St Columba Presbyterian Church Session Minutes, 11-14 July 1911 and 31 August 1913.
19 *Daily Telegraph*, 25 May 1886.
20 See the report of the social in the *Daily Telegraph*, 17 May 1892.
21 Census figures on church attendance for New Zealand 1886-1926 fluctuate between 22% and 34%. Hugh Jackson, 'Churchgoing in Nineteenth-Century New Zealand', *New Zealand Journal of History*, 17, 1, April 1983, pp.43-59. In 1926, the only year with information on the Taradale Town District, local attendance was 35% and the national average was 34%. *Census*, 1886-1926, Places of Worship, numbers attending services.
22 Fairburn, *The Ideal Society and Its Enemies*, p.185; G. T. Bloomfield, *New*

NOTES TO PAGES 98-110

      Zealand: A Handbook of Historical Statistics, Boston, 1984, p.110.
23 St Columba Presbyterian Church Session Minutes, 23 June 1909.
24 Martha Edwards, interviewed Taradale 30 January 1987.
25 In 1919 the Roman Catholic priest announced at Mass that '[s]chool will reopen tomorrow week <u>Monday</u> Feb 3rd - attendance of all children of school age most important. No children within anything like reasonable distance from a Catholic school may be sent to a <u>Godless</u> school - a very serious matter. If necessary sacrifices must be made for the sake of the children's faith.' Meanee Sunday Notices 1918-21, 26 January 1919. Emphasis in original.
26 *New Zealand Methodist,* 16 August 1890.
27 *New Zealand Methodist Times,* 15 November 1913.
28 Emily Jones, interviewed Taradale 29 August 1988.
29 Matthew Silk, interviewed Taradale 2 August 1988.
30 Henry Nolan, interviewed Meanee 14 February 1987.
31 Ernest Edwards, interviewed Napier 5 February 1988.
32 Bridget Tweed, interviewed Napier 12 February 1987.
33 See, for example, the report in *New Zealand Methodist,* 28 November 1891.
34 St Columba Presbyterian Church Session Minutes, 2 May 1919.
35 St Columba Presbyterian Church Bible Class Minute Book, 10 September 1930.
36 H. R. Jackson, *Churches & People in Australia and New Zealand, 1860–1930,* Wellington, 1987, p.164.
37 Louisa Plumb, interviewed Taradale 20 January 1987.
38 Patrick Stevenson, interviewed Taradale 12 February 1988.
39 Sophie Richardson, interviewed Hastings 7 February 1987.
40 Louisa Plumb, interviewed Taradale 20 January 1987.
41 Sophie Richardson, interviewed Hastings 7 February 1987.
42 Patrick Stevenson, interviewed Taradale 12 February 1988. The quotation can be found in Ch. 3.
43 Ownby, *Subduing Satan,* pp.182-93.
44 Michael Roper, interviewed Taradale 10 February 1987.
45 See Joe Lorigan, *The Park Sensations, A story of the Napier Park Racing Club and Famous Greenmeadows,* Napier, 1987, for a detailed narrative of the rise and fall of the Greenmeadows race track and club.
46 See, for example, the advertisement in the *Daily Telegraph,* 7 November 1892.
47 Lorigan, *The Park Sensations,* p.173.
48 See the collection of photographs in Lorigan, *The Park Sensations,* pp.103-5, 108-11.
49 *Daily Telegraph,* 19 November 1888. Many social historians have noted the existence of a monkey walk in other societies. Kathy Peiss, *Cheap Amusements: Working Women and Leisure in Turn-of-the-Century New York,* Philadelphia, 1986, refers to streets in each New York neighbourhood known to the young as places to be seen, p.59; Derek Thompson, 'Courtship and Marriage in Preston Between the Wars', *Oral History,* 3, 2, 1975, pp.39-44, discusses the 'monkey rack' in Preston, pp.42-3; Jerry White, *The Worst Street in North London: Campbell Bunk, Islington, Between The Wars,* London, 1986, locates Campbell Bunk's monkey parade as Seven Sisters Road, p.201.
50 Taradale School Headmaster's Log Book, 5 March 1893.
51 ibid., 6 May 1893.
52 ibid., 8 May 1893.
53 Michael Roper, interviewed Taradale 10 February 1987.
54 Joseph Barnett, interviewed Taradale 26 August 1988.
55 James Green, interviewed Taradale 13 May 1987.
56 Taradale Town Board Minutes, 20 June 1912 and 8 January 1914.

NOTES TO PAGES 110-120

57 N. J. Elliott, 'Anzac, Hollywood and Home: Cinemas and Film-Going in Auckland 1909-1939', MA thesis, University of Auckland, 1989, p.119.
58 ibid., p.88.
59 ibid., p.123.
60 Ellen K. Rothman, *Hands and Hearts: A History of Courtship in America*, New York, 1984, pp.264-6.
61 Margaret Marsh, *Suburban Lives*, New Brunswick, 1990, p.88.
62 See the figures on the rapid growth of radio receiving licenses from the 1920s in Bloomfield, *New Zealand*, p.261.
63 Omaranui Bowling Club Minutes, 24 August 1928 and 19 August 1930.
64 ibid., 29 October 1928 and 15 August 1929.

CHAPTER 7 *Feminine Leisure*

1 On female leisure and respectability see Andrew Davies, *Leisure, Gender and Poverty: Working-Class Culture in Salford and Manchester, 1900-1939*, Buckingham, 1992, pp.61-73, 141, 172.
2 Hannah Field, interviewed Taradale 20 May 1987.
3 Florence Rifle, interviewed Napier 5 February 1988.
4 On gossip as power and community for women see Melanie Tebbutt, 'Women's talk? Gossip and "women's words" in working-class communities, 1880-1939', in Andrew Davies and Steven Fielding, eds, *Worker's Worlds: Cultures and Communities in Manchester and Salford, 1880-1939*, Manchester, 1992, pp.49-73, especially pp.49, 54, 61.
5 Martha Edwards, interviewed Taradale 30 January 1987.
6 In 1892 George Bradley, Taradale's Saddlery Manufactory, advertised 'Ladies', Gents' and Boys' Saddles, Bridles, Breastplates, Bits, Spurs, Whips, and Thongs'. Girls did not even get a look in. *Hawke's Bay and East Coast Almanack and Business Directory for 1892*, Napier, 1891, p.6.
7 AJHR, 1916, E2 Appendix B, p.xviii.
8 Louisa Plumb, interviewed Taradale 20 January 1987.
9 Ernest Edwards, interviewed Napier 5 February 1988.
10 See the Roman Catholic Meanee Sunday Notices 10 August 1919-28 March 1920.
11 Alice Parke, interviewed Greenmeadows 1 September 1988.
12 On knitting and the Great War see Heather Nicholson, *The Loving Stitch: A History of Knitting and Spinning in New Zealand*, Auckland, 1998, Ch. 6.
13 Louisa Plumb, interviewed Taradale 20 January 1987.
14 Hannah Field, interviewed Taradale 20 May 1987. Hannah's brother, James Green, claimed that his mother had no interest in the races.
15 Grace Miner, interviewed Taradale 13 February 1988.
16 Hannah Field, interviewed Taradale 20 May 1987.
17 Joseph Barnett, interviewed Taradale 26 August 1988.
18 There is some evidence that Maori women went to the Taradale Hotel. See Taradale Police Diary of Duty, 17 October 1898.
19 *Daily Telegraph*, 19 February 1900.
20 Taradale Police Diary of Duty, 2 and 26 November 1895.
21 ibid., 1 November 1899.
22 ibid., 23 June 1901.
23 Brian Sutton-Smith, *A History of Children's Play: The New Zealand Playground 1840-1950*, Wellington, 1982, pp.151-280.
24 AJHR, 1890, E-1b, p.19; see also the Taradale School Committee Minutes, 11 July 1891. From 1891 teachers patrolled the Taradale School playground.

25 Library Committee 25 September 1903, General Committee Book, Taradale Town Board Records.
26 *Taradale Town District, By-Laws and Rules of Procedure*, Napier, 1913, p.57.
27 On not challenging parents' authority see Elizabeth Roberts, *A Woman's Place: An Oral History of Working-Class Women, 1890–1940*, Oxford and New York, 1984, p.11; Paul Thompson, 'The War with Adults', *Oral History*, 3, 2, 1975, p.30.
28 Kathleen Thomson, interviewed Napier 8 February 1988.
29 Alice Parke, interviewed Greenmeadows 1 September 1988.
30 Arthur Bishop, interviewed Taradale 30 August 1988.
31 Martha Edwards, interviewed Taradale 30 January 1987.
32 J. Garnham and G. Cowlrick, eds, *Ad Lucem: Napier Girls' High School 1884–1984*, Napier, 1984, pp.48-9, 54.
33 ibid., p.39.
34 Catherine Smith, 'Control of the Female Body: Physical Training at Three New Zealand Girls' High Schools, 1880s–1920s', *Sporting Traditions*, 13, 3, 1997, p.69.
35 *Hawke's Bay Almanack and Directory for 1909*, Napier, 1908, p.103.
36 Taradale School Headmaster's Log Book, 1 July 1908, 13 August 1908 and 31 August 1908.
37 ibid., 22 August 1911.
38 Taradale School Headmaster's Log Book, 23 February 1899 and AJHR, 1902, E-1b, p.20.
39 Taradale School Headmaster's Log Book, 16 March 1920.
40 On the gendered allocation of school space see Ruth Fry, ' "Don't Let Down the Side": Physical Education in the Curriculum for New Zealand Schoolgirls 1900–1945', in Barbara Brookes, Charlotte Macdonald and Margaret Tennant, eds, *Women in History: Essays on European Women in New Zealand*, Wellington, 1986, p.110.
41 In the New Zealand case these arguments are put well in M. A. E. Hammer, '"Something Else in the World to Live For": Sport and the Physical Emancipation of Women and Girls in Auckland 1880–1920', MA thesis, University of Auckland, 1990.
42 Garnham and Cowlrick, *Ad Lucem*, p.49.
43 ibid., pp.51-2, 89.
44 Mary Chamberlain, *Growing Up in Lambeth*, London, 1989, p.68, makes a similar point when discussing adolescent women in London's East End, between the wars.
45 Ellen Store, interviewed Greenmeadows 12 January 1987.
46 Louisa Plumb, interviewed Taradale 20 January 1987.
47 Kathy Peiss, *Cheap Amusements: Working Women and Leisure in Turn-of-the-Century New York*, Philadelphia, 1986, pp.56-76.
48 For the elite and middle class see Fiona McKergow, 'Fashion and Femininity: The Sartorial Experiences of Elite and Middle Class Women in New Zealand, 1905–1928', MA research essay, University of Auckland, 1991. Danielle Sprecher's study of inter-war fashion is not as class-bound, but her sources dictated a more middle- than working-class focus. Danielle Sprecher, 'The Right Appearance: Representations of Fashion, Gender, and Modernity in Inter-war New Zealand, 1918-1939', MA thesis, University of Auckland, 1997.
49 For a similar development among working-class women in London see Sally Alexander, 'Becoming a woman in London in the 1920s and 1930s', in David Feldman and Gareth Stedman Jones, eds, *Metropolis London: Histories and Representations since 1800*, London and New York, 1989, pp.245-71. On

New Zealand women and Hollywood fashions see Sprecher, 'The Right Appearance', pp.94-114.
50 Joseph Barnett, interviewed Taradale, 26 August 1988.
51 St. Columba Presbyterian Church Session Minutes, 27 July 1907 and 2 May 1919.
52 St. Columba Presbyterian Church, Young Women's Bible Class Minute Book, 18 April 1928.
53 Peiss, *Cheap Amusements*, makes a similar point about the heterosocial orientation of working-class women's leisure in turn-of-the-century New York, p.61.
54 Friendly Society Annual Returns, Ancient Order of Foresters, Redclyffe (Taradale), 1909, 1913, 1915, 1926. National Archives, AACS, 537/349b.
55 Friendly Society Annual Returns, Manchester Unity Independent Order of Oddfellows, Meanee (Taradale), 1925, 1927, 1928, 1929, 1930. National Archives, AACS, 537/42b.
56 Mary Ann Clawson, *Constructing Brotherhood: Class, Gender and Fraternalism*, New Jersey, 1989, p.179.
57 Greenmeadows Methodist Church, Greenmeadows Ladies' Guild Minutes, 3 October 1929.
58 ibid., 19 February 1930.
59 See the Greenmeadows Methodist Church, Trustees' Minutes, 14 December 1915 and 15 September 1924.
60 Louisa Plumb, interviewed Taradale 20 January 1987. The Women's Institute was renamed the Country Women's Institute some years after the end of this study.
61 *Home and Country: The Journal of the New Zealand Women's Institutes*, 1 April 1929, p.11; 10 June 1929, p.4.
62 Kathleen Thomson, interviewed Napier 8 February 1988.

CHAPTER 8 *Masculine Leisure*

1 On leisure and men's identity see Andrew Davies, *Leisure, Gender and Poverty: Working-Class Culture in Salford and Manchester, 1900–1939*, Buckingham, 1992, p.30.
2 John Higham, 'The Reorientation of American Culture in the 1890's', in John Weiss, ed., *The Origins of Modern Consciousness*, Detroit, 1965, especially pp.27, 32; E. Anthony Rotundo, 'Body and Soul: Changing Ideals of American Middle-Class Manhood, 1770-1920', *Journal of Social History*, 16, Summer 1983, pp.26, 28; Maurizia Boscagli, *Eye on the Flesh: Fashions of Masculinity in the Early Twentieth Century*, Colorado, 1996, especially Ch. 3.
3 Jock Phillips, *A Man's Country? The Image of the Pakeha Male – A History*, revised ed, Auckland, 1996, Ch. 3.
4 Bruce Kidd, 'Sports and Masculinity', in Michael Kaufman, ed., *Beyond Patriarchy: Essays by Men on Pleasure, Power and Change*, Toronto, 1987, p.255.
5 Taradale School Headmaster's Log Book, 11 July 1907.
6 ibid., 2 November 1917.
7 ibid., see, for example, 14 November 1919, 11 March 1921, 17 March 1922 and 3 November 1922.
8 ibid., 1 July 1908.
9 ibid., see, for example, 12 June 1909, 4 August 1920 and 25 February 1921.
10 ibid., 25 September 1920.
11 ibid., 5 June 1922.
12 ibid., 21 June 1921.
13 James Green, interviewed Taradale 13 May 1987.

14 Margaret Marsh, 'Suburban Men and Masculine Domesticity, 1870-1915', in Mark C. Carnes and Clyde Griffen, eds, *Meanings for Manhood: Constructions of Masculinity in Victorian America*, Chicago and London, 1990, pp.111-27.
15 Hannah Field, interviewed Taradale 20 May 1987.
16 *Daily Telegraph*, 23 May 1893 and 8 June 1893.
17 The first mention of Taradale cricket I have found was in the *Daily Telegraph*, 19 November 1896. The Taradale Hockey Club and the United Hockey Club, Taradale, are listed in the 1907 almanack.
18 For a fuller discussion of club membership see Caroline Daley, 'Gender in the Community: Women and Men in Taradale, 1886-1930', PhD thesis, Victoria University of Wellington, 1992, pp.208-9.
19 *Daily Telegraph*, 7 May 1889.
20 Phillips, *A Man's Country?*, especially Ch. 3.
21 Many of the records of Taradale's pre-1930 sporting bodies were either not retained or were destroyed in the February 1931 earthquake. The following discussion is based on newspaper reports, oral evidence, and extant material from various clubs.
22 Emily Jones, interviewed Taradale 29 August 1988.
23 William Cliff, interviewed Taradale 8 February 1988.
24 See Daley, 'Gender in the Community', pp.205-6, 208-9. On the egalitarian nature of rugby in New Zealand see Phillips, *A Man's Country?*, pp.90-1 and Geoff Fougere, 'Sport, Culture and Identity: The Case of Rugby Football', in David Novitz and Bill Willmott, eds, *Culture and Identity in New Zealand*, Wellington, 1989, pp.113-14.
25 *Hawke's Bay Herald*, 12 November 1890.
26 *Hawke's Bay Herald*, 17 May 1890.
27 Thomas Raven, interviewed Poraite 8 February 1987.
28 *Daily Telegraph*, 15 November 1886.
29 William Cliff, interviewed Taradale 8 February 1988.
30 James Green, interviewed Taradale 13 May 1987.
31 See Taradale Charge Book. The two borstal cases were on 12 January 1926 and 7 October 1930.
32 Taradale Diary of Duty, 4 March 1896.
33 Taradale Diary of Duty, 5 March 1899.
34 Taradale Diary of Duty, 14 November 1900.
35 Taradale Diary of Duty, 10 January and 2 February 1906.
36 Thomas Raven, interviewed Poraite 8 February 1987.
37 Henry Nolan, interviewed Meanee 14 February 1987.
38 Emma Needle, interviewed Napier 9 February 1987.
39 In 1908 an act was passed that made it illegal for a woman to hold a licence unless she was a widow; in 1910 it became illegal to supply liquor to 'any female Native, not being the wife of a person other than a Native'; in 1912 barmaids were made illegal; in 1916, under the War Regulation Amendment Act, women could be prohibited from purchasing liquor. This was based on the belief that lascivious women had been enticing soldiers back into their homes with the promise of alcohol.
40 For a discussion on men's status as consumers in this period see Mark A. Swiencicki, 'Consuming Brotherhood: Men's Culture, Style and Recreation as Consumer Culture, 1880-1930', *Journal of Social History*, 31, 4, 1998, pp.773-808.
41 Jane McNight, interviewed Napier 5 February 1988.
42 Kathleen Thomson, interviewed Napier 8 February 1988.
43 Henry Nolan, interviewed Meanee 14 February 1987.
44 Patrick Stevenson, interviewed Taradale 12 February 1988.

45 Taradale Diary of Duty, 11 November 1920.
46 *Daily Telegraph*, 24 June 1873, 10 July 1873, 14 July 1873, and *Hawke's Bay Herald*, 8 December 1873.
47 *Daily Telegraph*, 20 August 1886 and 17 February 1888.
48 *Daily Telegraph*, 9 August 1897.
49 Taradale Diary of Duty, 3 and 4 April 1918.
50 Fifty of the 124 men were on the electoral roll (40%), and only eight of the men involved owned land (6%).
51 Sharpe was dealing with the Early Modern period. See J. A. Sharpe, 'Enforcing the Law in the Seventeenth-Century English Village', in V. A. C. Gatrell, Bruce Lenman and Geoffrey Parker, eds, *Crime and the Law, The Social History of Crime in Western Europe Since 1500*, London, 1980, p.107.
52 The decision is known for 73 of the 'drunk in public' cases. In 22 instances these were to do with men on the electoral roll; the remaining 51 men had no known ties to the area. Of the 22 locals, 14 were convicted and fined up to £1 and one was fined more than £1, four were convicted and discharged, two were imprisoned, and one had his case dismissed. Of the non-resident men, 20 were convicted and fined up to £1, two were fined over £1, 26 were convicted and discharged, one had his case dismissed, one was convicted and ordered to come up for sentence, and one was remanded.
53 Alice Parke, interviewed Greenmeadows 1 September 1988.
54 Twenty-five men had prohibition orders requested for them. In ten cases the records do not indicate who requested the order, but in seven cases it was the wife, in four cases it was a male relative, in two cases the man himself requested the order, in one case a female relative other than a wife took out the order, and in one case a male friend requested the order.
55 Davies, *Leisure, Gender and Poverty*, p.30.
56 Ted Ownby, *Subduing Satan: Religion, Recreation, and Manhood in the Rural South 1865–1920*, pp.22-3.
57 James Green, interviewed Taradale 13 May 1987. To 'cave it' means to watch out for one another. I am grateful to Anne Else for explaining this to me.
58 George Davies, interviewed Taradale 9 February 1988.
59 Davies, *Leisure, Gender and Poverty*, p.37.
60 Richard Jackson, interviewed Taradale 4 February 1987.
61 P. H. J. H. Gosden, in *Self Help: Voluntary Associations in the Nineteenth Century*, London, 1973, argues that lodges 'owed their origins to the need felt by working men to provide themselves with succour against the poverty and destitution resulting from sickness and death', p.2. A similar argument pervades Nancy Swinburne Renfree, 'Migrants and Cultural Transference: English Friendly Societies in A Victorian Goldfield Town', PhD thesis, La Trobe University, 1983. Renfree argues that the provision of benefits and welfare measures led to the development and strength of the Odd Fellows and Foresters in nineteenth-century Victoria, rather than of non-welfare bodies such as the Masons.
62 Mark C. Carnes, *Secret Ritual and Manhood in Victorian America*, New Haven and London, 1989.
63 The combined figures for the MUIOOF, the AOF, and the HACBS indicate that 117 of 354 new members were minors (33%). The Masons' returns do not consistently give the ages of their members.
64 The combined figures for the MUIOOF, the AOF and the HACBS indicate that 245 of 354 new members were single (69%). The Masons' returns do not indicate marital status.
65 Erik Olssen, *Building the New World: Work, Politics and Society in Caversham 1880s–1920s*, Auckland, 1995, pp.36-8. The occupational categories for the

354 members of Taradale's MUIOOF, AOF and HACBS were:

	No. of Lodge Men	% of Lodge Men	% of All Men
Occupational Group 1	2	–	2
Occupational Group 2	21	6	7
Occupational Group 3	57	16	26
Occupational Group 4	103	29	19
Occupational Group 5	86	24	22
Occupational Group 6	85	24	24

66 Mary Ann Clawson, *Constructing Brotherhood: Class, Gender and Fraternalism*, New Jersey, 1989, has argued this for the American context; see especially p.15.
67 See Clawson, *Constructing Brotherhood*, pp.196-210, for a discussion on how women's auxiliaries in the United States negotiated and accommodated male power.
68 Taradale School Headmaster's Log Book, 15 March 1902.
69 See Taradale School Headmaster's Log Book, 1899-1902, and 1908 onwards, for references to military drill and the cadet corps, and Taradale School Committee Minutes 1901-02, 1908, and 1910, for their comments.
70 Richard Jackson, interviewed Taradale 4 February 1987.
71 *Daily Telegraph*, 22 November 1894.
72 Jeffrey P. Hantover, 'The Boy Scouts and the Validation of Masculinity', in Elizabeth H. Pleck and Joseph H. Pleck, eds, *The American Man*, New Jersey, 1980, pp.285-302.
73 Information regarding the names of office holders came from a variety of sources including town board records, school archives, friendly society annual returns, almanacs, newspaper reports and church archives. The following types of office holders were studied: JPs, Licensing Committees, Rivers Boards, Road Board, Cemeteries Committee, Library Committee, Jockey Club, Dramatic Club, Music Society, Temperance Organisations, Town and Suburban Racing Club, A & P Society, Taradale School Committee, Friendly Society officials, Rugby Club, Rifle Club, Polo Club, Cricket Club, Bowling Club, Hockey Club, Young Men's Mutual Improvement Society, Taradale Town Board, church officials and Great War committee members.
74 David Pearson, *Johnsonville: Continuity and Change in a New Zealand Township*, Sydney, 1980, p.79.
75 Of the 341 men who held the 545 offices, 233 men (68%) held only one office, 67 (20%) held two offices, 17 held three offices, ten held four offices, eight held five offices, one held six offices, two held seven offices, one held eight offices, one held nine offices, and one held ten offices. H. G. Oxley, *Mateship in Local Organization: A Study of Egalitarianism, Stratification, Leadership, and Amenities Projects in a Semi-industrial Community in Inland New South Wales*, St. Lucia, 1974, p.142, makes a similar point about the men holding office in the two townships he studied.
76 The marital status of 289 of the 341 men could be positively identified. Of those 289 men, 225 are known to have been married at the time they first held office, and 64 are known to have been single. For further information and discussion of this, see Daley, 'Gender in the Community', pp.228-30.
77 The age of 244 of the 341 men could be ascertained. Six of these men were minors. The breakdown by age of the remaining 238 is as follows:

Age	No. Office Holding Men	% Office Holding Men	% All Men
20-29	68	29	29
30-39	70	29	25
40-49	67	28	20
50-59	24	10	13
60+	9	4	12

78 The religious orientation of 198 of the 341 men could be identified. Anglicans comprised 46% of the office holders, and 48% of the general male population whose religious orientation is known; Roman Catholics accounted for 19% of the office holders, while 23% of the male population were Catholic; Presbyterians made up 22% of the office holders, and 22% of all males were also Presbyterian; and Methodists made up 12% of the office holders, and 6% of the male population. Other denominations accounted for the remaining 1% of office holders and 1% of the male population. These figures are slightly distorted since one of the categories of office holding considered is church officials. Few RC church officials could be traced. Once the religious orientations of the church officials are removed, the figures are Anglican 49%, RC 24%, Presbyterian 24% and Methodist 3%. In total 136 of the 341 office holding men were landowners (40%). Overall, 511 males owned land (27%). It should be remembered that the figure of 27% is taken from the entire male population, many of whom were too young to be landholders. In terms of occupation the figures are:

Occupation Group	No. of Office Holders	% of Office Holders	% of All Men
Occupation Group 0	8	2	-
Occupation Group 1	21	6	2
Occupation Group 2	37	11	7
Occupation Group 3	119	35	26
Occupation Group 4	74	22	19
Occupation Group 5	51	15	22
Occupation Group 6	31	9	24

For further discussion on these points see Daley, 'Gender in the Community', pp.230-33.

Conclusion

1 Ernest Edwards, interviewed Napier 5 February 1988.
2 For a more extensive refutation of Fairburn's atomisation thesis, see Caroline Daley, 'Gender in the Community: A Study of the Women and Men of the Taradale Area, 1886-1930', PhD thesis, Victoria University of Wellington, 1992, pp.10-16; Caroline Daley, 'Taradale Meets The Ideal Society and Its Enemies', *New Zealand Journal of History*, 25, 2, 1991, pp.129-46.
3 Elizabeth Bott, *Family and Social Networks: Roles, Norms, and External Relationships in Ordinary Urban Families*, 2nd ed, London, 1971, passim.
4 Rollo Arnold, *Settler Kaponga 1881-1914: A Frontier Fragment of the Western World*, Wellington, 1997, pp.308-15.

Bibliography

The bibliography is set out under the following headings:

1. Archival Sources
    a. Unpublished
        I. Private Papers
        II. Non-Government Archives
        III. Government Archives
    b. Published
        I. Official Papers
        II. Published Records and Institutional Publications
        III. Newspapers
        IV. Contemporary Directories and Published Material
2. Non-Archival Sources
    a. Books, Articles and Theses
3. Personal Communications
    a. Interviews

1. ARCHIVAL SOURCES

a. Unpublished

I. Private Papers

Account Book of Mr George Ridley's Wife, Private Collection
History of All Saints' Parish by Miss F. E. Davis, Private Collection
Notes by Mr W. B. Davis, Taradale Archive, Taradale Public Library
Some Early History of Taradale by W. B. Davis, Taradale Archive, Taradale Public Library
Taradale Country Women's Institute Highlights Through the Years, July 1925–1969 by Violet Seager, Taradale Country Women's Institute Collection
The History of Taradale by Zelma Hunt, Hawke's Bay Art Gallery and Museum Library, Napier

II. Non-Government Archives

All Saints Anglican Church Archives, Taradale:
    All Saints Sunday School Minute Book 1885–1898, SS1
    All Saints Vestry Minute Book 1882–1899, M3
    All Saints Vestry Minute Book 1900–1911, M4

BIBLIOGRAPHY

All Saints Vestry Minute Book 1923–1944, M5
List of Communicants 1885–1890, Folio 6
List of Members of the Church of England Contributing to the Stipend of All
   Saints Parish, Taradale, June 1893–1896, December 1896–1898, Folio 6

Greenmeadows Methodist Church Archives, Methodist Archives, Christchurch:
   Greenmeadows Members Roll 1910–1915, 5014
   Greenmeadows Ladies' Guild Minutes 1929–1931, 5014 (1)
   Register of Trustees, Volume 1—Trustees, Greenmeadows, 1888–1928
   Trustees' Minutes, 1915–1930

Hawke's Bay Education Board Archives, Napier:
   Annual Examination Reports, Taradale School 1915–1929
   Inspector's Report, Taradale School 1915–1926
   Inspector's Report, Meanee School 1894

Hawke's Bay Hospital Board Archives, Napier:
   Hawke's Bay and Waipawa Hospital and Charitable Aid Board for Hawke's Bay
      Old People's Home, Parke Island, Minutes 1910–31
   Hawke's Bay Hospital and Charitable Aid Board Finance Board Minutes
      1910–1917
   Hawke's Bay Hospital and Charitable Aid Board 'Levies' on Local Bodies 1910
   Hawke's Bay Hospital and Charitable Aid Board Minutes 1910–1923
   Register of Patients
   United Districts Charitable Aid Board Minutes 1893–1900
   United Districts Charitable Aid Board Minutes 1900–1907
   United Districts Charitable Aid Board Minutes 1907–1910
   Waipawa and Hawke's Bay Charitable Aid Board Minutes 1885–1892

Lodge Omaranui (Freemasons) Archives, Taradale:
   Lodge Omaranui No. 216 Registration Book 1920–30

Omaranui Bowling Club Archives, Taradale:
   Minutes 1927–1930

New Zealand Biographies, Alexander Turnbull Library, Wellington

Roman Catholic Archives, Cerdon, Wellington:
   Diary of Mr Anderson, 1894–1903, DNM 8
   Meanee Sunday Notices 1918–1920, DNM 2/12
   Meanee Sunday Notices 1920–1923, DNM 2/13
   Meanee Sunday Notices 1930, DNM 2/14
   Register of the Association in Honor of the Sacred Heart of Jesus established at
      Meanee During the Mission ending 25th of September 1894, ACC 21
   Reignier I (Box), 208/20

St Columba Presbyterian Church Taradale Archives, Hawke's Bay Art Gallery and
   Museum Library, Napier:
   Bible Class Minute Book 1929–1933
   Ladies Guild Minutes 1909–1913
   Ledger 1908–1937
   Ledger Relating to Minister's Stipend 1908–1925
   Managers Minute Book 1905–1912

BIBLIOGRAPHY

    Managers Minute Book 1912–1945
    Miscellaneous Loose Papers Re Church Finances 1908–1937
    Session Minutes 1895–1920
    Sunday School Minutes 1913–1938
    Young Women's Bible Class Minute Book 1926–1928

Taradale School Archives, Taradale:
    Taradale School Committee Minutes 1889–1918, 1925–1930
    Taradale School Headmaster's Log Book 1886–1924, 1928–30

Taradale Town Board Records, Napier City Council Archives:
    Church of England Cemetery Committee Minute Book 1885–1940
    Finance Committee Minutes 1917–1918
    General Committee Book 1897–1934
    Library Committee Minutes 1897–1904
    Lighting and Sanitation Committee Minutes 1918–1924
    Parks Committee Minutes 1918–1922
    Taradale Town Board Minutes 1886–1930
    Taradale Tramway Committee Minutes 1914–1915
    Town Hall and Library Committee Minutes 1918
    Works Committee Minutes 1917–1918

III. Government Archives

Friendly Societies Annual Returns, National Archives:
    Ancient Order of Foresters Annual Returns, Redclyffe (Taradale), 1886–1945, AACS, 537/349b
    Hibernian Australasian Catholic Benefit Society Annual Returns, St Patrick's (Meanee), 1910–1916, AACS, 537/613b
    Manchester Unity Independent Order of Odd Fellows Annual Returns, Meanee (Taradale), 1884–1954, AACS, 537/42b

Justice Department, Napier:
    Birth Records 1886–1930
    Death Records 1886–1930

Justice Files, National Archives:
    Napier Probates 1886–1930
    Testamentary Register, Napier 1876–1930, AAEC 638 74–78

Police Records, Taradale, National Archives:
    Charge Book 1909–1925, P TDL 3/1
    Crime Book 1899–1959, P TDL 6/1
    Diary of Duty 1888–1926, P TDL 2/1–9
    Summons Book 1891–1930, P TDL 4/1–2

Registrar General, Lower Hutt:
    Marriage Records 1886–1930

Valuation Rolls, National Archives:
    Taradale Borough 1.4.1905–31.3.1908, W1089, 2/32 Volume 1
    Taradale Borough 1.4.1908–31.3.1918, W1089, 2/32 Volumes 1 and 2
    Taradale Borough 1.4.1918–31.3.1934, W1089, 2/32 Volume 1

BIBLIOGRAPHY

b. Published

I. Official Papers

Appendices to the Journal of the House of Representatives, 1886–1930
A Return of the Freeholders of New Zealand, October 1882, Wellington, 1884
Census of New Zealand, 1886–1936
New Zealand Gazette, 1886–1930
New Zealand Official Year Book, 1893–1930
Statistics of New Zealand, 1886–1920

II. Published Records and Institutional Publications

1875–1975, A Century of Faith and Witness, All Saints' Parish, Taradale, Napier, 1976
Greenmeadows Methodist Church, 75th Anniversary 1888–1963, Napier, 1963
Lodge Omaranui No. 216: 50th Jubilee 1920–1970, Napier, 1970
Looking Backward Down the Years: Centennial History of St Columba Parish, Taradale, 1866–1966, Hastings, 1966
Otatara Pa Historical Reserve, Napier, 1983
St Marks Methodist Church, Greenmeadows–Napier, 1888–1988, Napier, 1988
Taradale CWI 60th Anniversary 1925–1985, Taradale, 1985
Taradale Rugby Football Club (Inc.) 75th Jubilee, 1898–1973, Napier, 1973
Taradale Town District, By-Laws and Rules of Procedure, Napier, 1913
Taradale Town District Jubilee 1886–1936, Souvenir Booklet, Napier, 1936
The Narrative of the Plains, Napier, n. d. (c.1919)
The Story of the Napier Police District, Waipukurau, 1986

III. Newspapers

Advocate, 1894–1900
Daily Telegraph, 1873, 1884, 1886–1930
Hawke's Bay Herald, 1873, 1876, 1885–1904
Home and Country: The Journal of the New Zealand Women's Institutes, 1929
Methodist Times, 1911–1916
New Zealand Methodist, 1888–1894
New Zealand Methodist Times, 1913–1914
Outlook, 1904–1909
Tablet, 1894

IV. Contemporary Directories and Published Materials

East Coast and Hawke's Bay Streets, Alphabetical and Trades' Directory, 1896, Napier, 1895
Harding's New Zealand Almanac, 1887–90, Napier, 1886–89
Harding's New Zealand Almanac; Diary, Year Book: East Coast Directory and Local Guide, 1886, Napier, 1885
Hawke's Bay Almanack and Business Directory for 1886, Napier, 1885
Hawke's Bay Almanack and Business Directory for 1889, Napier, 1888
Hawke's Bay Almanack and Business Directory for 1890, Napier, 1889
Hawke's Bay Almanack and Business Directory for 1894–98, Napier, 1893–98
Hawke's Bay Almanack and Directory for 1894, Napier, 1893
Hawke's Bay Almanack and Directory for 1896, Napier, 1895
Hawke's Bay Almanack and Directory for 1899, Napier, 1898
Hawke's Bay Almanack and Directory for 1900, Napier, 1899

BIBLIOGRAPHY

Hawke's Bay Almanack and Directory for 1905, Napier, 1904
Hawke's Bay Almanack and Directory for 1907–10, Napier, 1906–9
Hawke's Bay Almanack and Directory for 1913–16, Napier, 1912–15
Hawke's Bay Almanack and Directory for 1918, Napier, 1917
Hawke's Bay Almanack and Directory for 1920, Napier, 1919
Hawke's Bay Almanack and Directory for 1922–25, Napier, 1921–24
Hawke's Bay Almanack and Directory for 1927, Napier, 1926
Hawke's Bay Almanack and Directory for 1929, Napier, 1928
Hawke's Bay Almanack and Directory for 1930, Napier, 1929
Hawke's Bay and East Coast Almanack and Business Directory for 1891–93, Napier, 1890–92
Hawke's Bay Electoral Roll, 1887
Industries of New Zealand (Illustrated): An Historical and Commercial Review, Descriptive and Biographical, Facts, Figures and Illustrations. An Epitome of Progress: Business Men and Commercial Interests, Auckland, 1898
Napier and Hawke's Bay Streets, Alphabetical and Trades Directory, 1893–94, Napier, 1893
Napier Electoral Rolls, 1893–1928
The Cyclopaedia of New Zealand, Volume Six, Christchurch, 1908
Wise's Street Directory, 1885–1886
Wise's Street Directory, 1887–1888

2. NON-ARCHIVAL SOURCES

a. Books, Articles and Theses

Alexander, Sally, 'Becoming a woman in London in the 1920s and 1930s', in David Feldman and Gareth Stedman Jones, eds, *Metropolis London: Histories and Representations since 1800*, London and New York, 1989

Arnold, Rollo, 'Community in Rural Victorian New Zealand', *New Zealand Journal of History*, 24, 1, 1990, pp.3–21

Arnold, Rollo, *Settler Kaponga 1881–1914: A Frontier Fragment of the Western World*, Wellington, 1997

Bloomfield, G. T., *New Zealand: A Handbook of Historical Statistics*, Boston, 1984

Bock, Gisela, 'Women's History and Gender History: Aspects of an International Debate', *Gender & History*, 1, 1, Spring 1989, pp.7–30

Boscagli, Maurizia, *Eye on the Flesh: Fashions of Masculinity in the Early Twentieth Century*, Colorado, 1996

Bott, Elizabeth, *Family and Social Network: Roles, Norms, and External Relationships in Ordinary Urban Families*, 2nd ed, London, 1971

Boylan, Anne M., 'Growing Up Female in Young America, 1800–1860', in Joseph M. Hawes and N. Ray Hiner, eds, *American Childhood: A Research Guide and Historical Handbook*, Westport, Conn., 1985

Bradley, Harriet, *Men's Work, Women's Work: A Sociological History of the Sexual Division of Labour in Employment*, Cambridge, 1989

Brod, Harry, ed., *The Making of Masculinities: The New Men's Studies*, Boston, 1987

Brookes, Barbara, Charlotte Macdonald, and Margaret Tennant, eds, *Women in History: Essays on European Women in New Zealand*, Wellington, 1986

Brookes, Barbara, Charlotte Macdonald, and Margaret Tennant, eds, *Women in History 2*, Wellington, 1992

Butler, Judith, *Gender Trouble: Feminism and the Subversion of Identity*, London and New York, 1990

Butler, Judith, *Bodies That Matter: On the Discursive Limits of 'Sex'*, London and New York, 1993

Carnes, Mark C. and Clyde Griffen, eds, *Meanings For Manhood: Constructions of*

Masculinity in Victorian America, Chicago, 1990
Carnes, Mark C., *Secret Ritual and Manhood in Victorian America*, New Haven and London, 1989
Carrigan, Tim, Bob Connell, and John Lee, 'Towards a New Sociology of Masculinity', in Harry Brod, ed., *The Making of Masculinities: The New Men's Studies*, Boston, 1992
Chamberlain, Mary and Ruth Richardson, 'Life and Death', *Oral History*, 11, 1, 1983, pp.31–43
Chamberlain, Mary, *Growing Up in Lambeth*, London, 1989
Clawson, Mary Ann, *Constructing Brotherhood: Class, Gender and Fraternalism*, New Jersey, 1989
Coney, Sandra, ed., *Standing in the Sunshine: A History of New Zealand Women Since they Won the Vote*, Auckland, 1993
Cowan, Ruth Schwartz, *More Work for Mother: The Ironies of Household Technology from the Open Hearth to the Microwave*, London, 1989
Daley, Caroline, 'Gender in the Community: Women and Men in Taradale, 1886–1930', PhD thesis, Victoria University of Wellington, 1992
Daley, Caroline, '"He would know but I just have a feeling": Gender and Oral History', *Women's History Review*, 7, 3, 1998, pp.343–59
Daley, Caroline, 'Taradale Meets The Ideal Society and Its Enemies', *New Zealand Journal of History*, 25, 2, 1991, pp.129–46
Dalziel, Raewyn, 'The Colonial Helpmeet: Women's Role and the Vote in Nineteenth-Century New Zealand', *New Zealand Journal of History*, 11, 2, 1977, pp. 112–23
Dalziel, Raewyn, 'Emigration and Kinship: Migrants to New Plymouth 1840–1843', *New Zealand Journal of History*, 25, 2, 1991, pp.112–28
Davies, Andrew, *Leisure, Gender and Poverty: Working-Class Culture in Salford and Manchester, 1900–1939*, Buckingham, 1992
Edmond, Lauris, *Hot October: An Autobiographical Story*, Wellington, 1989
Ehrenreich, Barbara, *The Hearts of Men: American Dreams and the Flight from Commitment*, London, 1983
Elliott, N. J., 'Anzac, Hollywood and Home: Cinemas and Film-Going in Auckland 1909–1939', MA thesis, University of Auckland, 1989
Else, Anne, ed., *Women Together: A History of Women's Organisations in New Zealand/Nga Ropu Wahine o te Motu*, Wellington, 1993
Fairburn, Miles, *The Ideal Society and its Enemies: The Foundations of Modern New Zealand Society 1850–1900*, Auckland, 1989
Faragher, John Mack, 'History From The Inside-Out: Writing the History of Women in Rural America', *American Quarterly*, 33, 5, 1981, pp.537–57
Faragher, John Mack, *Sugar Creek: Life on the Illinois Prairie*, New Haven, 1986
Fields, Valerie, ed., *Women as Mothers in Pre-Industrial England*, London, 1990
Fougere, Geoff, 'Sport, Culture and Identity: The Case of Rugby Football', in David Novitz and Bill Willmott, eds, *Culture and Identity in New Zealand*, Wellington, 1989
Fry, Ruth, '"Don't Let Down the Side": Physical Education in the Curriculum for New Zealand Schoolgirls 1900–1945', in Barbara Brookes, Charlotte Macdonald and Margaret Tennant, eds, *Women in History: Essays on European Women in New Zealand*, Wellington, 1986
Fry, Ruth, *It's Different for Daughters: A History of the Curriculum for Girls In New Zealand Schools, 1900–1975*, Wellington, 1985
Garnham, J. and G. Cowlrick, eds, *Ad Lucem: Napier Girls' High School 1884–1984*, Napier, 1984
Gibbons, Peter, 'Non-fiction', in Terry Sturm, ed., *The Oxford History of New Zealand Literature in English*, Auckland, 1991
Gittins, Diana G., 'Marital Status, Work and Kinship, 1850–1930', in Jane Lewis, ed., *Labour and Love: Women's Experience of Home and Family 1850–1940*, Oxford, 1986

BIBLIOGRAPHY

Gosden, P. H. J. H., *Self Help: Voluntary Associations in the Nineteenth Century*, London, 1973

Groneman, Carol and Mary Beth Norton, 'Introduction', in Carol Groneman and Mary Beth Norton, eds, *'To Toil the Livelong Day' America's Women at Work, 1780–1980*, Ithaca and London, 1987

Gundersen, Joan R., 'The Local Parish as a Female Institution: The Experience of All Saints Episcopal Church in Frontier Minnesota', *Church History*, 55, 3, 1986, pp.307–22

Hammer, M. A. E., '"Something Else in the World to Live For" Sport and the Physical Emancipation of Women and Girls in Auckland 1880–1920', MA thesis, University of Auckland, 1990

Hantover, Jeffrey P., 'The Boy Scouts and the Validation of Masculinity', in Elizabeth H. and Joseph H. Pleck, eds, *The American Man*, New Jersey, 1980

Hardyment, Christina, *From Mangle to Microwave: The Mechanization of Household Work*, Cambridge, 1988

Higham, John, 'The Reorientation of American Culture in the 1890's', in John Weiss, ed., *The Origins of Modern Consciousness*, Detroit, 1965

Hoff, Joan, 'Gender as a Postmodern Category of Paralysis', *Women's History Review*, 3, 2, 1994, pp.149–68

Jackson, H. R., *Churches & People in Australia and New Zealand, 1860–1930*, Wellington, 1987

Jackson, Hugh, 'Churchgoing in Nineteenth-Century New Zealand', *New Zealand Journal of History*, 17, 1, 1983, pp.43–59

James, Bev and Kay Saville-Smith, *Gender, Culture and Power: Challenging New Zealand's Gendered Culture*, revised ed, Auckland, 1994

Jensen, Joan M., 'Cloth, Butter and Boarders: Women's Household Production for the Market', *Review of Radical Political Economics*, 12, 2, 1980, pp.14–24

Katz, Michael B., *The People of Hamilton, Canada West: Family and Class in a Mid-Nineteenth-Century City*, Cambridge, 1975

Kaufman, Michael, ed., *Beyond Patriarchy: Essays by Men on Pleasure, Power and Change*, Toronto, 1987

Kerber, Linda K., 'Separate Spheres, Female Worlds, Woman's Place: The Rhetoric of Women's History', *Journal of American History*, 75, June 1988, pp.9–39

Kidd, Bruce, 'Sports and Masculinity', in Michael Kaufman, ed., *Beyond Patriarchy: Essays by Men on Pleasure, Power and Change*, Toronto, 1987

Kimmel, Michael S., 'The Contemporary "Crisis" of Masculinity in Historical Perspective', in Harry Brod, ed., *The Making of Masculinities: The New Men's Studies*, Boston, 1987

Lake, Marilyn, 'Helpmeet, Slave, Housewife: Women in Rural Families 1870–1930', in Patricia Grimshaw, Chris McConville and Ellen McEwen, eds, *Families in Colonial Australia*, Sydney, 1985

LaRossa, Ralph, *The Modernization of Fatherhood: A Social and Political History*, Chicago and London, 1997

Lazerow, Jama, 'Religion and the New England Mill Girl: A New Perspective on an Old Theme', *New England Quarterly*, 60, 3, 1987, pp.429–53

Levesque, Andree, 'Prescribers and Rebels: Attitudes to European Women's Sexuality in New Zealand, 1860–1916', in Barbara Brookes, Charlotte Macdonald and Margaret Tennant, eds, *Women in History: Essays on European Women in New Zealand*, Wellington, 1986

Levi, Giovanni, 'On Microhistory', in Peter Burke, ed., *New Perspectives on Historical Writing*, Cambridge, 1991

Lorigan, Joe, *The Park Sensations: A Story of the Napier Park Racing Club and Famous Greenmeadows*, Napier, 1987

Macdonald, Charlotte, *A Woman of Good Character: Single Women as Immigrant Settlers* in *Nineteenth-Century New Zealand*, Wellington, 1990

Marsh, Margaret, 'Suburban Men and Masculine Domesticity, 1870–1915', in Mark C. Carnes and Clyde Griffen, eds, *Meanings for Manhood: Constructions of Masculinity in Victorian America*, Chicago and London, 1990

Marsh, Margaret, *Suburban Lives*, New Brunswick, 1990

Matthews, Glenna, *"Just a Housewife": The Rise and Fall of Domesticity in America*, New York and Oxford, 1987

Matthews, Jill Julius, *Good and Mad Women: The Historical Construction of Femininity in Twentieth-Century Australia*, Sydney, 1984

McGeorge, Colin, 'How Katy Did at School', *New Zealand Journal of Educational Studies*, 22, 1, 1987, pp.101–11

McGeorge, Colin, 'School Attendance and Child Labour 1890–1914', *Historical News*, 46, May 1983, pp.17–20

McGeorge, Colin, 'Schools and Socialisation in New Zealand 1890–1914', PhD thesis, University of Canterbury, 1985

McKergow, Fiona, 'Fashion and Femininity: The Sartorial Experiences of Elite and Middle Class Women in New Zealand, 1905–1928', MA research essay, University of Auckland, 1991

Mein Smith, Philippa, *Maternity in Dispute, New Zealand 1920–1939*, Wellington, 1986

Mein Smith, Philippa, 'Truby King in Australia: A Revisionist View of Reduced Infant Mortality', *New Zealand Journal of History*, 22, 1, 1988, pp.23–43

Modell, John and Tamara K. Hareven, 'Urbanization and the Malleable Household: An Examination of Boarding and Lodging in American Families', *Journal of Marriage and the Family*, 35, 3, 1973, pp.467–79

Molloy, Maureen, *Those Who Speak to the Heart: The Nova Scotian Scots at Waipu 1854–1920*, Palmerston North, 1991

Mooney, Kay, *History of the County of Hawke's Bay: Part II*, Napier, n. d. (c.1974)

Morgan, David H. J., *Discovering Men*, London and New York, 1992

Munro, Jessie, *The Story of Suzanne Aubert*, Auckland, 1996

Nicholson, Heather, *The Loving Stitch: A History of Knitting and Spinning in New Zealand*, Auckland, 1998

Nicol, John, *The Technical Schools of New Zealand: An Historical Survey*, Wellington, 1940

O'Sullivan, Kitty, *The Curse of the Greenstone Tiki*, Auckland, n.d. (c.1945)

Olssen, Erik, *Building the New World: Work, Politics and Society in Caversham 1880s–1920s*, Auckland, 1995

Olssen, Erik, 'Towards a New Society', in Geoffrey W. Rice, ed., *The Oxford History of New Zealand*, 2nd ed, Auckland, 1992

Olssen, Erik, 'Women, Work and Family: 1880–1926' in Phillida Bunkle and Beryl Hughes, eds, *Women in New Zealand Society*, Auckland, 1980

Olssen, Erik and Andree Levesque, 'Towards a History of the European Family in New Zealand', in Peggy G. Koopman-Boyden, ed., *Families in New Zealand Society*, Wellington, 1978

Osterud, Nancy Grey, *Bonds of Community: The Lives of F arm Women in Nineteenth-Century New York*, Ithaca and London, 1991

Ownby, Ted, *Subduing Satan: Religion, Recreation, and Manhood in the Rural South, 1865–1920*, Chapel Hill, 1990

Oxley, H. G., *Mateship in Local Organization: A Study of Egalitarianism, Stratification, Leadership, and Amenities Projects in a Semi-industrial Community in Inland New South Wales*, St. Lucia, 1974

Park, Roberta J., 'Biological thought, athletics and the formation of a "man of character", 1830–1900', in J. A. Mangan and James Walvin, eds, *Manliness and Morality: Middle-Class Masculinity in Britain and America 1800–1940*, New York, 1987

BIBLIOGRAPHY

Passerini, Luisa, *Fascism In Popular Memory: The Cultural Experience of the Turin Working Class*, Cambridge, 1987

Paxton, C. T., 'Childhood in New Zealand, 1862–1921: Child Labour and the Gradual Popular Acceptance of Primary School Attendance', MA thesis, University of Auckland, 1987

Pearson, David G., *Johnsonville: Continuity and Change in a New Zealand Township*, Sydney, 1980

Peiss, Kathy, *Cheap Amusements: Working Women and Leisure in Turn-of-the-Century New York*, Philadelphia, 1986

Penn, Donna, 'Queer: Theorizing Politics and History', *Radical History Review*, 62, 1995, pp.24–42

Phillips, Jock, *A Man's Country? The Image of the Pakeha Male—A History*, revised ed, Auckland, 1996

Pollock, Linda A., *A Lasting Relationship: Parents and Children Over Three Centuries*, Hanover, 1987

Popular Memory Group, 'Popular Memory: Theory, Politics, Method', in Richard Johnson, Gregor McLennan, Bill Schwarz and David Sutton, eds, *Making Histories: Studies in History Writing and Politics*, London, 1982

Portelli, Alessandro, 'The Peculiarities of Oral History', *History Workshop Journal*, 12, 1981, pp.98–107

Ramazanoglu, Caroline, 'What Can You Do With a Man? Feminism and the Critical Appraisal of Masculinity', *Women's Studies International Forum*, 15, 3, 1992, pp.339–50

Reay, Barry, *Microhistories: Demography, Society and Culture in Rural England, 1800–1930*, Cambridge, 1996

Renfree, Nancy Swinburne, 'Migrants and Cultural Transference: English Friendly Societies in a Victorian Goldfield Town', PhD thesis, La Trobe University, 1983

Riley, Denise, *"Am I That Name?" Feminism and the Category of 'Woman' in History*, Minneapolis, 1988

Roberts, Elizabeth, *A Woman's Place: An Oral History of Working Class Women 1890–1940*, Oxford, 1984

Ross, Ellen, 'Survival Networks: Women's Neighbourhood Sharing in London Before World War I', *History Workshop Journal*, 15, Spring 1983, pp.4–27

Rothman, Ellen K., *Hands and Hearts: A History of Courtship in America*, New York, 1984

Rotundo, E. Anthony, *American Manhood: Transformations in Masculinity from the Revolution to the Modern Era*, New York, 1993

Rotundo, E. Anthony, 'Body and Soul: Changing Ideals of American Middle-Class Manhood, 1770–1920', *Journal of Social History*, 16, Summer 1983, pp.23–38

Rotundo, E. Anthony, 'Boy Culture: Middle-Class Boyhood in Nineteenth-Century America', in Mark C. Carnes, and Clyde Griffen, eds, *Meanings For Manhood: Constructions of Masculinity in Victorian America*, Chicago, 1990

Ryan, Mary P., *Cradle of the Middle Class: The Family in Oneida County, New York, 1790–1865*, Cambridge, 1981

Samuel, Raphael, 'Local History and Oral History', *History Workshop Journal*, 1, 1976, pp.191–208

Samuel, Raphael, ed., *People's History and Socialist Theory*, London, 1981

Scott, Joan W., 'Gender: A Useful Category of Historical Analysis', *American Historical Review*, 91, 5, 1986, pp.1053–75

Scott, Joan Wallach, *Gender and the Politics of History*, New York, 1988.

Seccombe, Wally, 'Patriarchy stabilized: the construction of the male breadwinner wage norm in nineteenth-century Britain', *Social History*, 11, 1, 1986, pp.53–76

Segal, Lynne, *Slow Motion: Changing Masculinities, Changing Men*, New Brunswick, 1990

Segalen, Martine, *Love and Power in the Peasant Family: Rural France in the Nineteenth Century*, London, 1983

BIBLIOGRAPHY

Sharpe, J. A., 'Enforcing the Law in the Seventeenth-Century English Village', in V. A. C. Gatrell, Bruce Lenman, and Geoffrey Parker, eds, *Crime and the Law: The Social History of Crime in Western Europe Since 1500*, London, 1980

Smith, Catherine, 'Control of the Female Body: Physical Training at Three New Zealand Girls' High Schools, 1880s–1920s', *Sporting Traditions*, 13, 3 1997, pp.59–71

Smith-Rosenberg, Caroll, 'The Female World of Love and Ritual: Relations Between Women in Nineteenth-Century America', *Signs*, 1, 1, Autumn 1975, pp.1–27

Smith-Rosenberg, Caroll, *Disorderly Conduct: Visions of Gender in Victorian America*, New York, 1985

Somerset, H. C. D., *Littledene: Patterns of Change*, Wellington, 1974

Sprecher, Danielle, 'The Right Appearance: Representations of Fashion, Gender, and Modernity in Inter-war New Zealand', MA thesis, University of Auckland, 1997

Springhall, John, *Youth, Empire and Society: British Youth Movements, 1883–1940*, London, 1977

Springhall, John, *Coming of Age: Adolescence in Britain 1860–1960*, Dublin, 1986

Strasser, Susan, *Never Done: A History of American Housework*, New York, 1982

Sutton-Smith, Brian, *A History of Children's Play: the New Zealand Playground 1840–1950*, Wellington, 1982

Swiencicki, Mark A., 'Consuming Brotherhood: Men's Culture, Style and Recreation as Consumer Culture, 1880–1930', *Journal of Social History*, 31, 4, 1998, pp.773–808

Tebbutt, Melanie, 'Women's talk? Gossip and "women's words" in working-class communities, 1880–1939', in Andrew Davies and Steven Fielding, eds, *Worker's Worlds: Cultures and Communities in Manchester and Salford, 1880–1939*, Manchester, 1992

Tennant, Margaret, 'Natural Directions: The New Zealand Movement for Sexual Differentiation in Education During the Early Twentieth Century', in Barbara Brookes, Charlotte Macdonald and Margaret Tennant, eds, *Women in History: Essays on European Women in New Zealand*, Wellington, 1986

Tennant, Margaret, *Paupers and Providers: Charitable Aid in New Zealand*, Wellington, 1989

Thernstrom, Stephan, *The Other Bostonians: Poverty and Progress in the American Metropolis, 1880–1970*, Cambridge, 1973

Thompson, Derek, 'Courtship and Marriage in Preston Between the Wars', *Oral History*, 3, 2, Autumn 1975, pp.39–44

Thompson, Paul, *The Voice of the Past: Oral History*, 2nd ed, Oxford, 1988

Thompson, Paul, 'The War With Adults', *Oral History*, 3, 2, Autumn 1975, pp.29–38

Thomson, David, *A World Without Welfare: New Zealand's Colonial Experiment*, Auckland, 1998

Thorp, J. M., *The History of Tiffen Lodge, Avenue Road, Greemeadows, Hawke's Bay*, Napier, 1971

Tilly, Louise A. and Joan W. Scott, *Women, Work, and Family*, New York, 1978

Toynbee, Claire, *Her Work and His: Family, Kin and Community in New Zealand 1900–1930*, Wellington, 1995

Vigne, Thea, 'Parents and Children 1890–1918: Distance and Dependence', *Oral History*, 3, 2, Autumn 1975, pp.6–13

Walvin, James, *A Child's World: A Social History of English Childhood 1800–1914*, Harmondsworth, 1982

Welter, Barbara, 'The Cult of True Womanhood: 1820–1860', *American Quarterly*, 18, 2, Part 1, Summer 1966, pp.151–74

White, Jerry, *Rothschild Buildings: Life in an East End Tenement Block 1887–1920*, London, 1980

White, Jerry, *The Worst Street in North London: Campbell Bunk, Islington, Between The Wars*, London, 1986

BIBLIOGRAPHY

Wilson, Adrian, 'The Ceremony of Childbirth and Its Interpretation', in Valerie Fields, ed., *Women as Mothers in Pre-Industrial England: Essays in Memory of Dorothy McLaren*, London and New York, 1990
Wilson, J. G., *History of Hawke's Bay*, Dunedin and Wellington, 1939
Wimshurst, Kerry, 'Child Labour and School Attendance in South Australia 1890–1915', *Historical Studies*, 19, 1981, pp.388–411
Wright, Matthew, *Hawke's Bay: The History of a Province*, Palmerston North, 1994
Young, Michael and Willmott, Peter, *Family and Kinship in East London*, Routledge & Kegan Paul, London, 1957

3. PERSONAL COMMUNICATIONS

a. Interviews

Joseph Barnett, Taradale, 26 August 1988
Arthur Bishop, Taradale, 30 August 1988
William Cliff, Taradale, 8 February 1988
George Davies, Taradale, 9 February 1988
Ernest Edwards, Napier, 5 February 1988
Martha Edwards, Taradale, 30 January 1987
Hannah Field, Taradale, 20 May 1987
James Green, Taradale, 13 May 1987
Charles Horse, Taradale, 1 and 3 February 1988
Fred Jackson, Taradale, 16 February 1988
Richard Jackson, Taradale, 4 February 1987
Emily Jones, Taradale, 29 August 1988
Edward McLean, Greenmeadows, 21 January 1987
Jane McNight, Napier, 5 February 1988
Philip Manners, Taradale, 10 February 1987
Grace Miner, Taradale, 13 February 1988
Emma Needle, Napier, 9 February 1987
Henry Nolan, Meanee, 14 February 1987
Alice Parke, Greenmeadows, 1 September 1988
Ann Pearce, Taradale, 11 February 1987
Eliza Peterson, Awatoto, 22 January 1987
Louisa Plumb, Taradale, 20 January 1987
Theresa Pond, Greenmeadows, 3 February 1987
Sophie Richardson, Hastings, 7 February 1987
Florence Rifle, Napier, 5 February 1988
Thomas Raven, Poraite, 8 February 1987
Michael Roper, Taradale, 10 February 1987
Charlotte Rose, Taradale, 16 January 1987
Matthew Silk, Taradale, 2 September 1988
Harriet South, Taradale, 19 January 1987
Patrick Stevenson, Taradale, 12 February 1988
Sarah Stevenson, Taradale, 15 and 16 February 1988
Ellen Store, Greenmeadows, 12 January 1987
Kathleen Thomson, Napier, 8 February 1988
Bridget Tweed, Napier, 12 February 1987

Index

A Man's Country?, 4
A Woman of Good Character, 3
adoption, 20, 107
Ah Keong, W., 138, 156
alcohol *see* crime: alcohol related, drinking, hotels
Alley, Henry, 7, 8, 12
Anderson, Francis, 77, 136
Anderson, Sidney, 36, 37, 77, 136, 153
Arnold, Rollo, 33, 162

Badley, Duncan Le Quesne, 19
bankruptcy, 41-2, 82, 90
Barnett, Joseph, 93, 108, 119, 168
Barnes, Billy, 88
Bartlett, James, 94, 96
Bartlett, Jane (née Gilmour), 94
Baylis, Elsie, 70
Baylis, Frank, 70
Beatson, Mr, 37
Bennett, Frank, 44
birth, 9, 13-21, 42, 59-61
Bishop, Arthur, 121, 168-9
Blackmore, John, 81
Bock, Gisela, 5
Boer War, 6
Boland, Eliza, 21
Boland, Gladys Lilian, 21
Boland, James junior, 21
Boland, James senior, 21
Boland, Johanna, 21
Boland, Margaret, 21
Boland, Rose, 21
Bott, Elizabeth, 159
Bourke, Charles O'Donnell, 41
boy scouts, 93, 155, 158
Bradley, George, 148
Bradley, Harriet, 40
Brown, Henry, 153
Brown, Howard, 153
Brown, Philip, 153
Brown, William, 152, 153
Bryon, Charlotte, 42

Bryon, John, 42
Burness, Miss, 67
Burr, Alf, 155
Butler, Judith, 5
Button, Daisy, 126, 154

Cantelin, Eliza, 42
Cantelin, William, 42
Carter, Emily, 97
Carter, Walter, 97
Cattanach, Agnes, 16
Cattanach, Annie, 15
Cattanach, Charles, 16
Cattanach, Edith, 15, 69
Cattanach, Grace, 16
Cattanach, Jeannie, 62
Cattanach, John junior, 16
Cattanach, John senior, 15, 69
Cattanach, Phoebe junior, 15, 16, 19, 25
Cattanach, Phoebe senior, 15, 16, 69
Cattanach, William, 16
Caversham, 7, 33, 154
charitable aid, 34, 42-3, 90
Chinese, 9, 138, 154, 156
Clarke, Alfred Pickering, 19, 42
Clarke, Blanche, 19
Clarke, Eric Pickering, 19
Clarke, Keith Pickering, 19
Clarke, Leathley Pickering, 19
class, 5, 117, 148, 154, 162
Clawson, Mary Ann, 127
Clegg, Walter, 140
Cliff, William, 2, 76, 93, 130, 136, 140, 169
Collinge, Ann, 28
Collinge, Francis, 9, 27, 28
Collins, Cornelius, 41
community *see* local community
Condie, Annie, 28
Condie, David, 28
Condie, George, 28
Condie, Margaret, 28
Condie, Thomas, 28

INDEX

convent school, 8, 63, 99
courtship, 21, 106-10, 112, 157
Cox, Cecily (née Hindmarsh), 24
Cox, Vivian Walter, 24
crime, 34, 42, 43, 81, 90, 126, 140-1
   alcohol related, 41, 108, 119-20, 146, 147, 148-50
   boys and, 43, 79, 140, 145, 146, 161
   breach of by-laws, 31, 43, 141, 142
   infanticide, 25-6
   women and, 70, 120, 149
   see also larrikinism, police
Cunningham, William, 148

Dalziel, Raewyn, 13, 34
Davies, George, 37, 82, 84, 94, 151, 169
Davis, Ernest, 148
Davis, James, 148
death, 9, 13, 25 8, 42
Dineen, Hannah, 143
Dineen, John, 143
Dolbel brothers, 37, 77
Dolbel, Philip, 155
Dolbel, Phoebe, 117
Douglas, Alex, 81
drinking, 6, 41, 69, 70, 78-9, 84-5, 88, 108, 119, 133, 143-50, 154, 157
   women and, 119-20, 143, 150
   see also hotels
Drummond, John

Edser, Alice (née Pritchard), 14
Edser, Harry, 14
Edser, Mary Ann (née Pritchard), 14
education
   new women and, 6, 47, 62-4, 122
   see also convent school, Taradale School
Edwards, Arthur, 148
Edwards, Ernest, 58, 75, 80, 101, 116, 169
Edwards, Martha, 18, 48-9, 63, 98, 115, 121-2, 164-5
Egan, Charlotte (née Jeffares), 12
Egan, John, 12
Elliott, Nerida, 110
Ellison, Annie, 127
Engelbretsen, Mr, 121
ethnicity, 2, 5, 138, 148, 156, 162

Fairburn, Miles, 12-13, 28, 159
family, 2, 3, 6, 11, 12-30, 41, 43, 93, 94, 97, 111, 159, 160
   extent of family ties, 12, 13, 14-16, 22-3, 26-27, 29, 158, 159
   meaning of, 14, 16-21, 23-5, 27-8, 29
   men's reliance on male kin and networks, 6-7, 23-4, 30, 34, 53, 54, 75-8, 80, 84, 90, 135, 137, 148, 151, 152, 153, 159, 162
   underestimation of family ties, 13-14, 16, 22
   women's reliance on female kin and networks, 15, 16-18, 21-2, 29, 34, 43, 46, 53, 54-5, 59, 61, 66, 71, 83, 113, 115, 159
   see also birth, courtship, death, illegitimacy, marriage
Faragher, John Mack, 40
Farrelly, James, 43
Farrelly, Mary, 43
femininities, 3, 5, 7, 11, 29, 30, 59, 62, 70, 104, 139, 160, 161
   changing meanings of, 47, 68, 70, 71, 119, 127, 131, 160
   inter-generational challenges, 5, 6, 7, 62, 68, 71, 107, 114, 120, 122, 126, 127, 131, 133, 160, 162
   respectability, 47, 50, 68, 71, 114, 119, 120, 160, 162
   see also 'new women'
Field, Hannah, 21, 22, 49-50, 64, 108, 114, 119, 130, 136, 165
Fish, Reverend, 155
friendly societies, 43, 117, 130, 132, 151-4, 156, 157
   sick pay, 34, 43-4, 152
   women and, 126-7, 154, 162
Fussell, Elsie (née Harvey), 24
Fussell, Lieutenant F. N., 24
Fussell, Norman, 24

Gardiner, Arthur, 81
Gebbie, Louisa *see* O'Dowd, Louisa
gender, 2-7, 11, 29-30, 47, 72, 94, 96, 98, 105, 111, 127, 131, 156, 158-61
   see also femininities, masculinities, oral history: gendered content and form, power
geographical mobility, 5, 9, 14, 22, 24, 93, 129, 137, 138, 149, 154, 156, 162
Gibbons, Peter, 7
Gilberd, Henry, 41
Gilchrist, Mr, 139
Gilmour, William, 94, 96
Glenny, Mr, 57
Goddard, Annie, 28
Goddard, Charles, 28
Goddard, Florence, 107
Goddard, Mr, 57
Golding, Pat, 85
Golding, Ann, 151, 152
Golding, Annie (née Brown), 153
Golding, Arthur, 152, 153
Golding, Charles, 151, 153
Golding, Elizabeth, 151
Golding, James, 152, 153
Golding, Samuel, 151, 152, 153

INDEX

Golding, William, 151, 153
Gray, Hugh Radford, 19
Great War, 6, 44, 65, 117-18
Green, James, 94, 108, 119, 135, 140, 140, 151, 169
Greenmeadows Fruit Farm, 36, 37, 65, 77, 84
Guppy, Robert, 9

Halliwell, Charlotte Lily, 62
Halpin, Fanny (née Jeffares), 12
Halpin, William, 12
Hammond, Ann, 14
Hammond, John, 8, 155
Hareven, Tamara K., 58
Harpham, Annie, 67
Harpham, William, 8
Harris, Miss E., 127
Harris, Hiram, 97
Harris, Lucy, 127
Harris, Mary (née Corbin), 97
Harrison, Alfred, 152
Harrison, Alice, 14
Harrison, Edward, 14
Harrison, Eliza, 14
Harrison, Ethel, 14
Harrison, Henry, 14
Harrison, Jane, 14
Harrison, Mary, 14
Harrison, Thomas, 14
Hastie, David, 22, 154
Hastie, Eliza (née Howard), 22, 23
Hatton, Arthur, 26, 58
Hatton, Charlotte (née Pointon), 26
Heale, Arthur, 24
Heale, Nora (née Hindmarsh), 24
Hepburn brothers, 137
Hill, Henry, school inspector, 48, 80, 81, 120
Hindmarsh, Adrian, 24
Hindmarsh, Annie (Madeline), 62
Hindmarsh, Barbara, 62
Hindmarsh, Cecily, 62
Hindmarsh, Charlotte, 24, 62
Hindmarsh, Dorothy, 62
Hindmarsh, John, 24, 62
Hoani, 138
Hollis, Arthur, 148
Hollis, James, 148
Hookings, Mr, 155
Horse, Charles, 169-170
hotels, 8, 47, 75, 77, 78, 84, 85, 88, 108, 110, 119, 127, 133, 142-50, 154, 156
  see also drinking
household economy, 2, 3, 6, 11, 31-45, 73, 90, 143, 159
  see also work: unpaid
Howard, Edward, 15
Howard, Eliza senior, 97
Howard, Eliza junior, 97
Howard, Henry, 23
Howard, Marion, 23, 97
Howard, Mary Charlotte (née Harpham), 97
Howard, Samuel, 97
Howard, Violet (née McCutcheon), 15
Howard, William, 44
Hunt, Elizabeth, 42, 44
Hunt, John, 42, 44

illegitimacy, 15-16, 19-21, 25, 107

Jackson, Fred, 170
Jackson, Richard, 80, 151, 155, 170
James, Fred, 23
James, James, 41
James, Josephine (née Johnson), 23
James, Marjorie (née Johnson), 23
James, Lawrence, 23
James, William, 23
Jarvis, Bill, 152
Jarvis, Mark, 9
Jeffares, Bridget, 70
Jeffares, Charles, 12
Jeffares, Charles Villers, 19
Jeffares, Clarence, 12
Jeffares, Eileen (née Higgins), 12
Jeffares, Hannah (née Smith), 12
Jeffares, Isaac, 8, 12
Jeffares, Isaac junior, 12
Jeffares, James, 70
Jeffares, Jessie (née Taylor), 12
Jeffares, Joseph, 12, 150, 154
Jeffares, Mary Jane (née Villers), 12
Jeffares, Richard, 12
Jeffares, Robert, 12, 70
Jeffares, Rose (née Russell), 12
Jeffares, Tad, 141, 142
Jeffares, Thomas, 12
Jeffares, William, 12
Jenson, Joan, 57
Johnson, J., 39
Johnson, Margaret, 39
Johnson, Thomas, 38-9
Johnsonville, 7, 76, 155
Jones, Emily, 17, 61, 63, 67, 100, 137, 138, 165
Jones, Mrs, midwife, 18
Jones, Percy, 147

Kaponga, 7, 33
kin, 2, 6, 29, 30, 94, 159
  see also birth, family, marriage, death
King, Flewellen, 37

Lake, Marilyn, 54

INDEX

land
  ownership, 9, 31, 35-6, 45, 73, 82, 89, 132, 138, 156
  use, 7-8, 31, 33, 35, 36-8, 45, 75, 82-3
Lansdown, Frank, 77
larrikinism, 108, 112, 139-42, 143, 150, 156, 162
Larson, Berhardt, 69
Larson, Lena, 69
Lauchlan, Ada, 70
Lauchlan, Jane, 70, 71
Lawton, James, 147
leisure, 2, 3, 6, 11, 91-157
  Agricultural and Pastoral Show, 32, 54, 103-4, 111, 130, 159
  billiards, 75, 108, 133, 141-2, 143
  boys' play, 80, 133-6, 154-5
  churches and, 97-103, 111, 116-17, 160
  commercial, 92, 106-10, 130, 133, 143, 156
  communal, 91-106, 110-12, 130
  dances, 102, 107-8, 112, 141, 145
  dog trials, 103, 104-5
  girls' play, 115-16
  horse races, 105-6, 111, 119, 159
  hunting and fishing, 33, 80, 94, 133, 135, 136, 150-1, 155, 156, 159
  men's work allowing for leisure, 74, 80, 88-89, 90, 94, 132-3, 143, 156
  movies, 109-10, 126, 130, 160
  Omaranui Bowling Club, 111, 134, 136
  picnics, 93-6, 104, 105, 110, 111, 132, 134, 150, 159
  women's work as leisure, 32, 53-4, 99, 104, 113, 114, 118, 129
  see also boy scouts, friendly societies, hotels, Roskilda Tea Gardens, sport, women's organisations
length of residence
  see geographical mobility
LeRoy, Albert, 138
Leslie, James, 141
Leslie, Robert, 141
Lewis, Alf, 141
Linehan, Cornelius P., 119
local community, 2, 4, 7, 9, 34, 46, 71, 91, 96, 134, 154, 155, 158
  critique of, 7, 12-13, 28-9
  see also leisure: communal
lodges *see* friendly societies
Lord, Arthur junior, 21, 77
Lord, Arthur senior, 77
Lord, Gladys Lilian (née Boland), 21, 77
Lord, W., 77
Lord, W. junior, 78
Lord, William, 150, 154
Lowe, Catherine Wakeling, 19
Lowe, George Wakeling, 19

Lowe, Mabel Wakeling, 19
Lucas, George, 15
Lucas, Hannah, 15
Lucas, Henry, 15

Manners, Philip, 146-7, 170
Maori, 9, 84, 105, 138, 147, 148, 154
marriage, 9, 13, 21-5
Marsh, Margaret, 6, 110, 136
masculine domesticity, 6, 30, 110, 136, 161, 162
masculinities, 3, 4, 5, 6, 7, 11, 30, 73, 104, 108, 137, 160, 161, 162
  definitions of, 73, 82, 83, 86, 89-90, 133, 134, 139, 150, 151, 155, 157
  inclusive nature of, 7, 37, 72, 73, 76-8, 84, 88, 90, 131, 133, 136, 137, 154, 156, 157, 162
Martin, Ada, 117
McCutcheon brothers, 137
McLean, Edward, 37, 64, 86-8, 142, 170
McNight, Jane, 47, 53, 143, 165
McPherson, Janet, 120
Mechanics' Institute, 9, 120
Mein Smith, Philippa, 25
microhistory, 11
Miller, J. F., 37
Miner, Grace, 17, 21, 31, 64, 119, 130, 146, 165
Modell, John, 58
Molloy, Maureen, 13, 19
Moore, Alice, 94
Moran, Frank, 148
Moreland, Hannah, 70
Murnane, Bridget, 97
Murnane, Garret, 97
Murnane, Johanna, 97
Murnane, Mary, 97
Murphy, brothers, 9

Neagle, Mary, 28
Neagle, Richard, 9
Neagle, R. J., 78
Needle, Emma, 40, 60, 64, 142, 165-6
Nelson, Alfred, 16
Nelson, Ena, 16
Nelson, Lavinia (née Grinham), 16
New Plymouth, 13, 29
New Woman, 6
'new women', 6, 47, 67-68, 71, 114, 125-6, 127, 160, 162, 163
  see also education
Ngahoro, 138
Ngati Kahungunu, 8
Nicol, J., 37
Nicol, Miss M., 118
Nolan, Henry, 21, 78, 86, 101, 142, 144-5, 170

O'Dowd, Charles, 77
O'Dowd, Louisa (née Gebbie), 77, 91, 113, 114, 130, 131, 132
O'Dowd, Patrick, 77, 91, 113, 132, 153, 156, 157
Ogden, Harriet, 126
Olssen, Erik, 33, 154
oral history, 3, 10
　gendered content and form, 3, 10-11, 16-18, 21-22, 24, 29, 30, 47-56, 60-1, 64, 82, 87, 93, 96, 100-1, 102-3, 108, 112, 121-2, 139-40, 143-4, 146-7, 149, 156-7, 161, 162-3
O'Reilly, Ellen Margaret, 28
O'Reilly, Patrick, 28
Ormond, Eileen, 59
Ormond, James, 59
Ormond, Jessie, 59
Ormond, Mary junior, 59
Ormond, Mary senior, 59
Ormond, Patrick, 59
Ormond, William junior, 59
Ormond, William senior, 59
O'Shannassey, Pat, 147
Osterud, Nancy Grey, 70
O'Sullivan, Kitty, 77
Otatara pa, 8
Ownby, Ted, 93

Parke, Alice, 17, 37, 63, 65, 117, 121, 166
Peacock, Bessie, 62
Pearce, Ann, 17, 56, 61, 63, 166
Pearson, David, 76, 155
Peddie, Thomas, 9
Peterson, Eliza, 166
Phillips, Jock, 4, 134, 137
Plumb, Louisa, 21, 51, 53, 58, 65, 84, 99, 102, 103, 115-16, 118, 125, 129, 166
Plunket, 25, 131
Pointon, Edwin, 26, 76
Pointon, Mary Jane, 26
Pointon, Sarah, 70
police, 140-2, 145, 148-9
　Gartley, Constable Jim, 108, 140, 141, 142, 146
　McIvor, Constable, 149
　O'Halloran, Constable, 42, 142
　Riordan, Constable, 141
　Rutledge, Constable, 120
Pond, Theresa, 17, 18, 47, 55, 64, 65-6, 144, 166-7
Powdrell, Frank, 77
Powdrell, Harry, 77
Powdrell, Herbert, 77
Powdrell, Kate, 118
power, 4-5, 7, 71, 72, 73, 89, 114, 133, 137, 154, 155, 156, 157, 160, 162, 163

Preston, Fanny, 120
Pritchard, Alfred, 14
Pritchard, Elizabeth (née Harrison), 14
Pritchard, Mary Ann, 14, 16

Ramzanoglu, Caroline, 73
Randall, Amelia, 36, 37, 41, 65
Raven, Thomas, 48, 76, 84, 86, 139, 141, 171
religion, 5, 37, 91, 119, 147, 148, 152, 155, 156, 162
　Anglican, 8, 22, 24, 46, 57, 96, 97, 99, 102, 116, 136
　Bible Class, 96, 98, 100, 102, 103, 126
　Catholic, 8, 28, 37, 96, 97, 101, 117, 148
　church attendance, 96-97, 98
　Methodist, 8, 96, 99, 102, 103, 105, 116, 127, 128
　Presbyterian, 8, 22, 69, 97, 98, 100, 102, 103, 105, 116, 126, 155
　Sunday School, 96, 97, 98, 99-102, 126
　women's church groups, 97, 116-17, 127-8, 130
Rhodes, Irene, 62
Richardson, Sophie, 40, 46, 53, 63, 96, 103-4, 125, 167
Ridley, George, 57
Ridley, Sarah Jane (née Harpham), 57
Rifle, Florence, 47, 58, 84, 114, 143, 167
Rising, Alice, 70
Rising, May, 70
Roberts, Edward, 142
Robinson, Edward, 42
Robinson, Mary, 42
Roper, Michael, 171
Rose, Charlotte, 21, 25, 91, 167
Roskilda Tea Gardens, 108, 112
Rothman, Ellen, 110
Rowe, Albert, 77
Rowe, Mabel (née Irvine), 77
Rundle, Mary Ann, 15
Rundle, James, 15, 158
Rundle, John, 15
Rundle, Mary Ann, 15
Rundle, Miss, 123
Rymer, Ella, 62
Rymer, George, 8, 106, 147
Rymer, Isabel (née Harvey), 24
Rymer, Lizzie, 62

Scotcher, George, 141
Scott, Joan, 4, 29
Scullin, Anderson, 79
Seccombe, Wally, 34
separate spheres, 2
sex, 2, 5, 70, 106-8, 126
　before marriage, 19, 22

INDEX

contraception, 65-6
sexual double standard, 20, 107
see also illegitimacy
Sharpe, J. A., 149
Shugar, Miss, 2, 139
Silk, Matthew, 17, 61, 75, 83, 100, 137, 138, 171
Smith, Walter, 79
South, Harriet, 52, 58, 63, 65, 67, 124, 167
Spencer, Elizabeth Jerome, 128
sport, 110, 133, 134-9
   boys' sport, 134-7
   girls' sport, 123-4, 135
   men's sport, 133, 134, 136-9
   rugby, 123, 134-135, 136-9, 156, 157
   women's sport, 122-4, 131, 160
   see also leisure
Standing in the Sunshine, 3
Stansfield, Bert, 84
Steinmetz, Bartholomew, 37, 70, 86
Stevenson, Patrick, 31, 32, 78, 103, 104, 130, 146, 171
Stevenson, Sarah, 63, 84, 92, 167-8
Store, Ellen, 51, 52, 63, 125, 126, 168
Strachan, Alexander, 69
Strachan, Henrietta, 69
Sutton, Noel, 81
Sutton-Smith, Brian, 120
Swansegar, Dr Percy Carter Boddington, 51, 61
Sweeney, John, 126

Taradale School, 1, 2, 48, 69, 93, 107, 115-16, 120, 123-124, 133, 134-5, 139-40, 154-5, 156, 159
   attendance at, 78, 80-2
   dividing fence, 1, 3, 6, 93, 159
Tareha, Te Roera, 156
The Story of Suzanne Aubert, 3
Thompson, Robert, 153
Thomson, David, 43
Thomson, Kathleen, 20, 22, 51, 59, 63, 66, 131, 144, 168
Tiffen, Henry Stokes, 7, 8, 9, 36, 41
Tong, Noel Robert, 15, 158
Toynbee, Claire, 4, 29, 33, 70
Tracy, Julia, 41
Tuke, Reverend Charles, 9, 22, 153-4
Tweed, Bridget, 21, 59-60, 101, 168

Waiohiki pa, 9, 156
Waipu, 7, 13, 19, 23, 29
Wakelin, Edith (née Corbin), 97
Wakelin, Mark, 97
Walker, Henry
Wallace, Nurse, 16, 17, 18
Walsh, Mary, 70
Waterhouse, William, 36, 41, 77, 83
Wells, Nora, 70, 71
White, David, 79
White, Joseph, 81
Willan, Greenwood, 89
Williams, Mostyn, 85
Williamson, Clarice Mary, 62
Williamson, Mr, headmaster, 116, 122, 123
wills, 27-8, 40-1, 44
Wilson, Dillon, 81
Women in History, 3
Women in History 2, 3
Women Together, 3
women's organisations, 116-18, 127-31
   Mothers' Union, 114, 116, 117, 128, 131
   Women's Institute (WI), 59, 128-31
Wood, Dorothy Razell, 19
Wood, Joan Razell, 19
Wood, John Razell, 19
work, 31-90
   female work cultures, 65-7, 122
   helpmeet ideology, 34-5, 45, 46, 72
   importance of kin, 31-3, 34, 37, 46, 53, 54-5, 64, 66, 73, 75-8, 80, 83, 84, 90, 159
   male breadwinner ideology, 34, 35, 44, 45, 72, 73, 82, 90, 150, 159
   mutuality in, 34, 40, 72, 159
   sex-segregated, 40, 47-8, 51, 54, 58-9, 65, 136
work, paid
   boys, 80-2
   married men, 31, 32, 36-9, 44, 74-8, 82
   married women, 32, 54-9, 68-71
   single men, 32, 33, 44, 84, 86-8
   single women, 64-8, 75, 90
work, unpaid
   boys, 31, 32-3, 48, 49, 75-6, 78-9
   girls, 31, 32-3, 40, 47-8, 60, 78, 79, 124
   married women, 31, 32, 39-40, 46, 47, 49-59, 67, 74, 104, 113, 114, 138
   married men, 48-9, 53, 82, 83-4, 99, 136, 150
   reproductive labour, 59-61
   single women, 64, 97
World War I
   see Great War